Religion and Power

No Logos without Mythos

D1558834

DAVID MARTIN
London School of Economics, UK

ASHGATE

Published by
Ashgate Publishing Limited
Wey Court East
Union Road
Farnham
Surrey, GU9 7PT
England

Ashgate Publishing Company
110 Cherry Street
Suite 3-1
Burlington, VT 05401-3818
USA

www.ashgate.com

British Library Cataloguing in Publication Data
A catalogue record for this book is available from the British Library

The Library of Congress has cataloged the printed edition as follows:
Martin, David, 1929–
  Religion and power-no logos without mythos / by David Martin.
      pages cm
  Includes index.
  ISBN 978-1-4724-3359-6 (hardcover) – ISBN 978-1-4724-3360-2 (pbk.)
  – ISBN 978-1-4724-3361-9 (ebook) – ISBN 978-1-4724-3362-6 (epub)
  1. Religion and politics. 2. Religion–Philosophy. 3. Political science–Philosophy. I. Title.
  BL65.P7M348 2014
  201'.72–dc23

                                                                    2013051044

ISBN   9781472433596 (hbk)
ISBN   9781472433602 (pbk)
ISBN   9781472433619 (ebk – PDF)
ISBN   9781472433626 (ebk – ePUB)

Printed in the United Kingdom by Henry Ling Limited,
at the Dorset Press, Dorchester, DT1 1HD

RELIGION AND POWER

At last, a book from a leading sociologist about the real relations between religion, politics and violence. It sets the standard for future discussions.

Keith Ward, University of Oxford, UK

Not since the writings of R.H. Tawney have the sociological and moral imaginations been joined in such an eloquent defence of both reason and religion. Martin not only commits us to the most rigorous of reflections on religion and power, he also demands we engage with the power and authority of religion.

Adam Seligman, Boston University, USA

The complicated and very varied relationships between faith and power can only be understood by making comparisons between different societies and at different points in their history. This is the great strength of David Martin's analysis. His knowledge is wide and he compares with great skill. It is a refreshing change from the ignorant and purely ideological analyses provided by our born-again atheists in which faith inevitably renders malign the exercise of power and anyway must give way to a brave new secular and enlightened world. David Martin has shown both that religious convictions and religious institutions continue to be directly and indirectly important in shaping the uses of power and that the consequences of this vary both by which religion we are considering and by the way faith is embedded in and interacts with other aspects of the social order. In this latter respect faith is no different from secular political beliefs and values. Truly a masterpiece of comparative sociology.

Christie Davies, University of Reading, UK

This book offers new insights into the evolution of religion, and its complex relations to modern nationalism and politics, relations characterized by both borrowing and opposition. Attempts to mark a neat separation between religion and the secular do more to obscure what is going on in our world than clarify the moral issues we face. David Martin's careful analysis casts floods of light on the real world, in which no group is pure, and all honest agents have to face dilemmas, often agonizing. There is much more in this broad and stimulating book, including reflections on the continued significance of sacred spaces in contemporary cities, and their relations to each other.

Charles Taylor, McGill University, USA

There are few more contentious issues than the relation of faith to power or the suggestion that religion is irrational compared with politics and peculiarly prone to violence. The former claim is associated with Jürgen Habermas and the latter with Richard Dawkins. In this book David Martin argues, against Habermas, that religion and politics share a common mythic basis and that it is misleading to contrast the rationality of politics with the irrationality of religion. In contrast to Richard Dawkins (and New Atheists generally), Martin argues that the approach taken is brazenly unscientific and that the proclivity to violence is a shared feature of religion, nationalism and political ideology alike rooted in the demands of power and social solidarity.

to Izaak

Contents

PART III: RELIGION, POWER AND EMPLACEMENT

Acknowledgements

Chapter 1, 'Secularisation, Secularism and the Post-Secular: The Power Dimension', was given at Moscow State University in September 2013 and at Heidelberg University in July 2013. It was translated into German, and published in Russian and English in *Religion, State and Church in Russia and Worldwide* (Fall 2013).

A shortened version of Chapters 2–5 was published as 'Religion und Gewalt', in *Transit: Europäische Revue* 43 (Winter 2012/13), pp. 137–58. Chapter 5 was originally a short paper given in Vienna for the IWM conference on secularism in June 2012, chaired by Charles Taylor, at the Institut Français, Vienna.

Chapter 6, 'The Political Future of Religion', was prepared for a conference arranged by Villa Gillet, Lyons, in November 2012, and published on its website.

Chapter 7 on 'Nationalism and Religion: Collective Identity and Choice' was given as the Ernest Gellner Memorial Lecture for 2013, at the London School of Economics (LSE) in April 2013, and published in *Nations and Nationalism* i 20:1, January 2014.

Chapter 8, 'Charisma and Founding Fatherhood', was given at the nationalism conference of April 2011 at the LSE, and published in a shortened version in Vivian Ibrahim and Margit Wunsch (eds), *Political Leadership, Nations and Charisma* (Abingdon: Routledge, 2012) as Chapter 3, pp. 40–51. I am grateful to Routledge for permission to reprint.

Chapter 10 was published as 'Religión, política y secularización: comparaciones entre Europe del Oeste y del Este' in Rodrigo Muñoz, Javier Sánchez Cañizares and Gregorio Guitián (eds), *Religión, Sociedad Moderna y Razón Práctica* (Pamplona: EUNSA, 2012), pp. 15–31. It was also translated into Ukrainian for the purposes of the University of L'viv during my visit there in 2011.

Chapter 11 was given at the Ernst-Troeltsch-Gesellschaft Kongress in Munich in October 2011.

A shorter version of Chapter 13 was given at a conference on post-secularity held at Groningen University in 2009 and published in Arie Molendijk, Justin Beaumont and Christoph Jedan (eds), *Exploring the Postsecular: The Religious, the Political and the Urban* (Leiden and Boston, Mass.: Brill, 2010), pp. 345–62. I am grateful to Brill for permission to reprint.

Discussions related to the argument of this book are to be found in my two articles for the 2014 Wiley-Blackwell volumes on World Christianity edited by Michael McClymond and Lamin Sanneh: one deals with secularisation in Europe and North America and the other with Christianity, Western music and the return of the sacred.

Introduction

A major section of this book criticises 'New Atheist' rhetoric for its indifference to a social scientific understanding of the social role of religion, or maybe simple ignorance of it. This section also draws attention to the verbal violence displayed by 'New Atheists' when fastening the blame for violence on religion and claiming innocence for themselves.

Apart from its critique of the rhetorical strategies of contemporary 'New Atheists', this book has a radical and contentious thesis: the importance of analysing religion and politics in the same conceptual frame. We cannot discuss the place of religion in our public life as though we were dealing with irrational religion in the private sphere and rational politics in the public sphere. That procedure is as morally outrageous as it is scientifically untenable. I have summed up my case in the phrase 'No Logos without Mythos', meaning by that an irreducible core of narrative myth and a grammar shared by religion and politics *alike* over the last three millennia. I find my starting point in the narrative myths stimulated by the different angles of transcendence and different transformation scenes found in Karl Jaspers' notion of the Axial Age. I find them also in Max Weber's essays on religious rejections of the world as it presently *is*, in the light of a world *to come*, or as it was *once*, or as it resides immanently, or elsewhere. I focus on the *tensions* these angles of transcendence, these transformation scenes and these religious rejections, create in every social realm: the economic, the political, the erotic and the aesthetic. I know the criticisms of the Axial Age hypothesis put forward by my friend and colleague Jan Assmann, and I appreciate his emphasis on the key role of writing as storing memory, in a volume to which we jointly contributed. This criticism is based on his magisterial studies in Egyptology, and I am quite happy if the idea of an Axial Age understood as having defined temporal and cultural *locations* is taken instead to refer to axial *characteristics* of the kind discussed in Max Weber's essays.[1] It is the profound tensions in the

---

[1] Robert N. Bellah and Hans Joas, *The Axial Age and Its Consequences* (Cambridge, Mass. and London: The Belknap Press, 2012). Robert Bellah provides *the* key analysis of the irreducible role of narrative in his *Religion in Human Evolution: From the Paleolithic to the Axial Age* (Cambridge, Mass.: Harvard University Press, 2011).

spheres of politics, economics, art and sexuality that matter. They cluster around power, wealth, representation and the erotic.

A book about faith and power has to begin with the issue of secularisation because secularisation implies a steady decline in the power of religion. At various points I am obliged to provide summaries of my own theoretical understanding of the secularisation process, and I fear the repetitions are unavoidable. Secularisation introduces a major theme of the book: the partial shift in what we loosely call modernity from the expression of power, violence and the pursuit of peace, in religious modes, to expressions in the secular and secularised modes of nationalism and political ideology. The locus of violence shifts, not the violence itself.

I would add one further important point about modernity that follows from my postulated unity of the religious and the political and from the historical variety of secularising tendencies central to my general theory of secularisation, including in particular the contested role of Pentecostalism as an agent of an 'alternative modernity', that realises on a global scale the modernising potential of German-American Pietism and Anglo-American Methodism. In my own studies since 1986 I have presented Pentecostalism within the frame of alternative modes of secularisation and alternative modes of modernisation.

But the credentials of Pentecostalism are contested from an unrealistic perspective that imagines a rational and rationalised sphere of 'western' politics intermittently encroached upon by irrational and quasi-religious forces at the margin of a truly modern consciousness. This perspective is a self-deluding fantasy, contrary to the empirical evidence about the nature of our everyday political practice. Of course, we debate and rationally examine alternative causal sequences in matters of public policy. But the horizon within which our debates take place is informed throughout with non-rational understandings and choices, and sustained by modes of solidarity based on images and pictograms of 'the Other' and of the past and the future.

This self-deluding perspective allows us mentally to quarantine Pentecostalism as informed by charismatic and magical impulses, including charismatic authority, as though our rational debates about the most efficient means to secure our ends exempted us from those same impulses, including charismatic authority. Yet Pentecostals are notoriously pragmatic in their use of efficient means to secure given ends. They are technically proficient and organisationally pragmatic. The problem here relates to charisma itself, which is an ineluctable element in politics and religion alike and easily combines the impetuous flow of the spirit with magical thinking. The impetuous flow of the spirit in Pentecostalism constantly combines with magical thinking, and that offends against our *artificially purified* notion about our own genuine modernity.

If we only pause for a moment to consider how the supposed rationality of the market operates, then our exemption from the sphere of the non-rational ought to be an obvious delusion. If the operations of the market do not convince us of our delusions about our modernity then we have only to contemplate the social reality of nationalism seen as the supposedly 'modern' substitute for religion. Bernice Martin has made a parallel argument with respect to 'modern' individualism as contrasted with the 'permeable' self of Pentecostals open both to the incursion of the Spirit (or demonic spirits) and to the selves of others with whom they have relations. We in the West have an artificially purified and solipsistic notion of the western individual, when in reality this individual only exists within the modalities of interdependence and social solidarity.[2]

In the first chapter I summarise my initial critique of secularisation and my subsequent 'general theory' of secularisation, before considering more recent issues relating to secularism and the 'post-secular'. I am highly critical of recent writing on secularism and the post-secular, in particular the contribution of Jürgen Habermas. I conclude the first chapter with a brief sketch of changing modes and shifting foci of collective violence from the Middle Ages to the period of Absolute (or Enlightened) monarchy, and from nineteenth-century nationalism to twentieth-century political ideologies like Liberal Imperialism, Fascism and Communism. I could equally well have included the Roman Empire because I argue that, whatever the type of society, the agents of the 'conscience collective' (in Durkheim's formulation) are always liable to deploy massive violence against 'the Other', whether defined as heretic, traitor, political deviant or implicated in 'an axis of evil'. In short, the discourse that preceded the attack on Iraq as part of 'the axis of evil' and as harbouring weapons of mass destruction is to be understood in the same context as the attack on the Albigensians. In Ancient Rome, for example, the state religion was not imposed on subject peoples, and any number of cults were tolerated *provided* they paid respect to the aura of the emperor and the imperial cult, but extreme brutality was deployed to suppress internal revolts and meet external threats. Whatever the more or less moral justifications adduced for violence, its dynamics and its attendant discourses are remarkably similar from the imperialism of ancient Rome to the liberal imperialism of today. Not only do I reject the supposed contrast between

---

[2]   Bernice Martin, 'Tensions and Trends in Pentecostal Gender and Family Relations', in Robert Hefner (ed.), *Global Pentecostalism in the 21st Century* (Bloomington: Indiana University Press, 2013, Chapter 4, pp. 115–48).

rational politics and irrational religion, but I also stress the underlying dynamics of power, solidarity and violence exercised against the Other *whether the dominant ideology is Christianity, nationalism or Communism.* The geopolitical dynamics of power discussed in the final chapter on Western Eurasia illustrate a striking continuity all the way from Russian Orthodoxy to scientific atheism, and from Ivan the Terrible to Soviet Russia.

The next four chapters critically examine contemporary discourses associating religion *in particular* with the use of violence. Just as the discourse associating religion with the use of violence, notably in the time of the 'Wars of Religion', involves a liberal claim to historical innocence, so the Marxist understanding of the violence of liberal imperialism in its turn involves a claim to historical innocence. Today a similar claim to historical innocence is made in the name of science by 'New Atheists' claiming that religion is not only superstition but uniquely prone to appeal to force. These four chapters focus on this claim as put forward by Richard Dawkins and by others loosely associated with the 'New Atheists'. They seek to illustrate the paradoxical indifference displayed by these protagonists of science to a social scientific understanding of a notoriously complex issue. Instead they deploy a moralising rhetoric, presumably because it avoids the real complexities of the issues involved.[3] It has all the polemical advantages of 'cheap and dirty' journalism.

Chapters 6 to 11 discuss the intersection of the religious and the political and seek to demonstrate the extent to which religion and politics need to be analysed in the same conceptual frame. Chapter 6 descries the political future of religion and suggests that future has a *longue durée* ahead of it, especially given the persistence of sacred 'centres' attracting the respect and reverence of the

---

[3]   A.C. Grayling has said that the case against faith schools can be summed up in two words: Northern Ireland ('A.C. Grayling on Faith Schools', www.youtube. com/watch?V=4UuSJJB9u-A, accessed April 2013). But, of course, issues cannot be decontextualised without analysis of the particular socio-historical conditions obtaining in Northern Ireland. One has to begin with the clash between British liberal imperialism and Irish secular nationalism, and the differential access to power, status and wealth enjoyed by rival groups distributed in different ratios across a territory demarcated by an arbitrary boundary. Then one has to look at the role of faith schools where these conditions do not obtain. Bully-boy polemic of the kind deployed by Grayling offends against the canons of rational debate and scientific comment, and either these are not understood or they *are* understood; and I am not sure which should shock us the most, the ignorance or the moral insouciance. Maybe the social scientific approach could be more easily grasped by A.C. Grayling were anyone to claim that the case against atheism was summed up in two words: Ukrainian famine. Once grasped, it might then be possible to move from the pleasures of indignation to the satisfactions of understanding.

majority. It is in this chapter that I develop furthest the theoretical perspective informing the book as a whole, picking up from the discussion in Chapter 5 about kinds of truth and sketching the relation between the kind of truth elicited by sociology and the kind of truth re-presented, uncovered and exposed by theology. I develop Weber's arguments about the spectrum of axial religions, their inter-relation and the different kinds of grammar that they generate. (The arguments in Chapters 5 and 6 were developed at the same time as I finalised the Prospect and the Retrospect of my intellectual autobiography *The Education of David Martin* in the late summer of 2012.)[4]

Chapter 7 adopts a contrasting approach by discussing the dialectic of automatic belonging (ethnic and territorial) with personal choice, and by elaborating the dialectic of religion and nationalism, in particular where religion and nationalism virtually fuse in the cultural defence of a territory and where transnational religion, for example Pentecostalism, challenges birthright membership in the Church-nation. Chapter 8 likewise focusses on nationalism and religion and analyses the many binary distinctions, like Charisma and Founding Fatherhood, shared by religion, nationalism and political ideology. I try to exhibit the common grammar of religion, nationalism and political ideology.

Chapter 9 focusses on the crossover between religion and politics as that emerges from the current debate about the actual role and the appropriate role of religion in the public sphere of politics It draws attention to the persistent confusion of normative and descriptive accounts of that role and criticises the notion that politics is rational whereas religion is irrational. You cannot divide up the social world in that way. The social world is a unity. As in earlier chapters, I stress the characteristics shared by religion and politics, such as ritual role-playing and rituals of commination. Chapter 10 concludes the middle section of the book with an exercise in comparison between religion and politics in South-Eastern Europe and South-Western Europe: areas inflected by very different patterns of secularisation. The different patterns of secularisation follow from very different histories and they produce very different relations between religion and politics. Chapter 11 tries to show how a common language (or mythic structure) is shared alike by religion, nationalism and politics through an exploration of the potent ambiguity of 'Jerusalem', England's second national anthem. It presents the argument of the whole book in concentrated form and provides the heart of what I want to say. Inevitably some material with respect to the Axial Age has to be repeated here in condensed form.

---

[4]   *The Education of David Martin: The Making of an Unlikely Sociologist* (London: SPCK, 2013).

The final four chapters are tentative sketches for what might have been a much more extended argument about the relation of religion and power to places and spaces, especially high places and sacred spaces. Chapter 12 provides a thematic introduction to these sketches by exploring the basic grammar of Christianity as that is realised in the tension between the City of God and the City of Man and in the tension between the kingdom of God translated into the Church (whether national or international) or translated into the radical sect. It also explores the emergence of a major transformation of that grammar in the early modern period when voluntary forms of Christianity hived off from the state and from the all-encompassing territorial collective, and often (for example in early nineteenth-century English Nonconformity) embraced a pacific commercial ethos equally opposed to ecclesiastical establishment and to the military and aristocratic notions of honour. This thematic introduction includes a brief outline of the distinction between centre and periphery because that distinction provides a key conceptual tool for any attempt to understand how power relations are inscribed in high places and sacred spaces.

Chapters 13 and 14 try to realise spatially my 'general theory' of secularisation, and focus in particular on the concept of functional differentiation whereby different social spheres, like education and welfare, emerge from the overarching sacred canopy of religion and occupy their own quasi-sacred space. These chapters are problematic, in part because it is not easy to know what to include and what to exclude. Nevertheless they fit well with the current interest in 'materialising' religion, especially in urban ecology, and I have risked including them. Chapter 15 brings together most of the themes treated earlier: it is a spatial-temporal realisation of secularisation and de-secularisation, ethno-religion and voluntarism, organised around the distinction between centre and periphery. It illustrates the geopolitical constants of violence over time and cultural space, whether the governing ideology is Christianity in the Orthodox style, Enlightened autocracy as practised by Catherine the Great or scientific atheism as practised by Soviet Russia.

Chapter 1

Secularisation, Secularism and the Post-Secular: The Power Dimension

I am not summarising the current debate over secularisation, secularism and the post-secular. I am not even recounting the long-term history of that debate, though that would be very well worth doing because much of it is obscured in current discussions. If it were a history I would have to begin with the crucial contributions of Peter Berger and Thomas Luckmann, and discuss the role of summary articles and commentaries like those by Karel Dobbelaere and Olivier Tschannen. My aim here is different. I focus on my own role in the sixties of the twentieth century in setting out the first critique of secularisation and in creating the first general theory of secularising processes as these are inflected by variable histories (or in recent parlance 'path dependency'). I do this principally because the initial construction of theories involves instructive and strategic decisions we all have to make at some time or other. These decisions are rooted in very different methodological perspectives within sociology as well as very different understandings of history and of its importance for sociology.

To begin with I pivot this exercise on the difference between my own work at the London School of Economics and that of Bryan Wilson at Oxford. I do this precisely because the difference was informed by different sociological methodologies and by different understandings of history. I could have referred to the contributions of many other colleagues, Grace Davie and Linda Woodhead, for example, but I want to focus on what in those early stages of theory construction was a striking contrast of approach. Bryan Wilson gave form and substance to what Steve Bruce refers to as 'the standard theory' of secularisation. Steve Bruce is a major contemporary protagonist of the standard theory within the British sociology of religion, and as a positivist and modernist enterprise it remains as viable today as it was when formulated by Bryan Wilson. It makes sense of a lot of data, particularly in Western Europe. This 'standard theory' received a comprehensive statement in Wilson's *Religion in Sociological*

Perspective (1982), though it originated as far back as 1966.[1] It calls on a battery of associated concepts like rationalisation, bureaucratisation, modernisation, societalisation, privatisation and functional differentiation. My approach was not in the positivist and modernist mode, but phenomenological and dialectic. I mean that I was interested in the structures of religious consciousness as well as empirical trends and correlations, and in the grammar of faith as that underwent transformations in society as a *whole*, not just in the sector conventionally identified as religious.

Doubts about Privatisation and Rationalisation: A Holistic Approach

I did not pay much attention to the battery of concepts deployed by Wilson – apart from functional differentiation, which had a long history in sociology – and I was particularly dubious about privatisation, though I also had reservations about the extent of rationalisation. In the course of what follows I shall try to explain these doubts and reservations about privatisation and rationalisation. In my own approach to secularisation I was interested in dispositions of power among elites and counter-elites, including intelligentsias. Dispositions of power assume the public presence of religion rather than privatisation. Of course, I analysed *common* empirical trends; but I also focussed on how these were inflected by very different contexts (for example, the American city was not like the European city) and inflected by very *different* configurations of power.

These configurations were structured by relations between religious majorities and minorities, and between centres and peripheries. Majorities at the centre of society usually enjoy greater access to a more (or less) centralised state than minorities on the peripheries. Of course, there are also configurations of power, for example the Alawis in Syria, where minorities exercise power over majorities through the state, or where states have ruled over or incorporated countries where the majority practise a different religion. One thinks of British rule in Ireland and Russian rule in Poland. I foregrounded Church–state relations, some of which might be formally recognised, as in England, while others simply involved the preponderant power exercised by a majority tradition, as is the case with Protestantism in the USA or Catholicism in France and Brazil. Such an approach necessarily required an analysis of nationalism, given that the rise of nationalism often fused with aspirations for independence within a multicultural

---

[1]   Bryan R. Wilson, *Religion in Secular Society* (London: Watts, 1966); *Religion in Sociological Perspective* (Oxford: Oxford University Press, 1982).

empire. A great deal turned on whether religion played a positive role or a negative role in the birth of the nation. A great deal also turned on how religion related to *different* national versions of the Enlightenment: some opposed to religion, as in France, some not, as in England and America. There were some countries, for example Brazil, where neither nationalism nor Enlightenment mattered that much. Nationalism and Comteanism in Brazil were confined to the elite precisely because the state exercised little central control and left a weak Church to provide the substance of collective consciousness.

My main theoretical tool was functional differentiation. Functional differentiation is a concept sometimes associated today with Luhmann, though it goes back to Parsons, Simmel and Durkheim, and it refers to the increasing autonomy of spheres of social activity – like politics, administration, education and welfare – from ecclesiastical oversight and theological discourse.[2] I regarded it as a major element in the processes of secularisation. But functional differentiation need not imply privatisation. Indeed, it could just as easily mean that religion was partly freed from the functions of social control and legitimation to contribute critically to public debate. That is precisely what the Christian Churches in Western Europe and North America have done, and done increasingly, from the 1890s up to the present day. Talcott Parsons thought differentiation freed religion to pursue its own proper ends.

Privatisation did not figure in my analysis, partly because the British experience would lead one to suppose quite the opposite: in Britain religion became *increasingly* active in political critique as it grew less important for legitimation. My approach postulated a number of basic historical patterns in which political systems and religious systems reflected each other and intersected. My focus was not religion or politics but the politico-religious nexus. It was my sense of that nexus that informed my doubts about the degree of rationalisation governing our everyday political practice. Steve Bruce, while continuing to accept the privatisation thesis, has at the same time argued in *Politics and Religion* (2003) that religion matters politically.[3] The sociology of religion only makes sense when pursued in close dialogue with political sociology, as well as with international relations and with the kind of history that combines religion and politics in a holistic analysis of power, including the uses, occasions and triggers of violence

---

[2]   Rudolf Stichweh, 'The History and Systematics of Functional Differentiation in Sociology', in Mathias Albert, Barry Burzan and Michael Zürn (eds), *Bringing Sociology to International Relations: World Politics as Differentiation Theory* (Cambridge: Cambridge University Press, 2013, pp. 50–70).

[3]   Steve Bruce, *Secularization. In Defence of an Unfashionable Theory* (Oxford: Oxford University Press, 2011); and *Politics and Religion* (Cambridge: Polity, 2003).

as discussed below. Analysed in a holistic way religion becomes as central for the
sociological enterprise today as it was for the classics 100 years ago. That is why
I have always turned to cognate disciplines, not only politics and international
relations but also social geography and anthropology, and to discussions of
tradition and change, centre and periphery, as pursued by scholars like Edward
Shils.[4] One would not dream of discussing religion in Northern Ireland or the
Caucasus, or for that matter Pentecostalism in Brazil, without calling on history,
political sociology, international relations, social geography, migration studies
and regional and local ethnography. With the reappearance of the nomad,
and the contemporary return of the folk-wanderings as the new version of
the 'internal proletariat', migration studies acquire increased importance. One
cannot imagine an analysis of religion in Armenia or Syria that does not deal
with borders and migrations, massacres and revolts, minorities and majorities,
policies of divide and rule by the imperial governments of multicultural empires,
and international relations between Russia, Turkey, Azerbaijan, Iran, France and
the United States.

Once the sociology of religion emphasises 'privatisation', it can gravitate
rather too easily to a marginal position within the social sciences, apart from
the largely historical exercise of analysing the supposedly critical difference
between a religious past and a secular present, or between traditional society
and modernity. The sociology of religion becomes reduced to analysing what
happens to religion with the great transition from the traditional to the modern,
and to picking over what fragments of the past remain. A crucial problematic
at the time I began my work was signalled by Daniel Lerner's 1958 book *The
Passing of Traditional Society*.[5] Certainly I was interested in identifying when
one might properly speak of a society entering modernity, which was very
early in England and very late in Albania, though I remained distinctly wary of
modernisation theory. My colleague Bryan Wilson accepted the marginality
of our subject and wondered why people were interested in it unless they were
working out a personal problem. That was one reason why he concentrated
on small sects regarded as relics of traditional religious community which
had persisted into the rationalised present. The sociology of religion was
a sideshow given what he regarded as the declining social significance of
religion. However, that observation introduces another complication because

---

   [4]   Edward Shils, *Tradition* (Chicago: Chicago University Press, 1981); *Center and
Periphery: Essays in Macrosociology* (Chicago: Chicago University Press, 1975).
   [5]   Daniel Lerner, *The Passing of Traditional Society: Modernizing the Middle East* (New
York: Free Press, 1958).

declining social significance is entirely compatible with increased critical activity in the public sphere.

Secularism Then and Now

This brief exercise in intellectual history introduces my discussion of secularisation, secularism and the post-secular. I did not regard secularism as a quasi-universal process leading to the privatisation of religion. I saw it as an ideology that *prescribed* privatisation and actively excluded religion from the public sphere, notably in France, Russia and Turkey. In my critique of secularisation I identified secularism as one of the crucial ideological loadings and normative prescriptions built into the master concept of secularisation. Ideological prescription easily masquerades as sociological description, especially when you recollect that much of sociology itself was part of the modernisation project. Of course we could have a descriptive 'middle range' theory of secularisation such as I attempted to devise, but one needed at the same time to identify the grand prescriptive project in which it was too often embedded. Secularism was that grand prescriptive project. Moreover, the sheer militancy of modernisation, secularisation and privatisation in the course of the French, Russian, Turkish and Chinese revolutions indicated the importance of religion, not its enfeebled irrelevance. What is departing from the stage of history in the course of a natural development does not need to be violently pushed by ideologues who consider ideology and violence uniquely associated with religion.

Today secularism has changed its meaning. Secularism now refers to several different things simultaneously: a secular attitude indifferent to religion; the process of disentangling religion from state power; *and* the ideology that promotes this disentanglement. To make matters even more complicated, the ideology seeking to promote the disentanglement of state and religion can be religiously motivated, as it was in early modern Baptist movements and nineteenth-century English Nonconformity.[6] Secularism understood as disentanglement *can* be a Christian project. In part the recent change of meaning reflects lay usages in the media. It also reflects debates in philosophy that extrapolate from the emancipation of philosophy from theology to the emancipation of politics from

---

6   Jonathan Parry, 'The Disciplining of the Religious Conscience in Nineteenth-Century British Politics' in Ira Katznelson and Gareth Stedman Jones (eds), *Religion and the Political Imagination* (Cambridge: Cambridge University Press, 2010, pp. 214–34).

religion in what Jürgen Habermas calls a 'post-metaphysical age'.[7] Once again the *normative* project of freeing politics from the incursions of the irrational and atavistic was presented as a quasi-universal *empirical* trend.

This is where the intervention of José Casanova in his *Public Religions in the Modern World* (1994) was critical.[8] Casanova analysed the role of religion in several contemporary countries to show its massive political relevance as a marker of de-privatisation or (the emphasis is mine) a *new appreciation* of the political relevance of religion. After all, the post-war European project had been built on foundations laid *inter alia* by the USA and the Vatican and by the creation of Christian Democratic Parties dominating European politics up to the demise of communism. It is difficult to conceive how major segments of intellectual opinion could elide the role of Catholics like Konrad Adenauer, Alcide de Gasperi, Robert Schuman and even (though his Catholicism was less salient) Jean Monnet in the creation of the European Union. How was it possible to forget the appeal to the legacy of Charlemagne or the role of the Catholic Church in Hungary in 1956 and in Poland throughout the post-war period, or the role of the churches in focussing social criticism during the Thatcher government in Britain or the continuing influence of the Social Gospel in the USA? The privatisation thesis depended on forgetting or eliding the obvious.[9] That is why part of my analysis turns on the varying roles played by intelligentsias in defining the situation rather than analysing what was actually happening.

As already indicated, by the 1990s secularism had come to refer to a generalised indifference to transcendent perspectives and to the various ways in which the Church *should* be separated from the state, as well as the ways in which the Church had *in fact* been separated from the state. 'Ought' and 'is' travelled in tandem. And, of course, there had been major movements throughout the nineteenth century in favour of 'free churches in free states'

---

[7]   Jürgen Habermas, *Between Naturalism and Religion: Philosophical Essays* (Cambridge: Polity, 2008).

[8]   José Casanova, *Public Religions in the Modern World* (Chicago: University of Chicago Press, 1994).

[9]   I am not sure why the privatisation thesis appeared so persuasive. Maybe some intellectuals extrapolated from their own view of the irrelevance of religion to assumptions about its role in the public sphere, or confused the diminishing role of religion as a source of political legitimacy and validation (in Europe) with a diminishing contribution on the part of religious thought to the great public issues of the day. A parallel blindness occurred in development theory, which until recently also assumed the irrelevance of religion to development. See Dena Freeman (ed.), *Pentecostalism and Development: Churches, NGOs and Social Change in Africa* (Basingstoke: Palgrave Macmillan, 2012), especially Deena Freeman, 'The Pentecostal Ethic and the Spirit of Development', pp. 1–38.

and these had been heralded at an early stage in the USA by Thomas Jefferson's 'wall of separation' between state and church.[10] It is important to remember that this wall was enacted to *protect* the 'free exercise' of religion, and by no means privatised religion or deprived it of political relevance. Free exercise ensured access to the public square. That has been its effect in the USA, and that implies that if you want to neutralise religion you should nationalise it like Peter the Great and Frederick the Great and make it part of the state apparatus. And yet, in the highly influential work of the German philosopher Jürgen Habermas secularism referred to the privatisation of religion as a precondition of the democratic secular state. As a member of the Frankfurt School, Habermas was concerned, after the destructive irrationalities of the Nazi period, to establish the space of politics as an arena of reasoned debate. One would have expected on the contrary that Nazism would alert one to the irreducible power of the non-rational in politics. I repeat what I have already said in my Introduction about our *artificially* purified notion of the rationalised character of western politics.

I found the idea that politics represents an arena of rational debate very surprising. I was, for example, influenced by Georges Sorel, who recognised that political discourse is riddled with myths and incantations. Whatever merit the idea of a rational politics might have had as a prescription, as a description of how politics is actually practised it is as remote from reality as the idea that religion had been privatised. It would be more convincing to describe the space of politics as occupied by a herd of easily panicked political animals. Politics may be a vocation as described by Max Weber, or it may be the systematic organisation of hatreds as described by Henry Adams, but it is certainly about appeals to populist instincts in peace and war and about who rules the polis in whose interest.

Yet Habermas decreed that religious views could only be admitted if they conformed to shared rational standards, and this requirement was taken seriously enough to stimulate responses, like Roger Trigg's *Religion in Public Life: Must Faith be Privatized?* (2007),[11] seeking to show that religious arguments could be rational. I should stress again that this normative requirement put forward by a philosopher was very different from sociological observation of the process of differentiation. It was also very different from the historical documentation of the separation of ecclesiastical norms from enactments of public law designed to cover all citizens, whatever their beliefs, or from the erection of a 'wall of

---

[10]   James F. Harris, *The Serpentine Wall: The Winding Boundary between Church and State in the United States* (London and New Brunswick: Transaction, 2013).

[11]   Roger Trigg, *Religion in Public Life: Must Faith be Privatized?* (Oxford: Oxford University Press, 2007).

separation' in the USA. It infringed the right of all citizens, including those who held religious beliefs, to give voice to their convictions and interests in the public realm. Of course, priests and pastors should not tell people how to vote, but even believers and church representatives have a right to be heard in their own language, though they would do well to remember the language of those they seek to persuade. The key religious questions – 'Who is my neighbour?' or 'Who is my sister, brother, mother?' or 'What are the general conditions governing commitment and covenant?' or 'What follows from concepts like human dignity and respect for creation?' – translate easily into any language. *All* contributors to debate, and not solely those who contribute from a religious perspective, need to consider how they are heard as a matter of basic political prudence. To make matters yet more complicated, it is clear that some politicians take special care of religious sensibilities precisely *because* they privately dismiss them as irrational. Far from excluding them on the grounds that they are irrational, they take great care to accommodate them, and even to exploit them, as a matter of common prudence. Secular politicians in Brazil learn the language of Pentecostals to secure votes. One has only to think of how Slobodan Milosevic deployed the language of Serbian religious nationalism to retain power.

Post-Secularity: An Otiose Source of Confusion

In due course Habermas shifted to a position whereby religious actors might contribute under certain conditions. One suspects he was responding to such interlocutors as Charles Taylor and Joseph Ratzinger, as well as to the global revival of Islam and the advent of sizeable Muslim minorities in Western Europe demanding their right to be heard according to standard liberal criteria. This change Habermas confusingly labelled 'post-secularity'.[12]

It was echoed in public comment by influential books proclaiming the *Revenge of God* (1994) or *God is Back* (2009) at the very same time as major analysts in Britain reiterated what Steve Bruce referred to as the standard theory of secularisation.[13] In 2001 Callum Brown published *The Death of Christian*

---

[12]   Jürgen Habermas, 'Notes on Post-Secular Society', *New Perspectives Quarterly* (Fall 2008, 25: 4, pp. 17–29).

[13]   Gilles Kepel, *The Revenge of God: The Resurgence of Islam, Christianity and Judaism in the Modern World* (Cambridge: Polity, 1994); John Micklethwait and Adrian Wooldridge, *God is Back: How the Global Rise of Faith is Changing the World* (New York: Penguin, 2009).

Britain and in 2002 Steve Bruce published *God is Dead.*[14] God is simultaneously back and dead. As I had never believed that religion had been banished to the private sphere, the supposed advent of post-secularity looked like yet another mythic projection reflecting what had been perceived, maybe even hoped for, rather than any observable process. It seemed paradoxical to label a period when religious institutions were losing ground and the religious influence on voting behaviour diminishing as post-secular. I make one further observation. I had repeatedly pointed out how embedded the categories of religion and the secular were in European history and Christian discourse, but this point was only generally recognised when taken up by others, in particular when post-colonial scholarship, notably the seminal contributions of Talal Asad, drew attention to the power dimension in the construction of the constituent categories in the secularisation debate.[15] William Cavanaugh has also underlined the way the binary distinction between religious and secular was constructed in the early modern period.[16]

The Critique and the General Theory

I turn now to my initiation of a critique published in 1965 and of a general theory of secularisation published first in 1969, and in detailed form in 1978. The dates matter because recent summaries of the secularisation debate often place critique and theory considerably later. My critique came out of a particular situation and a specific experience in post-war Britain. At the beginning of the sixties the religious condition of Britain remained relatively stable, though on the cusp of change. Apart from that I was confronted by the ruling assumptions of sociology at the London School of Economics based on the models of classical sociology. Of course, there had been many investigations documenting the weaknesses of the British churches, and I was well aware of them. But they were not cast in the large-scale theoretical frameworks found in continental social thought, above all the assumptions about secularisation found in Marx, Weber, Comte and Durkheim, or even the assumptions of the English evolutionary tradition

---

[14]   Steve Bruce, *God is Dead: Secularization in the West* (Oxford: Wiley/Blackwell, 2002); Callum G. Brown, *The Death of Christian Britain: Understanding Secularization 1800–2000* (London and New York: Routledge, 2001).

[15]   Talal Asad, *Formations of the Secular: Christianity, Islam, Modernity* (Stanford: Stanford University Press, 2003).

[16]   William Cavanaugh, *The Myth of Religious Violence: Secular Ideology and the Roots of Modern Conflict* (New York: Oxford University Press, 2009).

of Herbert Spencer and Lionel Hobhouse. English social thought is averse to grand schemes of evolutionary or revolutionary change, in spite of the influence of taken for granted notions of progress and social amelioration. In Britain even secularisation is undramatic. Nevertheless in the toe-hold which sociology had established at the London School of Economics secularisation was assumed if not explicitly theorised, and religion was dismissed as epiphenomenal, so sociologists concentrated on the mechanics of social amelioration, like social mobility. Not only was religion disappearing, it was also merely a reflection of real forces.

I had read Comte on the stages that lead to the positivist era of political change carried out under the aegis of social science, and rejected it. Comte was technocratic rather than democratic, and I believed politics to be about fundamental choices and visions as well as the Blue Books of social science and administration. Technical rationality in pursuit of social goals administered by so-called experts veers towards tyranny, whereas the symbolics of genuinely democratic politics veer towards the non-rational. Nothing in my idiosyncratic intellectual formation outside the university led me to organise history in dramatic terms of progressive ages and stages leading to the rational administration of things rather than conflicting political visions and their associated dilemmas and costs. I had absorbed thinkers like Pitirim Sorokin and Oswald Spengler, who saw history very differently from those who thought in terms of progressive stages. I had read writers like Nikolai Berdyaev, Georges Sorel and Norman Cohn, who saw Marxism not as the epitome of science applied to society but as secularised millenarianism. I had read authors like Jacob and Yonina Talmon, who regarded Marxism and nationalism alike as secular messianism and who analysed what they called 'totalitarian democracy'. My research focus had been on visions of peace as related to millennial expectation, including exemplary and eschatological violence, from the middle centuries of the first millennium BC to the peace movements before and after World War Two. All these scholars argued that politics is imbued with non-rational motives and motifs. I repeat: so much for comprehensive rationalisation.

I treated concepts like the Millennium and the Messianic Age as *simultaneously* religious and political both in the past *and now*. That is crucial because I was very wary of the notion of the Great Transition from the traditional to the modern espoused by some of my colleagues, for example, Ernest Gellner. I suspected scenarios based on *from* then *to* now. The religious and the secular existed in a continuing dialectic that engendered any number of transformations. For example, the expectation of the kingdom of God brought divine transcendence down to the *saeculum*: God with us. The conversion of the kingdom into a church, assimilated in the centuries after Constantine to the imperatives of political power, subjected Christianity to a profane and secular dynamic. The grammar of the binary distinction that divided the religious from the secular was radically unstable and subject to any number of transformations.[17] From my reading of Ernst Troeltsch I envisaged the uncompromising, unworldly and exclusive sect, the compromising, worldly and inclusive church, the voluntary free denominations and the mystical group as having political analogues. From my reading of Reinhold and Richard Niebuhr I derived a notion of the dialectic of faith and culture and the relation of the faith to the imperatives of power between states as well as within them.

The politics of protest from the twelfth century onward drew on a long religious tradition of the 'righteous rebel' and redemptive martyrdom.[18] Closer to home, the politics of conscience drew on a mutation of nineteenth-century Evangelicalism.[19] Whereas some of my colleagues envisaged a transition *from* the religious *to* the political, I regarded their politics as so much secularised religion and I saw the two domains of politics and religion as *constantly* interacting. The fields of religion, nationalism and political ideology are informed by the same concepts: for example, charisma and Founding Fatherhood; by the same dynamics of martyrdom, commemoration and purification; and by a precisely parallel creation of boundaries demarcating insider from outsider. Heresy could morph into treason and treason into political deviation with parallel excommunications, show trials and programmes of cleansing and extermination. Heresy, treason and political deviation considered as modalities of power all generate violence. That is why the built-in dynamics of power and violence are so central to the analysis of the forms of secularisation, and why this chapter concludes with a historical sequence that moves from heresy to treason to political deviation.

I repeat: I was suspicious of the transfer of teleology to seemingly secular history, especially ages and stages. I felt an affinity with von Ranke in his rejection of teleological history and sympathised with his famous dictum that 'Every age is immediate to God'. I saw sociology as too often subverted by over-

---

[17]   David Martin with Rebecca Catto, 'The Religious and the Secular', in Linda Woodhead and Rebecca Catto (eds), *Religion and Change in Modern Britain* (London and New York: Routledge, 2012, pp. 373–90).

[18]   Garry Runciman, 'Righteous Rebels When Where and Why?' in Bellah and Joas, *The Axial Age and Its Consequences*, pp. 317–34.

[19]   Melvin Richter, *The Politics of Conscience: T.H. Green and His Age* (London: Weidenfeld and Nicolson, 1964).

organised history, whereas history was polymorphous, cunning and perverse. Secularisation was precisely the kind of concept where description could be hijacked by transferred teleology. In my critique I indicated three ways in which the descriptive content of secularisation could be hijacked by ideology: rationalism, Marxism and Existentialism. The pioneers of Enlightenment preened themselves as the Party of Humanity, but they expropriated the religious metaphor of light and announced the Age of Reason and light emerging from the era of superstition and darkness. They condemned the past and subsumed it for their own benefit, and they sought to inaugurate universal peace by exterminating the last vestiges of religion as well as establishing the cult of reason.

If the inclusion of Existentialism now seems surprising one has to remember that in the post-war years Existentialism invaded England, largely in its French and (often) atheist version, though there was also a theological variant going back to Kierkegaard. The Existential annunciation of the autonomous self and 'Man come of Age' fed into the cultural mutations of the late sixties and consigned to history Schleiermacher's conception of religion as 'absolute dependency'. Philosophical and theological ideas – in particular God as the Ground of Being and religion as Ultimate Concern, as well as Thomas Luckmann's *The Invisible Religion* (1967), based on anthropological self-transcendence – fed an interest in implicit religion outside the churches and eventually surfaced as 'spirituality' and as Troeltsch's mystical religion.[20] There was also a burgeoning interest in the kind of speculative sociological theory associated with the Frankfurt School because it raised questions about the way religion both obscured and legitimated oppressive social structures, and promoted liberation, which anticipated a theology of liberation. Perhaps one may identify all this as the Germanic contribution, even when filtered through the USA and the 'death of God' theologians. It certainly unnerved the churches.

I expanded and developed my initial critique of secularisation partly in response to 'the standard model' as formulated by Bryan Wilson, but also taking into account other standard moves in the construction of secularisation. Bryan Wilson analysed secularisation as the replacement of communal solidarity based on religion by rationalised impersonal bureaucracy, as well as a process of functional differentiation as faith concedes its role in education and welfare to the state and the clergy concede status to alternative providers. Religion in his view loses 'social significance' and retires to the private realm. As I have already

---

[20]   Thomas Luckmann, *The Invisible Religion: The Problem of Religion in Modern Society* (London: Macmillan, 1967).

indicated, I was as dubious about sociological schemata based on contrasts of past and present – like traditional and modern, or Durkheim's mechanical and organic solidarity or Tönnies' *Gemeinschaft* and *Gesellschaft* – as I was about ages and stages. I questioned the automatic deployment of what I called nouns of process such as privatisation, rationalisation, bureaucratisation, societalisation, marginalisation and the master concept of modernisation.

I also noted that where religion survived, theory might have recourse to the idea of *artificial* retardation as if one had the kind of privileged access to the 'natural' direction of history. For example, I contrasted what I might call the Anglo-American/German-American mode of entry into 'modernity', based on a cooperation between Enlightenment and Methodist/Pietist religion (and on Weber's discussion of the small sects in America *not* the Protestant Ethic) with the French model based on a conflict of faith and Enlightenment.[21] But the former, which allowed religion access to a future, could be dismissed as an 'artificial retardation' and the latter as the natural course of events. So far as I was concerned there was no natural course of history and any idea of 'the inevitable' deserved all the opposition it could get. Of course, those who promoted the idea of 'the inevitable' could never have imagined the return of the Orthodox Church in Russia as the source of Russian identity or the triumph of the Koran and Pentecostalism in the Majority World.

Apart from ideas about the natural versus the artificial direction of history, the boundaries of concepts could be manipulated opportunistically, as when the 'apparent' religiosity of the USA was treated as 'internally secularised' following analyses like that of Will Herberg in *Protestant, Catholic, Jew* (1955) that suggested the *real* religion of the USA was America itself.[22] This insight was in itself plausible, but once you engage in a reductionism that discerns the real forces below the apparent surface you are prey to theoretical speculations that defy empirical verification. You can distinguish the real from the apparent as well as knowing the natural direction of history. Durkheim's theory of religion

---

[21] Not only did German Pietism influence British Methodism but it also ran alongside Methodism in the USA through massive German emigration. This is discussed in the most recent work on Pietism, such as Douglas Shantz, *An Introduction to German Pietism: Protestant Renewal at the Dawn of Modern Europe* (Baltimore: The Johns Hopkins University Press, 2013). The characteristics Shantz notes with regard to Pietism are shared with Methodism and Pentecostalism and associated with the advent of modernity: female agency, voluntarism, pragmatism, lay initiative, biblicism, mission, migration, perfectionism, individualism, pluralism, personal experience, emotion, mutual assistance.

[22] Will H. Herberg, *Protestant, Catholic, Jew: An Essay in American Religious Sociology* (New York: Doubleday, 1955).

as the ideal form of the Social is very suggestive but it remains a philosophical speculation. In any case, once you invoke notions like real religion and internal secularisation you have to use your criteria and vocabulary consistently over historical time and cultural space, so that you could easily identify the papacy in 1220 or Victorian England in 1870 as 'internally secularised'.

That raised the further question of your historical starting point for telling the story of *the* move from *the* religious to *the* secular. Too often narratives of secularisation utilise what I have called a handy historical tripod, one leg in our own modernity and the other two in the mid-thirteenth century at the height of the urban revolution and medieval Catholicism, and in the mid-nineteenth century at the height of the Industrial Revolution and 'Victorian Evangelicalism'. These narratives fail to enquire how far motives and behaviour were highly secular in times well before the Industrial Revolution: for example early eighteenth-century England, North America and Germany prior to the take-off of the various Awakenings.

Once you shift your criteria opportunistically, your schemata for contrasting a religious past with an irreligious modernity are in trouble, and you easily build irreligion into your definition of modernity. Contemporary Cairo can be dismissed as not *really* modern just because it is religious. Weber's work on the Protestant Ethic generated huge and fruitful debate about the functional equivalents of Protestantism elsewhere as well as relegating Protestant religion to a temporary phase in a rationalising process; but it also had the effect of privileging a particular path to modernity at the expense of other paths. Protestant history provided the history of *our* entry into *our* modernity. Moreover, there was a problem about the construction of time lines based on measuring the 'same' phenomenon over time, say, baptism, when the meaning of baptism alters radically. Metrics are crucial but they have to take into account how subjective meaning changes over time.

A Middle Range Theory of Secularisation

I accompanied my conceptual critique by the construction of a 'middle range' theory of secularisation deploying functional differentiation as a theoretical tool, and assuming that secularising tendencies were inflected by variable histories (now renamed 'path-dependency') and switched this way or that by 'crucial events' like the English Civil War and the American and French Revolutions. There were various elements that had to be assembled and integrated: basic theoretical assumptions like the role of variable history, for example crucial events and whether Enlightenment and the rise of nationalism colluded or collided with religion; analytical tools like functional differentiation; and a battery of empirical trends and data related to status, class, profession, degree and type of urbanisation. Above all I had to construct categories based to a large extent on power relations. These included the role and influence in a given culture of the intelligentsia and the teaching professions; the relation of religion to the organisation of parties and unions; the weight exercised by religion or by different religious bodies considered as pressure groups with variable proximity to power; and the degree of integration or differentiation between clergy and influential professional groups. They included the balance of power between a core area and peripheries which might have a different religious complexion, like Alsace or the American South; the degree to which power and communications were centralised or sclerotic so that elites could or could not mould the loyalties of subaltern strata; and the nexus of power between administrative elites and the security forces.

There are many 'lay' intuitions about fundamental differences of culture that bear on the construction of the relevant categories for a comparative analysis of religion and secularisation. There are quite plausible generalisations about the major cultural differences between Italy and Germanic lands north of the Alps, or between Western Europe and Eastern Europe, or Europe as a whole and the USA. As it turned out, these initial characterisations were useful; and there also seemed to be major cultural divides between North and South, East and West. Topography and geographical distance were correlated with cultural difference: mountain areas are religiously different from the cities of the plain, for example, in offering refuge to hard-pressed minorities; and some cities have areas that offer havens where migrants can gather for mutual support. In the event, I concluded that Protestant, Catholic and Orthodox cultures were systematically different, that they followed different patterns of secularisation and that they exhibited different modes whereby religion was or was not embedded in culture. I also concluded that when you cite a given characteristic, like individualism, as necessarily leading to secularisation much depends on the cultural *Gestalt*: individualism might have different consequences in a society like the USA where voluntary religious pluralism is dominant.

I also assumed on general sociological grounds that there were systematic links between all the elements in a particular cultural pattern. For example, an industrial wool town like Huddersfield in the north of England would exhibit a particular enterprising spirit, be hospitable to a faith based on voluntary membership and self-help like Methodism and have a lively associational life including brass bands and choral societies. That is a cultural *gestalt* on a small scale. The same applied to France once peasants had been converted into Frenchmen. Mass choral singing had a very different and far more political character in nationalist enlightened France and nationalist Italy than in England. Opera in Italy was popular and political, whereas in England massed choirs could be the voice of the religiously excluded. Of course, one cannot take notions of cultural integration too far. History is specific and contingent, and sociology is idiographic as well as nomothetic. History and sociology alike require the reading of signs as well as the calculations of metrics.[23]

But one does at least look to see what systematic linkages exist and how far they exhibit a particular character and colouring. I began by noting the significant differences between Protestant (and non-revolutionary) England and Catholic (and revolutionary) France as a key to very different patterns of secularisation. I also followed the strategy of Karl Marx in contrasting the different kinds of revolution in the key Western European countries: of England, with its industrial revolution; France with its political revolution and Germany with its cultural revolution. I distinguished multicultural empires from monocultural states; states that ruled over others (like England and Russia) from those that were oppressed (like Ireland and Poland); those with virtual religious monopolies (Italy) from those with duopolies (Germany); and those with varying degrees of voluntary pluralism (England and the USA). In the event I worked with a combination of whether a culture was Protestant, Catholic or Orthodox; with whether it was monopolistic, duopolistic or pluralistic; and whether it was super-ordinate or subordinate, taking into account regional and micro-nationalisms like Croatia as well as oppressed nations.

When it came to the comparison of England and France it seemed England was characterised by 'mere secularity', whereas France, particularly in the later stages of the Third Republic, was characterised by secularism in the sense of a militant rejection of religion *as such*. French secularism stimulated French Catholics to create the key data resources of the sociographic tradition known as *sociologie religieuse*, just as Dutch 'pillarisation' into separate socio-religious groupings stimulated the analysis of their collapse and subsequent secularisation.[24] French secularism dated back to the appropriation of faith by absolute monarchy and the absolute rejection of monarchs and priests by the

---

[23]   H.A. Hodges, *The Philosophy of Wilhelm Dilthey* (London: Routledge, 1952).

[24]   Jonathan Clark, *The Language of Liberty 1660–1832: Political Discourse and Social Dynamics in Anglo-American Worlds* (Cambridge: Cambridge University Press, 1994). Clark emphasises the presence of religious motives in the American Revolution.

Jacobin wing of the French Revolution. By contrast, the radical strain in English politics had roots going back to the religious protest of the Peasants' Revolt of 1381, but more immediately to the mixture of religious and political motifs present in the English revolutions of 1642 and 1689. The difference between France and England was given theoretical expression by the French historian Elie Halévy when he claimed that the rise of Methodism saved England from violent revolution on the French model. How far Halévy was right is much disputed, but his insight had a wide range of potential application; for example, the rise of Pentecostalism all over the 'Global South' could provide a religious alternative to violent revolution.

According to Jonathan Clark, the English Revolution was completed by the American Revolution, with its comparable mixture of religious and political motifs; and I argued, following Halévy, that this Anglo-American model (with extensive roots in German Pietism) is associated with the emergence of religious voluntarism and provides the global alternative to the French model.[25] I studied Pentecostalism as an extension of my work on secularisation to the global context, initially to Latin America and then to Africa, to pursue the issues raised by Halévy on the religious alternative to secular revolutionary violence and the issues raised by Weber on the economic ethic of the 'small sects' of the USA. As already indicated, I wanted to show how many alternative ways there were to modernity, unless you defined religion as *essentially* pre-modern. There really are several different routes. I stressed the route to modernity that included Pietist, Methodist and Pentecostal religion as a major component. That is a key element in my whole approach to secularisation. But there is also the Catholic Counter-Reformation route. After all, the major agency of development in much of Africa is the Catholic Church.

I had argued initially that the world was not predestined to reproduce the laicist secularism of France or the 'mere secularity' of Sweden. By the same token, alternative forms of modernisation might arise in Latin America and Africa. The supposed association of modernity with secularity, let alone non-violence, is contingent not necessary, especially once you observe the violence of the 'secular' regimes of the Islamic world. This is why I found S.N. Eisenstadt on 'multiple modernities' as significant as José Casanova on 'de-privatisation.[26]'

---

[25]   Elie Halévy, *A History of the English People in 1815 (3)* (Harmondsworth: Penguin, 1938); David Martin, 'Pentecostals: The Great-Grandchildren of Martin Luther', in der Reformationgesichtlichen Sozietät der Martin-Luther-Universität Halle-Wittenberg (ed.), *Spurenlese: Kulturelle Wirkungen der Reformation* (Leipzig: Evangelische Verlagsanstalt, 2013, pp. 245–60).

[26]   S.N. Eisenstadt, 'Multiple Modernities', *Daedalus* (Winter 2000: 129, pp. 1–30).

Moreover, Eisenstadt also argued that the radical millenarian tradition of Christianity had resurfaced in Jacobinism.[27] That was highly contentious, but it could well be related to Nicolai Berdyaev's claims about the origins of Russian communism and to Geoffrey Hosking's comment that the appalling suffering endured by the Russian Orthodox Church represented the clash of a secular messianism with a Christian messianism.[28]

The difference between England and France and between the French and Anglo-American revolutions can be related to the distribution of other cultural motifs. The distribution of peace movements and of the politics of conscience loosely corresponds to the distribution of religious voluntarism in Anglo-American cultures. The *levée en masse*, the centrality of the army and the relative absence of a politics of conscience correspond roughly to the revolutionary tradition in France, Russia and Turkey, and in Cuba and North Korea.[29] This stimulates us to ask why in Russia the army was central to the Soviet system, whereas now Russians identify with both the army and the Church in what some see as a process of de-secularisation, in spite of low levels of institutional practice. In Turkey it may be that the army is conceding a central place to the mosque, again in a process of de-secularisation. The standard theory of secularisation would deal with these seeming reversals as the partial return of the violently repressed, just at it deals with the global expansion of Pentecostalism as an interim phenomenon resulting from the breakup of organic local communities and the release of millions of migrants from close-knit, highly mediated and hierarchical modes of control.

Returning to the French–British comparison one could look at the role of the army in French imperialism and the role of the navy in British imperialism. Instead I prefer to point to the variable power of the intelligentsia in Anglo-American, French and continental European societies generally. The term 'intellectual' emerged in France at the time of the Dreyfus case when the Dreyfusards legitimated their protest at his wrongful trial by citing their credentials, just as the word 'ideologue' also emerged in France to express Napoleon's dislike of his opponents.[30] The idea of the 'intellectual' contrasts with the earlier formulation

[27] S.N. Eisenstadt, *Fundamentalism, Sectarianism, and Revolution: The Jacobin Dimension of Modernity* (Cambridge: Cambridge University Press, 1999).

[28] Geoffrey Hosking, 'The Russian Orthodox Church and Secularization', in Katznelson and Stedman Jones, *Religion and the Political Imagination*, pp. 112–31.

[29] Daniele Conversi, 'Modernism and Nationalism', *Journal of Political Ideologies* (February 2012, 17: 1, pp. 13–34).

[30] Stefan Collini, *Absent Minds: Intellectuals in Britain* (Oxford: Oxford University Press, 2005).

by Coleridge in England of the notion of a 'clerisy', with roots in Anglicanism, and with the notion of '*Bildung*' in Germany, with roots in Pietism.

When an intellectual stratum self-consciously emerged in England in the early twentieth century, for example in Lytton Strachey and the Bloomsbury group, it looked to France; and one might add that it still represented a mutation of the 'politics of conscience' in an aesthetic and/or rationalist version. Even so, writers like Charles Péguy or Charles Maurras or Georges Sorel are distinctive products of a French cultural world, not an Anglo-American one. The themes we need to develop here relate to the secular analogues of the saint and the prophet: the romantic aura of authority accredited to the political opinions of poets and novelists; the heroic revolutionary destiny attributed to the scientist or, in the case of Thorstein Veblen, to the engineer by comparison with the idle 'leisured class'.[31] The contemporary versions of the romantic aura of political accreditation, especially since the sixties, are found in the media elite and its pursuit of a secular agenda. Of course, that agenda may well have some justification, for example in contemporary Ireland, but that is a different issue. In Brazil, for example, the 'erudite' enjoy privilege in a racially hierarchical society behind a facade of racial innocence and use an anti-American nationalist rhetoric to de-legitimate the rise of kinds of religious voluntarism not under their patronage. Karl Mannheim's idea of the 'relatively unattached' intelligentsia in at least his earlier writings is yet another myth.[32]

I conclude with two observations relevant to my thesis about placing the secularisation debate in the context of relations of power, including power relations between states as well as within them, and about setting the issue in the context of the contingencies of history over a wide range of examples in cultural space as well as over the long durance of historical time. The first observation concerns the use of *critical* comparisons of cultural complexes rather than piling up transnational metrics *grosso modo*. I have regular recourse to the case of Lithuania.[33] All the Baltic States are ethnically nationalist, but in Latvia and Estonia the relation of religion to ethnicity is negative, resulting in very low levels of practice, whereas in Lithuania it is positive and practice is

---

[31]   Thorstein Veblen, *The Engineer and the Price System* (New York: Viking, 1934). Veblen spoke of the role of the technician in Soviet society.

[32]   Iris Mendel, 'Mannheim's Free-Floating Intelligentsia: The Role of Closeness and Distance in the Analysis of Society', *Studies in Social and Political Thought* (March 2006, 12, pp. 30–52).

[33]   Milda Ališauskienė and Ingo W. Schröder (eds), *Religious Diversity in Post-Soviet Society: Ethnographies of Catholic Hegemony and the New Pluralism in Lithuania* (Farnham: Ashgate, 2012).

quite high. All three states are comparable in terms of existential security, which is a variable often cited as the key to degrees of religiosity. For Steve Bruce in *Politics and Religion* this evidence supports the standard theory of secularisation because the degree of religious vitality depends on what role it plays in cultural defence, though it is worth recollecting that religion has *always* to some extent doubled for other social elements, for example the legitimation of the absolute monarchies of early modernity that we use to provide our 'religious' base line,[34]

It is at any rate clear that the variation among the Baltic States is bound up with different histories rather than different levels of existential security used as the critical variable governing degrees of secularisation in the widely quoted study by Pippa Norris and Ronald Inglehart.[35] I have long been interested in the difference between religious practice in Bulgaria and Romania, particularly since under communism in the sixties sociologists claimed that Bulgaria was well on the way to becoming a fully secularised society, apart from some backward social sectors. I do not think the explanation lies in different levels of existential insecurity. In the same way, one might ask how far the difference between the secular traditions of the Limousin and the religious traditions of Alsace can be explained by different levels of existential security rather than history. I can well believe that Sweden is more existentially secure and secular than Ghana according to the work of Norris and Inglehart, but the examples that occur to me from international and inter-regional comparisons ought to make us cautious about existential insecurity as a general explanation of difference. Existential insecurity strikes me as a rather vague category derived from off-the-peg explanations of religion.

History is our constant resource in questioning generalised trends *from* this condition *to* that condition, and the characteristic sociological over-organisation of historical data. The historian Jonathan Clark has sharply criticised the secularisation thesis and the positivism associated with it.[36] Hugh McLeod leads us to ask just how irreligious was the working class in the English Industrial Revolution; Keith Thomas to ask how religious was society at the dawn of the modern era four or five centuries ago; and Charles Taylor to ask whether the immense changes of the last half millennium can be subsumed within what

---

[34]   Bruce, *Politics and Religion*.
[35]   Pippa Norris and Ronald Inglehart, *Sacred and Secular: Religion and Politics Worldwide* (Cambridge: Cambridge University Press, 2004).
[36]   Jonathan Clark, 'Secularization and Modernization: The Failure of a Grand Narrative', *Historical Journal* (2012, 55: 1, pp. 161–94).

he calls 'a subtraction story' whereby religion constantly concedes ground to secularity and secularism.[37]

Persistent Configurations of Power

I want to conclude with a consideration of different configurations of power in different types of society to bring out what I regard as persistent shared structural characteristics. For that purpose I shall compare cultures over the last 800 years, from the 'religious' past to the 'secular' present: thirteenth-century Catholic Europe, the period of the formation of the nation state, nationalism over the last two centuries, and militant secular political ideology over the same period. The questions we need to ask concern the relevant medium of social solidarity and control, and the potential for violence wherever membership of a particular social category provides differential access to power, wealth and honour. In my examples I draw attention to the different criteria of inclusion and exclusion and of access to power, not to whether 'religion' is or is not pervasive or tolerant,

In thirteenth-century Christendom the criteria of exclusion were defined by heresy, and charges of heresy provided the dominant medium whereby the powerful identified a dangerous Other and vied with powerful Others for survival and pre-eminence. According to R.I. Moore in *The War on Heresy* (2012), the category of heresy was far from central in the first millennium of Christianity, and the existence of large numbers of Albigensian heretics as distinct from Christians seeking Evangelical simplicity is very dubious.[38] The danger represented by dualist heresy was a construction of ecclesiastical discourse derived from the schools of Paris in an overall struggle for power involving nobles and ecclesiastics, above all in the area between the Loire and the Garonne.

Coming to the early modern period, the state, often in the person of the absolute monarch, absorbed religion to make it the medium of social control, centralisation and legitimacy. The state constructed 'the Other' and engaged in campaigns of excommunication and expulsion. William Cavanaugh in *The Myth of Religious Violence* argues that far from the nation state being the happy solution to the 'wars of religion' supposedly characterising early modernity, it was the unhappy cause of them. He cites Charles Tilly: 'War made the state, and the

---

[37]   Charles Taylor, *A Secular Age* (Cambridge, Mass.: Belknap/Harvard University Press, 2007).

[38]   R.I. Moore, *The War on Heresy: Faith and Power in Medieval Europe* (London: Profile, 2012).

state made war.'[39] There were numerous factors involved in the 'wars of religion', including the state's attempt to collect taxes from an unwilling populace and to deal with the resistance of local elites to centralised control. The category of the 'wars of religion' that emerged at this time constitutes part of the founding myth of the innocent secular liberal state whereby Enlightened, rational and peaceful people confront violent, irrational religious others, particularly in the course of imperial and neo-colonial expansion. Enlightened Liberalism needs an unenlightened Other; and the myth of the *special* ability of religion to introduce irrationality and division lies behind our construction of the debate about the role of religion in contemporary society. William Cavanaugh rejects all argument that relies on ideas about what is really religious or really Christian. Vali Nasr puts forward a similar argument in his *Islamic Leviathan* (2001).[40] He reminds us that the state can do nothing for good or ill without hegemony and a source of social solidarity as distinct from sheer brute force. Islamism is the process of employing Islam for the purposes of state power and varies from country to country. There is no such thing as 'true Islam' apart from its use to undermine political rivals. In fragmented societies Islam provides the state with a medium of control and a way of exerting some control over Islamic dissidents by incorporating them, though this can have the awkward consequence of installing them at the heart of government.

If we turn to nationalism as discussed by Daniele Conversi we find rather different constructions of the Other, but the same dynamics of centralisation, survival and expulsion. Deploying the problematic set out by Conversi, we can trace the theme of purification through all the ethnic expulsions and the cultural and physical eliminations of recent centuries, from the treatment of Native Americans up to the Turkish Revolution and the neo-paganism of Nazi Germany.[41] If we turn finally to political ideology it becomes clear that ordinary politics, even in the most liberal democracies, are not governed by reason: we need only think of the comminatory language of thuggery, terrorism and vandalism indiscriminately deployed against opponents. I could have taken my examples from British, Dutch, Belgian, French or American Liberal Imperialism and all the barbarities each of these imperial systems committed against the Other, often in the name of the Enlightened distinction between the barbarous and the civilised. Instead I take what Geoffrey Hosking has to say about the

---

[39]   Cavanaugh, *The Myth of Religious Violence*, p. 163.

[40]   Vali Nasr, *Islamic Leviathan: Islam and the Making of the State* (Oxford: Oxford University Press, 2001).

[41]   Conversi, 'Modernism and Nationalism'.

clash between secular messianism and Orthodox messianism in Soviet times, and the elimination of persons so that they either ceased to exist symbolically or were exterminated physically.[42] Excommunication is characteristically executed on the body or on material objects with high symbolic value: in late medieval Europe inquisitors ensured that the bodies of dead heretics were dug up for burning; in late modern Europe nationalist Serbians ethnically cleansed Bosnian Muslims by acts of extreme violence against their bodies, and burned down mosques; in Russia in Soviet times the agents of the state and its ideology not only murdered dissidents but also turned churches into storehouses or blew them up, and even on one occasion lined up sacred icons to shoot them as signs of resistance to collectivisation.

In the creation of non-persons the key weapons lie in how you manipulate boundaries and the way you shuffle the meaning of words. Throughout this chapter I have drawn attention to the key role of definitions and how you construct the boundaries of concepts. Here it is as well to remember the dictum of Humpty-Dumpty in the English children's classic *Through the Looking Glass*: 'The question is,' said Alice, 'whether you can make words mean so many different things.' 'The question is,' said Humpty-Dumpty, 'which is to be master – that's all.'

---

[42]   Hosking, 'The Russian Orthodox Church and Secularisation'.

PART 1
Religion, War and Violence

Chapter 2
The Problematic

How could Christianity, which in its foundation documents has no honour code and categorically rejects reciprocal violence, become implicated in what it most vehemently rejects? How could the text of the Sermon on the Mount become the Sacred Scripture of the crusaders without the evident contradiction sparking a social convulsion or the direct and unequivocal repudiation of Christianity by the principalities and the powers? How could aristocracies based on blood ties and feudal obligations of service owed by serf to lord tolerate a liturgy that in the *Magnificat* daily promises to 'put down the mighty from their seats' and exalt 'the humble and meek'? How could merchants bent on accumulating wealth at all costs regularly recite a Scripture which sends the rich 'empty away' and preaches 'good news' to the poor? To Christians who take the New Testament seriously, the facts of Christian history pose a moral problem that can become surprisingly acute. We should not be surprised at that. The main reason Christians find Christian history such a moral problem is because they are Christians.

To sociologists Christian history poses no problem at all because the exigencies of power in different situations and in different types of society inflect and deflect the religious template built into the 'official' ideology of dominant elites. What else? The religious template appears to be radically unsuitable for a society based on a rigid social hierarchy and a warrior ethic, yet the hierarchy of the Church to a large extent mirrors the social hierarchy at large and supports a code of chivalry that in principle accepts the warrior ethic. The New Testament remains 'on the books', ceremonially elevated as the highest moral authority of a civilisation, and that means that elements of its radical iconography are incorporated in the iconography of power. The cross, once a sign of a convicted felon thrust outside the city, becomes a sign that claims dominion over the *orbis terrarum*. Galilee has become Christendom.

Of course, the original sign language remains in place as a 'sign of contradiction', to be picked up by those who have eyes to see and ears to hear, especially perhaps on the margins of society; but its impact will be partially confiscated, muted and reinterpreted, and those aspects of Sacred Scripture relatively amenable to the exigencies of power and hierarchy will be selectively emphasised. Almost I apologise for pointing out what ought to be obvious yet is not at all obvious because these self-evident facts of a very extensive assimilation to a warrior ethic and a feudal hierarchy (or, to take a later instance, an extensive assimilation to the burgeoning commercial cultures of Amsterdam and London) are cited against Christianity *as such*, including its radical template. The history of the most comprehensive revolution in history is cited against itself.

What happened in the late Roman Empire, East and West, in the Middle Ages, and in early modernity, is just what you would expect given the stark realities of our biological inheritance, and above all given the dynamics of wealth and power and the social solidarity of Us versus Them. Political necessity will for the most part, *but not entirely*, override a Gospel message opposed to violence and all that is entailed by 'great possessions', and sequester just those images and texts from Sacred Scripture that suit its purposes. What remains crucial is not the extent to which the Gospel message is overridden but the extent to which it remains on the books to be read, recited and sometimes heeded. Even kings can hear and within the limits of their warrior code heed the message, as when Athelstan in tenth-century England sought penance and absolution for his violent disposal of a royal rival. Assimilation is inevitable, but an alternative has been written into the script of a civilisation beyond erasure. For the rest feudal kings and lords will select those narratives that extol the 'God of battles' and the mighty deeds of 'the Lord's Anointed'; expansive early modern monarchies will select images of the supposedly expansive and prosperous monarchies of David and Solomon; early modern republicans will turn to a covenant relation between God and the People based on unhappy experiences of the institution of kingship recorded in Scripture concerning Saul or Ahab or Jeroboam ('the man who made Israel to sin'); and some people, often but not always on the margins, will proclaim the equality of all made in the image of God, share goods in common and reject the *ius gladii*.

I have already given the obvious answer to my initial questions, but it has scant chance of being taken on board because it runs athwart powerful ideological narratives that presuppose the *intrinsic* implication of religion in violence, not to mention injustice and repression. These narratives load the 'blame' onto religion for what is built into the exigencies of social organisation under various constraints, and treat religion as a scapegoat for what on any realistic assessment is bound to happen. Indeed, some of those who load the blame on to religion are themselves notable advocates of realism about the likely course of human affairs. That is why towards the conclusion of my argument I give an account of the ideological narratives on which critics of religion, both realist and utopian, draw. At the same time one can hardly expect western intellectuals to give up these narratives when they provide such an endless source of historical self-congratulation, historical innocence and personal righteousness.

So my first question about Christianity's fall from grace into violence generates my second question. Why does such a large segment of the western intelligentsia continue to propagate an ideologically saturated account of the problem of religion and violence when it poses no problem at all? The problem exists precisely for Christians who have not taken the measure of everything implied by the survival of the fittest, or who are at the very least not reconciled to it. It also exists for those secular people who are so unconsciously imbued with the hopes of a better world set forth in the Gospel (and elsewhere) that the realities of the human condition as revealed by history and social science, let alone biology, make the whole world seem out of joint. That is just what the Christian Gospel does both for those who believe and for those who find in the facts of Christian history incontrovertible reason not to believe. Of course, there is one explanation that would seriously truncate my argument. If we set aside sheer intellectual incompetence and conscious malpractice on the part of those who load the onus of human misery onto a phantom entity they denominate 'religion' (as though unconscious of how the term is embedded historically and indifferent to its incoherence), we are left with reluctance on the part of natural scientists and the arbiters of opinion to understand the problems and practices of sciences that do not project missiles or manipulate genes. Sociology shows that what happened historically is just what you would expect to happen; but sociology is not sufficiently understood or taken on board for a 'most favoured' narrative blaming religion to be dumped on the rubbish heap of failed explanations and distorted representations.

The obvious answer to my first question about the historical distortion of the Christian Gospel lies in the varying relationships of Christianity to particular historical situations, particular modes of social organisation and different kinds of power. You cannot treat the relation of Christianity to war and violence as a constant. Any statement about Christianity in general in relation to violence, let alone about religion in general, is liable to verbal sleights of hand, ideological misrepresentation and circular arguments. That is why I discuss below the problem of rhetorical 'sentences', by which I mean opinions encapsulated in minute linguistic packages demarcated by a subject, verb and object, as these are deployed in public debate. These packages are vehicles for the concentrated dissemination of the 'most favoured' ideological narrative and have little if anything to do with scientific discourse in either the natural or the social sciences.

The answer to my second question about the dominance and persistence of ideological narratives that lay much or even most of the onus for the violence of human history on 'religion' is more complicated and less easy to put across. These narratives – so useful, normative and emotionally satisfying to western elites, and so inimical to any sociological understanding of the relation of religion to violence – have themselves to be situated and contextualised in terms of historic struggles for dominance, above all in France. It is this French narrative I highlight in the concluding section of this particular sequence of discussion.

No wonder these ideological narratives appear more obviously true than my obvious sociological answer, and no wonder my all-too-easy answer is so difficult to get across. It does not fit a wider story. What intelligent person would forgo the effortless rhetorical advantage of excoriating and demanding the excision of the remnants of Christian civilisation in the cause of *peace* on earth and goodwill among peoples, as well as in the name of scientific truth and public virtue? Who would give up the pleasures of proclaiming unique historical innocence and assuming the mantle of a moral heroism allied to an intellectual honesty and superiority, particularly in the role of the knower, the scientific hero? Who would relinquish so simple and at the same time so *moral* an answer to a contentious question, only to get lost in an interminable and indeterminate enquiry in a social scientific discipline for which your average humane warrior for the truth has neither understanding nor respect?

There is another blockage in the way of accepting a social scientific answer to the question of religion and violence. It is that this same most favoured narrative includes a sub-narrative about the rationality of the public sphere within which such issues are debated and the 'most favoured narrative' disseminated. Two delusions would have to be jettisoned simultaneously, and that is far too much to expect if you have any realistic assessment of human affairs. The virtual domination of the public sphere with ideologically saturated narratives is self-evident whatever ideal visions and philosophical disquisitions one might propose as to what *ought* to be the case. The public sphere is demonstrably not an arena for the free passage of rational discussion and conversation between equals. On the contrary, it has become an arena for sensational and personalised 'news', for mediatised razzmatazz further debased by the advent of new technology and for gladiatorial polemics encapsulated in just the kind of sentences I propose to analyse. The rational content of conversation in the public sphere is time and again no more than an exchange between celebrities granted special licence on account of irrelevant credentials, and in the context of discussions about 'religion' and violence the credentials of a natural scientist, Richard Dawkins, provide the most obvious case in point.

When it comes to religion and violence, or Christianity and violence, context is all, or nearly all. There are several critiques of Christianity, including one by Nietzsche that dismisses it as the religion of slaves and of slavish compassion for the underdog. Nietzsche's view can be set aside because there is much to be said for it. Only two critiques are worth taking up for our purposes here. One critique dismisses Christianity as politically passive and quietist, and therefore indifferent to the necessary virtues of soldier and citizen in defence of the polity or the human right of the citizen to wage revolutionary war against tyrants. The other critique dismisses Christianity as chronically inclined to exceed the requirements of legitimate defence by supporting aggressive wars, sometimes in the cause of 'Christian civilisation', sometimes in the cause of confessional states like Poland and Sweden or of nations loosely defined as Christian, like the USA. To ask why there are two such contradictory critiques implies the answer. Whether Christianity is dismissed as too aggressive or too passive in part depends on whether it is defined as the ideological mainstay of a civilisation or nation state, or as a voluntary group. Christianity began as the latter and became the former, and therefore reflected the modes of power and forms of violence characteristic of the social contexts in which it was embedded.

In the case of the Roman Empire, Christianity can be dismissed by enlightened rationalism, for example by Edmund Gibbon in his *Decline and Fall of the Roman Empire*, as leaving to others the defence of civilisation against barbarism and replacing civic virtue in the here and now by an intolerant and superstitious asceticism focussed on the world to come. In the case of the warring city states of the Renaissance, the peaceable enclaves of Christian monasticism can be decried by the representatives of the Prince as evading the duties incumbent on citizens and encouraging an effeminate and ignorant preoccupation with 'another world'. The state churches of the Renaissance period took the same attitude to the voluntary Christian groups that emerged on the radical wing of the Reformation. In Article 37 of its Thirty-Nine Articles of Religion, the Church of England explicitly condemned those who refused to take up arms at the command of the magistrate and 'serve in the wars'. Article 37 and Article 38 condemning community of goods together remind us of the issues constantly raised in the radical Christian tradition, including, of course, the Radical Reformation.

In the developing world today some forms of Christianity, for example Pentecostalism, can be accused of failing to take up arms against oppressive regimes by people who in other contexts accuse Christianity of being all too prone to legitimate violence. According to Claudio Véliz (in a personal communication), a great many women in Latin America were very fed up with the macho posturing of their irresponsible menfolk. They were attracted to Pentecostalism because it replaced the violent street with the peaceful commensality of the domestic table. Some men were only too relieved to become domesticated and put their Kalashnikovs in storage, roughly following the pacific vision of Isaiah where spears are converted into pruning hooks. Different historical and cultural contexts generate different narratives about Christianity and violence. These will change markedly in the course of the transition from a pagan empire to the Catholic civilisations of the Middle Ages and the Renaissance, and in the course of the transition from the early modern confessional state to the kind of global voluntarism represented by Pentecostalism. Serious discussion of religion and violence demands systematic cross-cultural comparison, yet that is almost entirely lacking in contemporary debate. Cross-cultural comparison according to norms well established since J.S. Mill is the *sine qua non* of serious debate, yet all we have is the indiscriminate citation of instances taken out of context solely to serve the purposes of an ideologically predetermined conclusion.

I pivot my discussion on the emergence of an aggressive 'New Atheist' critique of religion that privileges the negative narrative over the positive, and does so from a 'scientific' viewpoint which contravenes every norm of social scientific investigation. That forces me to engage to some extent with the difference between statements made by natural scientists about the physical and biological worlds and statements made by social scientists about the human world. The difference between the scientific intentionality appropriate to socio-historical issues and the scientific intentionality appropriate to natural phenomena is crucial, and yet it is systematically elided. Indeed, the social sciences are abused precisely because they adopt a scientific intentionality and methodology appropriate to their subject matter. The human world can only be understood *scientifically* if you understand means and ends, meanings, motives and intentions as these are variably realised in widely different contexts. The arguments about causation appropriate to social science operate according to a different *ceteris paribus* clause to those of natural science because social science has to deal with subjectivity and, *therefore*, with the sheer specificity and contingency of history and historical location. Social science must cope with meaningful narrative.

Yet, as already indicated, the 'New Atheists' persist in citing assorted instances of religion and war taken indifferently from different periods, different types of society and different situations, irrespective of context, provided they illustrate their claims. This represents bad faith on a massive scale, and yet it is applauded as the exploits of a modern Mr Valiant-for-Truth. The 'New Atheists' pay scant attention to the constructed and historically embedded nature of the categories deployed, notably 'religion' and 'science', and they successfully avoid any nuanced scrutiny of the *degree* and *kind* of religious involvement in war and violence, as that varies, say, between the Knights Templar in 1320 and the Quakers and others who founded the first Peace Societies in 1816. Above all they fail to enquire why, say, Christianity and Buddhism embrace non-violence in their origins and foundation documents, and yet embrace violence elsewhere with what might seem to be unseemly enthusiasm, apart from the banal observation that when Christians or Buddhists come to power they change their tune. The observation is worse than banal because those Christians who eventually came to occupy the seats of power in Rome in the centuries after Constantine were not the same people, nor did they come from the same social stratum, as those persecuted under various emperors from Nero to Diocletian.[1]

It is distinctly odd when a public debate by 'scientists' conforms to the quick fixes, rhetorical ploys and gladiatorial confrontations between celebrities characteristic of the public sphere. Perhaps this is because these contributions to public debate seek to firm up slack atheist identities rather than advance social scientific understanding. It is almost equally odd that the animus manifested against religion on the grounds of its violence appears to derive from a standpoint that takes the Sermon on the Mount as the baseline for criticism. This is what I mean by the unconscious assimilation of the perspectives of the Christian Gospel by self-conscious secularists who take on board precisely the disjunction that Gospel generates between what we might hope for and what we indubitably observe. I do not for one moment suggest that 'New Atheists' like Richard Dawkins believe in the Sermon on the Mount as a rule of life for themselves, though they clearly regard it as one of the least 'offensive' texts in Scripture. I mean that they *talk* as though they, and all other enlightened persons, agree that war is an *unequivocal* evil along lines that approximate classical Christian pacifism and which may even draw persuasive power from the prestige enjoyed by the Sermon on the Mount.

They do this without any rational consideration of the proper occasions of war, whether in defence of civilisation against barbarism, in revolt against tyranny or in defence of the state against international predators.[2] Worse, they proceed in insouciant indifference to the findings of science. Given their pretensions this is peculiarly offensive. The natural science of biology proclaims the struggle

---

[1]   Peter Brown, *Through the Eye of a Needle: Wealth, the Fall of Rome, and the Making of Christianity in the West, 350–550 AD* (Princeton: Princeton University Press, 2012).

[2]   Nigel Biggar, *In Defence of War* (Oxford: Oxford University Press, 2013).

for survival to be an empirical norm of the biological and social world alike, so that there can be nothing empirically surprising or morally outrageous about its prevalence in all the discourses of power, religious or otherwise. It is richly paradoxical that 'New Atheists', in particular Richard Dawkins, should document *empirically* the inevitability of the struggle for survival, and even in some cases proclaim the (dubious) malign inevitability of religion, and at the same time complain *morally* about these quasi-natural phenomena as though they believed in the doctrine of free will and had never heard of Kant's famous dictum that 'ought implies can'. This is like screaming moral abuse at a car for refusing to start: it is as infantile as it is unrealistic. Unless 'New Atheists' are willing to set out in depth what they regard as the proper occasions of war, for example in defence of peace, this amounts to moral free-loading and free-wheeling on an impressive scale. They are like individual snipers firing opportunistically from hidden positions, and acknowledging no principle of internal consistency. Impact is all.

When people in the name of science ignore the norms of social science and fail to specify the proper occasions of violence, they further debase public debate. Public debate licenses the verbal violence of 'scientific' celebrities and encourages them to maraud at will beyond the sphere of their competence. My argument examines the rhetorical moves made by participants in public debate, in particular the 'New Atheists'.

With regard to the special character of the social sciences (understood as the pre-eminent site for any serious discussion of religion and violence) I argue that they include provinces of meaning that exhibit the *distinctive* truths of human and social existence. These are the concern of all the social sciences, of history, art and literature, *and* of the theologies of the major world religions. I make no apologies for referring unequivocally to truths that fall outside the natural science model as 'truths' in spite of all the dogmatic statements that endeavour to restrict truth claims to one mode of natural scientific observation and in spite of the pan-relativism adopted by some exponents of post-modernism.

There are forms of observation that illuminate vast ranges of carefully sifted experience or paradigmatically summarise and re-present the realities of the human condition, and there are other forms of observation and paradigmatic summaries that mis-represent that experience and distort those realities. The former I count as true, the latter as false. Moreover, it should not be that difficult to devise a spectrum running from extended observation to paradigmatic re-presentation together with some indication of the way criteria of judgement require appropriate modification as one moves from one end of the spectrum to the other. Some of those modifications relate to a further spectrum of major importance that runs from exempla centred on collective entities and exempla focussed in varying degrees on the individual. One needs to modify criteria of judgement as one moves from (say) the violent *collective* reactions of Hungarians and Serbs to what they perceive as paradigmatic historic defeats; to Schiller's play *Wallenstein* where *individual* characters are both agents and victims of the multitudinous sources of violence in the 'wars of religion'; and then to the *dramatis personae* of the Passion story focussed on Christ as both *individual* agent and victim. True re-presentation includes specific situations and individuals which dramatically focus the paradigmatic action. One of the classic complaints about Christianity focusses on 'the scandal of particularity', but there is no such scandal outside the specific domain of abstracted reason and generalised empirical observation. History includes the particular, and it includes the general understood most comprehensively and profoundly in the particular.

Distorted observation, and partial or mis-representation, define what is not true. In short, the concept of truth cannot be abandoned in the human sphere any more than it can be abandoned in the sphere of natural science. The concept of criticism is unintelligible without it, and the intellectual task is to give an account of its modes. One has to ask how an account of corruption and of its corrosive consequences in politics and economics differs from the account of the corrosive and tragic effects of, say, jealousy such as you find in Shakespeare's *Othello* or from the account of the moral deteriorations and likely tragic denouement following from the pursuit of untrammelled power at all costs such as you find in Goethe's *Faust*. One has also to consider the truths about humanity and about the corruptions of power that are uncovered and discovered in the moral confrontations and likely tragic consequences that flow from the embrace of unflinching moral integrity and non-violence as these are depicted in the Gospels. I explore the varied *kinds* of truth shared by all the non-positivistic disciplines and choose eventually to focus on the kind of truth exhibited by the moral template of non-violence found in the foundation documents of Christianity, above all in the narrative of the Passion. I examine that narrative, as it derives directly from the Sermon on the Mount, because together the Sermon and the Passion story help generate the quite *distinctive* problematic of violence in Christian societies.

They do so precisely because the New Testament runs counter to the necessities of the struggle for survival exposed by both the social and the biological sciences. Internecine struggles and associated codes of face and honour constitute a default position in human history and present no problem, yet they are contradicted by the non-violent Christian template or repertoire. *Struggle can be taken for granted, whereas non-violence requires explanation.* The non-violence of the Sermon on the Mount as it is followed through and realised in the narrative of the Passion is scarcely the easiest aspect of Christianity to take on board given the obvious consequences of its adoption for the maintenance of a civilised or reasonably peaceful existence, or indeed for the continued existence of Christianity itself in a Europe threatened by hostile invaders for well over a millennium.

It is not in the least surprising that Christianity devised strategies of negotiation, compromise and assimilation as it spread in societies characterised by discourses of power and codes of honour. On the contrary, the history of Christianity – including all the objectionable inferences drawn from this or that element in the biblical narrative, say, about the nature of woman or sexuality, some of it based on the vast corpus of false and primitive science – follows precisely the course you would expect. You simply need to grasp the type of society in question and its stock of approved knowledge and to trace how that interacts with a religion whose original repertoire puts such a fundamental query against the raw realities of power.

In examining the process of negotiation, compromise and assimilation between the original repertoire and the kinds of face and honour found in different kinds of society, I focus on feudal monarchy and early modernity and the transition between them. Inevitably the Christian Church between 1250 and 1700 turned to those parts of its Scriptural repertoire most compatible with the types of society in which it exercised power, and found them most often in the Old Testament, though texts in Paul and the Pastoral Epistles also proved serviceable. Apart from the enactments of liturgy, which were in any case shrouded by a classical language, the presentation of Christianity was often loaded towards the Old Testament, so that rulers fashioned their self-understanding in the image of Solomon, David, Hezekiah or Josiah. Appropriations of the figure of Christ crucified by monarchs and ecclesiastics were much less popular because less plausible and persuasive, except when deployed at tangents that ignored the stripping away of the human dignity of Christ by the legally constituted authorities in 'Church' and state. The Godly Prince of the Renaissance ruling *jure divino* found scant gratification in the role of a convicted felon.

The Sequence of Discussion

My discussion is divided into three. First I examine the nature of the debate on religion, war and violence, in particular the distorted relation between the

The Problematic 43

logic of the social sciences and the rhetoric of public debate. I try to expose the disparity between the rhetoric of the main participants, particularly those who have become celebrities in the anti-religious cause, and what would be required by sociological enquiry. I make two moves. I foreground the miniaturised violence and verbal pugilism on display in the conduct of the debate. I then place this violence in the wider perspective of the *endemic* role of violence at every level of social interaction, from the most general, where nations struggle over territory, to the intimate duels and the parades of dominance over territory we find in domestic relations.

In my second section I develop the points I made earlier about the many varieties of truth aside from the truths promoted by natural science, at least when it is misgoverned by the restrictive protocols of philosophical positivism. Positivism is an add-on but is often implied by the approach of the 'New Atheists' when scorn is poured on all the varieties of observation, representation and truth-telling that do not conform to the natural science model. These other varieties of truth are found within the social sciences *and* in all the humanities – including history, literature, the arts *and* theology – and they are part of the defence of all these disciplines, especially theology, against contemporary kinds of attack framed in terms of alien criteria. One might in a preliminary way describe them as the truths of human existence, characterised by narrative and by the contingency of history. I need to repeat what I earlier indicated. The *exempla* I offer in this second section illustrate the kinds of truth found in historical and tragic drama, and the kind of truth about non-violence and violence uncovered and discovered in the kerygmatic Christian narrative of the Passion. They show that the moral integrity intrinsic to that narrative, from the initial announcement in the Sermon on the Mount to what is *almost* foreordained in the Passion, runs counter to 'the grain of the universe' as articulated by natural, biological, social and psychological science: Newton, Marx, Darwin, Freud, Machiavelli and Nietzsche.

In my third section I shift the discussion to the ideological sources of the debate about violence and religion and to the modes of argument intrinsic to these ideological sources. I contrast rival narratives about religion and violence, first those of the French and the American Enlightenments, and second those of Protestants and Catholics. I show how contemporary critiques adapt motifs selectively from negative aspects of these narratives and combine them with a revised version of the nineteenth-century opposition between fundamentalism and science. These critiques often pivot around the difference between the empirical provisionality of science and the non-empirical reliance on authority, especially the stabilised authority of texts made possible by the invention of alphabetic scripts, presumed to be characteristic of certain kinds of religion. I say 'certain kinds of religion' because stabilised texts are a late development and distinctly atypical in the *longue durée* of history, even though the axial religions of the last three millennia, with their sacred or normative texts, are now numerically dominant. This point is implicit in Pascal Boyer's *Religion Explained* where he shows that the religious forms of the Axial Age, in particular monotheism, are quite unrepresentative of religion in general, at least as he chooses to define it as the hyper-detection of agency in the interests of survival.[3] Those forms of religion that might plausibly underwrite the idea that religion is to be 'explained' as the hyper-detection of agency have only a modest overlap with those forms that are stabilised in sacred texts accorded unique authority.

Curiously, there are forms of fundamentalist Christianity which believe that faith provides information about natural causation within the same universe of discourse as natural science. We have the strange spectacle of struggles between standard science and 'Creation science' equally based on false premises about the nature of Christianity: the blind 'New Atheists' wrestle with the blind 'Creationists', and they both stand and fall together as they stumble into the ditch.

I suggest that all our life choices and commitments, not simply those of religion, are non-empirical, and that these include the optimistic secular meta-narrative of progress.[4] I cite various kinds of rhetorical manipulation, for example where rhetorical protagonists point to supposedly obvious instances of the involvement of religion in violence without further analysis of historical and cultural context. I conclude with two passages, one concerned with the conditions of justified war, and the other with the difference between the role of religion in archaic civilisations and in the Axial Age where the emergence of different angles of transcendence on the world creates meta-narratives within the major world religions in varying degrees contrary to 'the grain of the universe' as exposed by the biological and social sciences. Confucianism, Buddhism, the Indian scriptures, Islam, Judaism and Christianity all embody different angles of transcendence that provide varied vantage points to review the world as it is from different perspectives, for example the perspective of 'the kingdom of God', and have to engage in different modes of negotiation with the structures of power.

---

[3]   Pascal Boyer, *Religion Explained: The Evolutionary Origins of Religious Thought* (London: Vintage, 2001).

[4]   Brad Gregory, *The Unintended Reformation: How a Religious Reformation Secularized Society* (Cambridge Mass.: Harvard University Press, 2012).

Chapter 3

The Rhetorical Issue of Sentences about Religion and Violence

Just as the scrutiny of kinds of truth is central to my argument, so is the scrutiny of sentences where the 'essentially contested' category of 'religion' plays the role of a 'subject' to which some inherent characteristic x and some likely consequence y is attributed. In ordinary discourse, including debate over religion and violence, we take such sentences for granted, whereas they are highly problematic. That matters for two closely connected reasons. The first relates to the way we conventionally label 'religion' as a definable and delimited entity when it is nothing of the kind. The second relates to the way the illusory 'entity' denominated religion is saddled for polemical purposes with *specific* characteristics and consequences which are in reality shared by *all* the varied discourses of power. For example, campaigns and rituals of purification are the common currency of religion, political ideology and nationalism.

As in the case of purification rituals, the saddling of religion with *specific* characteristics *shared* by all the discourses of power is a prime example of that kind of rhetorical falsehood. When we articulate a sentence claiming that an entity we identify as 'religion' *is* this or *does* that, we are not so much making an empirical statement covering a set of interrelated characteristics, as offering a stipulative definition of *what we understand religion to be* for the purposes of a particular argument based on a rhetorical wrestling match fixed in advance to deliver a foregone conclusion. Polemicists not only take the part for the whole, but assume what is to be proved, cite examples out of relevant context, manipulate criteria to serve their purposes, forget that statements are provisional, and deploy *odium theologicum*. By definition scientists do not do this. When it comes to issues of religion and war Richard Dawkins is a polemicist, and one who does not care how much he contradicts himself provided he can get away quickly with the sudden thrust. One moment he claims that he (helped on by the revelatory impact of the religious violence of 9/11) has put to flight the dwindling powers of superstition, while the next moment he expresses alarm at their menacing recrudescence.

Take, for example, the constantly reproduced sentence from Chapter 11 of *The Selfish Gene*: 'The meme for blind faith secures its own perpetuation by the simple unconscious expedient of discouraging rational enquiry.'[1] This is an elegant and seemingly simple sentence that appears to nestle innocently within a scintillating wider argument. For the average incurious atheist it provides the pleasurable assurance of very special exemption from the deadly virus infecting the intellectual operations of those routinely dismissed as 'believers', including presumably people like Leszek Kołakowski and Alasdair MacIntyre. But put logical and empirical pressure on the sentence and it oozes problems. You need to know first whether specifically 'blind faith' is a subcategory of faith, or alternatively inheres in the very idea of faith. The context strongly implies the latter – that faith is by definition inherently blind; but if that is so, the postulated consequence of a 'meme' for blind faith in terms of resistance to rational enquiry is likewise true merely by definition. The meme inserted in the sentence in order 'unconsciously' to reproduce this unhappy condition as an entity, equipped with quasi-agency, is effectively a *deus ex machina*, doing no empirical work. The context also implies that blind faith is an inherent property of religion when blind faith is either a dubious and abusive metaphor for a condition affecting an extraordinary variety of types of commitment, or else it functions to define *all* these types of commitment as 'religious'. Clarity about these complicated matters is not helped when Richard Dawkins routinely claims that Christians do *not* believe what they are signed up to (a useful tactic for initially disconcerting Christian debating partners), and that faith is *culturally* acquired (rather than biologically through memes) by the 'child abuse' of early religious socialisation. The only way to get at the truth of these matters is by recourse to evidence. Historically we know, as Alec Ryrie has reminded us, that Christianity has been rather too inclined to offer reasons for faith.[2] But there is a vast amount of contemporary evidence that religious or spiritual attachments come in many modes, most of them subject to some more or less thoughtful consideration, and that the distribution of such attachments – high, for example, in Poland, vanishingly small in the former East Germany – depends on historical conditions for religious attachment or identification that vary massively depending on whether you are east or west of the Oder–Neisse line. In short, the *deus ex machina*, aka the meme, is as good as dead.

---

[1]   Richard Dawkins, *The Selfish Gene* (Oxford: Oxford University Press, 1976, p. 198).
[2]   Alec Ryrie, *Being Protestant in Reformation Britain* (Oxford: Oxford University Press, 2013).

In the framing of rhetorical sentences we may in an entirely arbitrary way define religion as that which in essence causes wars, or we may arbitrarily define religion as that which *in essence* binds society in solidarity. Then we can combine the two and marginally increase the exiguous empirical component by defining religion as that which binds society together and, *therefore*, causes wars. The word 'therefore' adds to the empirical content and at least tells you that social solidarity among Us generates the seeds of conflict with social solidarity among Them, though this observation is far too generalised to be of much empirical use. It is too generalised precisely because religion is very far from the only entity that binds society together and therefore causes wars. The link between the solidarity of Us and conflict with Them is genuine but it takes numerous forms, not all of them religious, and there are many forms of religion to which it is irrelevant. That is what I mean when I say that what we conventionally call 'religion' is polemically singled out as moral scapegoat for characteristics that inhere in all the discourses of power and solidarity.

No wonder social scientists are so wary of loose statements about hypostasised 'entities' like 'religion' and insist on attaching a massive qualifying rubric. None of the verbal concepts of sociology can be treated unproblematically as a bounded 'entity' constructed on a crude version of the natural science model. The semantic depth and historically inflected nature of concepts in the social sciences drives a deep ditch between them and the natural sciences. Some natural scientists maraud across the ditch without having the faintest suspicion they are trespassing on ground they *systematically* misunderstand. The settled modes of operation native to the natural science side of the divide, such as metrics, have a strictly limited purchase across it. In social science metrics are pointers and circumscriptions to be deployed with a proper caution about the seemingly solid and historically stable entities they purport to measure.

I am interested in sentences, arguments and styles of public rhetoric concerning religion, war and violence. Unless we recognise how these operate we lack a baseline to move the argument forward. We have to become properly conscious of how locutions and discourses about religion, war and violence veil their tautological, moral and polemical character behind statements with only the most exiguous empirical purchase. Acquiring that consciousness depends on the scrutiny of concrete examples, some of which are here provided by Richard Dawkins, though mostly not itemised since they are easily accessible on the Internet. I have also looked at the arguments of other 'New Atheists' like the late Christopher Hitchens, Sam Harris, A.C. Grayling and Michael Martin.

Examining the Smallest Possible Unit of Argument

I now examine the smallest possible unit of polemical assertion 'religion causes wars' understood as a core statement of position by Richard Dawkins. A relatively early instance of this kind of blanket assertion encapsulated in embryonic linguistic form can be found in an interview with Dawkins conducted on 22 January 1995 by Sue Lawley for the BBC radio programme *Desert Island Discs*. I refer to it here because it provides a perfect illustration of what I shall identify as the hit-and-run technique, where a huge assertion is made without any fear it will be taken up and subjected to analysis. However, the core assertion made in *Desert Island Discs* is not simply an off-the-cuff locution made in a moment of gross intellectual carelessness. In essence 'religion causes wars' has been repeated by Dawkins in many other contexts. His reported speeches and *obiter dicta* as found on the internet under the auspices of the Richard Dawkins Foundation show little of the provisionality he believes intrinsic to science.

The locution 'religion causes wars' exemplifies a technique constantly used when time is too short for a considered comeback. It represents a standard hit-and-run raid on the vast storehouse of history where the assailant utilises an extremely loose trope embedded in the ideological narratives I examine later. A glove has been thrown down with no real danger that the challenge will be taken up in extended combat. If the partner in this game were seriously to take up the challenge he or she would break the unspoken rules of the game. The verbal assailant achieves a cheap victory and is away before anyone can mobilise.

The Uses and Misuses of Natural Scientific Authority

One has to ask just how Dawkins gets away with it, and the answer lies in the deployment of irrelevant authority to disseminate a particular ideological narrative. The technique works because Richard Dawkins carries around the authority ascribed to the natural scientist. Of course, 'religion causes wars' is not a natural scientific statement but a quasi-social scientific bluff which anyone with the slightest knowledge of social science knows to be empty of empirical content. A socially constructed accreditation as a natural scientist, constantly trumpeted by its beneficiaries to secure uncritical reception of assorted opinions of all kinds, allows a loose ideological trope to masquerade as a social scientific statement. Yet hardly anyone registers shock because this particular ideological trope is so much taken for granted through sheer iteration that it has been 'naturalised' as possessing empirical purchase. Statements can be taken 'at face value' as obviously true through iteration and reiteration. Yet this technique for establishing falsehoods is identified as intrinsic to *religion*. The scientist pontificates without reproof on the basis of a generalised authority, whereas the *ex cathedra* statements of real popes are quite properly liable to exposure as ridiculous. The self-styled scientist breaks the first rule of scientific procedure by taking for granted what is to be proved, and engages in statements about *the* source of violence which are themselves violent speech acts, as in *An Atheist's Call to Arms* to 'wage war' on religion.

Speaking Daggers: Endemic Violence

We find violence everywhere, not just in violent struggles for supremacy between tribes and nations but also at the domestic level. Violence is endemic in each and every type of context. No wonder Christianity takes its global logo from a paradigmatic act of unjust violence committed against an innocent man. In Shakespeare's *Hamlet* we have an example of apparently senseless violence between nations. The Prince sees an army about to go into battle over a strip of barren land 'that hath no profit in it but the name'. Some social scientists might understand this as a struggle over territory with high symbolic value but no material benefit. 'Face' is a sufficient motive in itself, and 'face' is normally expressed in words. Words are potentially lethal, so that even a comma out of place can generate extreme violence and potential annihilation.[3] For others, the symbolic value has been 'referred' from its real point of origin in the territorial imperative and/or in material benefits and interests. This is a false distinction because symbol, socio-biological imperative and material gain are mutually reinforcing. Nevertheless, the *casus belli* is focussed in the symbol, whatever material forces lie behind it.

Domestic relations are like international relations. Nora in Ibsen's *A Doll's House* is the human equivalent of symbolically occupied territory, kept vacant of all intrinsic character by the dominating imperatives of infantilised 'womanliness' imposed by her husband, Torvald. Her final bid for autonomy *forces* her to leave Torvald's 'doll's house' because she can 'no longer live in the house of a stranger who does not know her'. The symbolic idea of womanliness fuses with the assertion of material control over the 'territory' of her person. This turns sexual

---

[3]   Brian Cummings, *The Literary Culture of the Reformation: Grammar and Grace* (Oxford: Oxford University Press, 2002).

mutuality into quasi-rape carried out by an occupying force, and Torvald invokes 'religion' to provide symbolic cover for the patriarchal and territorial imperative.

Violence in domestic relations is committed *inter alia* through speech acts as well as territorial enclosure, and speech acts are as a class replete with violence. To quote again from *Hamlet*, we 'speak daggers' though we 'use none'. The same verbal pugilism is evident in debates over religion and violence by 'New Atheists' like A.C. Grayling and Christopher Hitchens. The general dynamics of power represented by control of the field apply to debate, to the usurpation, domination and liberation of territory in the domestic sphere, and to acts of war to secure strips of real territory. Miniaturised verbal violence has been normalised beyond comment, and it enjoys a special licence in debates about religion and violence.

I now examine how the authority of 'the natural scientist' is deployed in debate on public issues that lie outside its remit specifically to bring out the *special* character of social science. The natural scientist claims to exercise authority on the basis of a philosophy restricting 'truth' to statements generated according to a positivist *modus operandi* and a delimited natural scientific intentionality. It seems not to matter that this philosophy is excluded by its own criterion of truth. Yet it can be protected by a blank refusal to recognise the boundaries of science or by declaring that science has made philosophy redundant. Not so. What is to count as truth is highly problematic and extends far beyond the restricted area governed by positivist protocols.

Any contention that these protocols can be straightforwardly extended to the social sciences is implausible. Yet some social scientists apparently adopt the positivist position, even though their practice is bound to be inconsistent outside an artificially restricted range of subject matter. Those who restrict the accolade of objective analysis to the operation of material forces and those who restrict it to what can be measured drastically reduce the range of issues that can be discussed 'scientifically'. The ideological sources of these restrictions in Marxism and positivism are in fact incompatible, but that does not prevent some social scientists combining them in practice. Charles Taylor has subjected these restrictive protocols to comprehensive criticism, for example in his work on Merleau-Ponty and Gadamer.[4]

Social scientific truth is saturated in language and in semantic auras embedded in historical and cultural usages. Moreover, I have already indicated there are many *kinds* of truth relevant to scientific discourse about religion, war

---

[4]   Charles Taylor, 'Understanding the Other: A Gadamerian View on Conceptual Schemes', and 'Language Not Mysterious?', in *Dilemmas and Connections: Selected Essays* (Cambridge Mass.: Belknap/Harvard University Press, 2011, pp. 24–38 and 39–55, especially p. 40).

and violence. The problem canvassed here only appears intractable because some social scientists are themselves tempted to engage in loose tropes embedded in standard ideological narratives, and because the public sphere is to a high degree saturated in such narratives. Indeed the public sphere lives *off* them and lives *by* their seeming naturalisation. Given they are constructed on the basis of ideological organisations of history constantly contradicted by the sheer contingency of history, they are versions of the Indian rope trick held aloft in the public sphere because they represent its constitutive fictions. If one wanted to be paradoxical one might even label them 'religious'. After all, they conform to the definition of religion as that which binds society together. This is precisely the situation that has led some thinkers to declare there is nothing beyond the Indian rope trick and that consequently there is no such thing as truth when it comes to our standard ideological narratives. On the contrary, there are many truths of different kinds.

The Deconstruction of Taken For Granted Power Relations

I am deconstructing the miniaturised power relations of public debate to show what they share with power relations in general, up to the level of figures of authority accorded limited licence to pronounce and aggressively to denounce, whether they are popes or 'scientists' or other persons sheltered by 'a little brief authority'. These malpractices are inaudible to the naked ear, and therefore uniquely effective. Yet sometimes the inaudible can be detected loud and clear. When Christopher Hitchens added the subtitle *How Religion Poisons Everything* to his book *God Is Not Great* he made explicit what is elsewhere implicit.[5] The subtitle is eye-catching nonsense. Yet hardly anybody says so, and Hitchens is granted the licence and even the adulation of a hero of free thinking and free speech. Instead of the barely registered thrust of the hit-and-run raid, Hitchens confronts us with verbal strutting where the alpha male protagonist beats his breast to secure attention. He deploys speech acts to convey the maximum aggression and defy anyone to risk intellectual annihilation. This is how a serious and extremely complicated issue is degraded into a populist punch-up to 'catch the ears of the groundlings'. The alpha male exhibits contempt in the aggressive style exhibited in prize fights and exchanges between combatants in tournaments conducted under the feudal code of honour.

---

[5]   Christopher Hitchens, *God Is Not Great: How Religion Poisons Everything* (New York: Twelve, 2007).

Both Christopher Hitchens and A.C. Grayling are prone to acts of gross verbal aggression that use expressions of contempt to intimidate the Other and decry their intellectual status. Hitchens backs up exaggerated expressions of contempt with quick and elegant thrusts to the solar plexus. The style of A.C. Grayling drips contempt, as when he dismisses Christians as 'away with the fairies', meaning that they are retarded at the level of deluded children. Grayling is ever ready to expound a truncated and extremely simplified historical narrative based on the key transition *from* religious ignorance *to* true scientific knowledge. It is a typical from/to construct illustrated by his contemptuous dismissal of biblical writers as 'ignorant goat herds'.

The moment debate includes an interlocutor who understands the contours of the issue in question the rhetorical approach has to change. The protagonist can neither carry out a quick underhand thrust before disappearing down an alleyway nor brazenly strut his stuff across the boards. When Richard Dawkins debated with Archbishop Rowan Williams on 23 February 2012, he set out his case in cautious depth and exhibited sweet reasonableness. His self-presentation as an apostle of reason required him to exemplify his self-assigned role. A contemptuous approach could only damage the cause of sweet reason. No killer punch can be delivered under the conventions and courtesies governing this kind of exchange and within so extended a time frame. This is partly because the protagonist is not exploiting a monopoly or an intellectual inequality, and partly because there are cruces in the argument where participants articulate assumptions beyond which it is impossible to go. On the one side these assumptions might include a positivist articulation of the limits on what are to count as meaningful statements and on the other side some exposition of the nature of historicity and associated semantic complexities. In this debate a crux occurred where the archbishop, following the classic affirmations of Christian theology, said that God is 'not an extra to be shoehorned into the universe'. Dawkins failed to see what that implied for his contention that God understood as a variable – a God particle, say, operating within the ensemble of variables – does no discernible work. A transcendent God is not an immanent factor alongside other factors to be assigned a causal role with a designated range of essentially 'mysterious' effects.

The Logic of Social Science and the Rhetoric of Public Debate

I now return to the statement 'religion causes wars' to bring out the logic of social science and the rhetoric of public debate, and the extent to which logic and rhetoric interweave. I need to establish in more detail what I understand by social science and the integrity of its procedures, not least because the findings of social science circulate as part of the accepted currency of public debate *without* being understood as a distinctive scientific practice. Social science requires careful conceptual clarification, historical contextualisation and a tentative and provisional approach. Social scientists eschew statements about a supposed 'entity' known as 'religion' in favour of initial hypotheses about what might be *more or less* likely to follow on the basis of a given set of beliefs – say, the Quakers or the Assassins – in given historical and social contexts. In those contexts they would try to elicit what Karl Popper called 'the logic of the situation'. This approach is entirely alien to the way people swap views in ordinary conversation and to the conventions of public debate over the role of religion *as such* in relation to conflict in general, or the specific role of religion in particular contemporary conflicts. A social scientist veers between intellectual shock over the display of sheer ignorance about the relevant social scientific approaches and moral shock over culpable indifference to them.

Interrogating Further the Core Component

'Religion causes wars' is a banal statement of 'the obvious' which can only become empirically productive when related both to historical and cultural context *and* to a general enquiry into the sources and dynamics of human conflict *as such* from the emergence of the species to the present day. In itself the statement is inert and uninformative. It is banal precisely because it is isolated from the almost infinitely complicated context of human conflict. That is the only arena in which it might eventually acquire a modicum of empirical force, by which time it would be qualified almost out of recognition. The claim is both an obvious truth of casual small talk and utterly ridiculous in the way so many 'obvious' truths of everyday conversation are ridiculous. No one who has even begun to think about what religion is, and enquired with some degree of systematic seriousness into the multitudinous sources of human conflict, can fail to see that taken in isolation this standard banality, articulated in a casual speech-act, conveys no information whatever. It is the question posing as an answer.

By purporting to convey information when it does next to no empirical work it conforms to what we mean by a falsehood, not as a conscious intention to deceive but by being misleading. Of course, once a speaker understands just *how* misleading such 'obvious' statements are when taken in isolation, and acquires some knowledge of the broader contextualisation required by any genuinely scientific procedure, what had been merely misleading becomes deliberate falsehood. Since we must absolve Dawkins from any intention to deceive, we conclude he simply does not know what can and cannot be said from a social scientific viewpoint. He is immunised from susceptibility to moral discomfort about making morally saturated statements under 'scientific' auspices.

An Alternative Version of the Obvious

I next draw attention to another version of 'the obvious' that sharpens the question raised by 'religion causes wars' by pointing to *almost* equally obvious facts that render it dubious. I say almost equally obvious because we have already noticed that 'religion causes wars' is so much part of a hegemonic narrative that it usually secures acceptance without conscious scrutiny. I take this second version of the obvious from Marilynne Robinson, and I observe that her contribution is animated by proto-scientific curiosity and can only be generated once the taken for granted has been subjected to conscious scrutiny. What she has to say represents stage two in the formulation of a question because it puts the obvious in question, whereas the first stage took for granted precisely what needed to be questioned.

I take my example from the Introduction to Robinson's *Absence of Mind*, a book which presents a wide-ranging critique of the positivist and consciously modernist thought represented by Dawkins and the other 'New Atheists'.[6] I am here interested only in the way she deals with a variant on the core component just discussed, which slightly enlarges the empirical range of the question by dealing with the contention that 'conflict arises out of religion, more *especially* out of religious difference'. Her next move is formally rhetorical but also proto-scientific. She says that people who hold the view that conflict arises out of religion 'would do well to consult Herodotus, or to read up the career of Napoleon'.[7] She deploys 'the obvious' *strategically* by widening the range of

---

[6]   Marilynne Robinson, *Absence of Mind: The Dispelling of Inwardness from the Modern Myth of Self* (Terry Lectures) (New Haven and London: Yale University Press, 2010).

[7]   Robinson, *Absence of Mind*, pp. xi–xii.

reference. She points out that highly generalised statements about what religion 'causes' are based on far too narrow and indiscriminate a basis of cultural and historical reference and comparison.

But then she adds that 'this thesis about the origins of conflict is novel in the long history of the debate over human origins which has typically argued that conflict is natural to us, as it is to animals and is, if not good in an ordinary sense, at least necessary to our biological enhancement'.[8] This is precisely the point I made in Chapter 1 where I underlined the oddity of claiming that conflict is endemic to humans *and* uniquely the fault of religion, *and* to be morally deplored. Having stirred up doubt by extending the range of comparison Marilynne Robinson points up just this potential contradiction. If Darwinian and Freudian explanations treat conflict as natural and built-in it seems odd to maintain that conflict has something specially to do with religion, or, indeed, to complain about it morally any more than one complains morally about tsunamis. She then points up another contradiction, which is that those who load the onus of conflict onto religion often deplore it *both* as fomenter of oppression and violence *and* as promoting dysgenic compassion. The latter is, of course, Nietzsche's criticism. This parallels the contradiction between those who accuse Christianity of political aggression and those who accuse it of political quietism. 'Religion' does incompatible things. Marilynne Robinson has not engaged in a fully fledged social scientific approach to conflict, but she has drawn attention to awkward facts and curious contradictions.

---

8   Robinson, *Absence of Mind*, p. xii.

Chapter 4
Modes of Truth and Rival Narratives

One of the principal objections to religion turns on exclusive truth claims seemingly embedded in the main world religions, and the consequences these claims entail for peaceful coexistence. Yet the concept of truth, and the concept of falsehood, emerged in a very late phase in the development of religious consciousness, and cannot be predicated of religion in general. Moreover, the concept of truth is a two-edged sword wielded not only to confound the worshippers of idols, maybe by exemplary violence, but also to establish the idea that there are criteria, including criteria that can be turned critically and prophetically against those who expound them. The issue is important because these criteria relate to *kinds* of truth and falsehood very different from those in the natural sciences, even though there may be a genealogical connection between the late emergence of the idea of religious truth and the even later emergence of the idea of scientific truth. It is a paradox that the critics of religion present themselves as exponents of the unequivocal truth of the established findings of natural (and biological) science to the exclusion of other modes of truth-telling. They too rejoice in exclusive truth claims and in a self-image as warriors, heroes and martyrs in the cause of an aesthetically satisfying beauty inherent in the truth of things as they really are. In recent times religious people have suffered a great deal from the zeal of those who restrict truth-telling to the type of truth represented by the natural, biological and social sciences. The concept of truth is a two-edged sword in *every* context, not just in the context of religious affirmations.

I have earlier suggested there is a multiplicity of kinds of truth and of non-naturalistic chains of consequence, for example in literary narrative, especially tragedy, and in history, as against the missionary zeal of those committed to the univocity of truth. The kind of non-naturalistic truth-telling found in Christianity, as well as in Buddhism and to some extent the other axial religions, runs against the grain of the realities exposed in particular by biology but also by social science. These sciences show that the struggle for dominance and its associated codes of honour and face constitute the default position of human society, alongside and as a *consequence* of the imperative of social solidarity.

Christianity distances its followers, particularly those who pursue its precepts consistently, from the empirical givens of 'the world' understood as a realm governed by what the New Testament calls 'the principalities and powers'. The chronic disparity inherent in a world temporarily under the government of 'Satan' generates the concepts of temptation and evil: hence 'lead us not into temptation but deliver us from evil'. Curiously enough this borrowed concept of evil is central to the moral judgements passed against religion by Richard Dawkins. The 'New Atheists' extract the concept of evil from its religious matrices, without noticing either its origins or its blatant incompatibility with their own philosophical positivism. Moreover, they have located a prime source of evil in the very prophetic tradition which initially exposed it through the embrace of transcendence. They naively suppose things would be so much *better* were the evil of religion removed and the natural benevolence and happy consciousness of man allowed to express itself and to flourish, even though according to their own scientific premises man is driven by the struggle for survival and haunted by religious fantasies that infect his consciousness with all the power of a destructive virus. This makes sense of the moral excoriation of religious believers. It also makes sense of the implausible optimism of the 'atheist bus' travelling around London with its message 'There probably is no God – now relax and enjoy your life', and of an optimistic programme of material redemption secured by the power and technical domination of science worthy of Auguste Comte.

Non-naturalistic discourses are not based on hypostasised entities like religion but on the impacted richness of the verbal sign according to particular historical and cultural contexts, and on the internal 'logic of the situation'. I now turn to the modes of truth-telling embedded in these discourses, including the discourse of Christianity. I look first at truths relating to religion and violence embedded in the story of the Passion central to the Christian Gospel. Christianity embodies its 'truth' in dense signs within impacted and multilayered narratives, for example, the cross understood as a dense sign at the heart of the story of the Passion. At issue here is the kind of truth exhibited in the kerygmatic narratives of a faith like Christianity. Truth of this kind does not conform to those kinds of mutually exclusive truth based on a discourse centred on discrete empirical entities and their properties.

Christian truth is based on a narrative (and its associated signs) that exhibits a moral centre of gravity generating a more immediate and organic spectrum of interpretative potentials and a more remote and incidental range of appropriations according to different situations and types of society, of which feudalism is one, early modernity another and industrial capitalism yet another. The distinction between organic and incidental cannot be demarcated by abstract and rational criteria, but only by tracing the courses of different socio-moral logics and their mutual relations and elective affinities. And what that means can only be made clear by concretely tracing the 'logic' of the organic potentials, and then the logic of the incidental appropriations. That is a delicate task quite different from stipulative definitions of what is to count as real or true Christianity.

We are not dealing with true or false in that irrelevant sense, but with overlapping logics – some of which are tightly related and others much less so. Once you understand what is meant by a centre of moral gravity you realise that these comprise a limited set and that they overlap in a manner that is far from mutually exclusive. The very notion of mutual exclusivity belongs to an alien kind of truth, and that means it really is very simplistic to argue that the field of 'religion' (meaning here the specifically axial religions) is *inherently* rife with incompatible truth claims. Alternative centres of moral gravity such as we find in Islam and Confucianism are indeed markedly different from each other, but they nevertheless overlap and interpenetrate.

Within each of the different centres of moral gravity there are varying articulations of the space between timeless Being and of Becoming as experienced by humans under the pressures of time, especially shortness of time and expectations of eschatological judgement. The major traditions contain elements of both, and one may perhaps point to a maximum difference between a Christianity concerned with moral trajectories of Becoming under the pressures of shortness of time and modes of Chinese thinking that arrest time in the pleasures of moral and aesthetic contemplation. The Christian tradition oscillates between anticipations of a kingdom achieved by the power of God and very occasional attempts to eliminate structures of hierarchy and power through the exemplary violence of revolution, whereas Chinese traditions seek simultaneously to control and legitimate hierarchy and violence through a concept of harmony which requires the hidden compulsions of self-control. This creates different balances between Being and Becoming within these two traditions. In the Christian case there are interim resting places for the experience and exploration of benevolent Being which may either take the form of aesthetic contemplation or the devotional techniques of the ascetic tradition. These visits to what in *The Pilgrim's Progress* (1678) Bunyan calls 'the delectable mountains' are not final resting places but refreshments and assurances about what may be attained when the spiritual warfare of the earthly pilgrimage comes to its final conclusion. The pilgrimage of faith and hope will involve tragic encounters with despair, guilt, pathos and bathos over the distance between what is aimed at and what is achieved, generating a drama of judgement and forgiveness, and chronic falls into the abyss of non-Being. This kind of spiritual drama of Becoming is relatively rare in Chinese civilisation.

What is crucially different about the centres of moral gravity comes out most clearly in relation to discourses of power and violence. These discourses lie so deeply embedded in human society that the contrast between them and 'non-naturalistic' centres of moral gravity such as we find in the New Testament will yield the maximum illumination of the problems at issue. I now turn to the Christian centre of moral gravity in the Passion narrative to elicit the relations it generates, organically and incidentally, to discourses of power. I have a particular interest in the tension between everything implied by non-violence in the Sermon on the Mount, as that is realised in the Passion narrative, and the honour code at the heart of feudalism and, of course, at the heart of many other types of society. The explicit prohibition of an honour code in Christianity can be rephrased as its distinctive understanding of the integrity of the non-violent Christian subject. The integrity and consistent moral responsibility of the non-violent Christian subject embodied in Jesus makes the relation of Christianity to societies where 'honour' is central particularly tense. The tension demands strategies of negotiation and interim reconciliation.

This goes beyond the Weberian account of tensions within the economic, political, aesthetic and erotic spheres to explore the pressures on self-fashioning exercised by shortness of time and imminence of judgement. According to the Gospel (John 9:4), 'the night is coming when no man can work', but in the meantime we work furiously to give an account of ourselves to redeem 'the waste sad time/ Stretching before and after.'[1] Clive James in his poem 'Dreams Before Sleeping' summons up his losses and disasters in lapidary accounts of how you may lie on 'the bed of nails you made' and transfigure your tragedies and failures into lasting poetry.[2] This is the aesthetic solution some people pursue for the whole of their lives. The logic of these silken threads of moral consequence is quite different from the hard chains of material causation found in natural science.

Art and literature in Christian civilisations are chronically concerned with the deteriorations that follow from lapses in consistent moral responsibility and with the apparently trivial and inadequately motivated first steps that eventually stumble into a moral abyss where the Christian self becomes alienated from itself

---

[1]   T.S. Eliot, 'Burnt Norton', in *Four Quartets* (London: Faber, 1945).
[2]   Clive James, 'Dreams before Sleeping', in *Nefertiti in the Flak Tower: Collected Verse 2008–2011* (London: Pan Macmillan, 2012, pp. 46–7).

and God. Interim bargains are made that appear to exact limited immediate costs but imperceptibly accelerate into monstrous moral debts that can neither be faced nor sustained. Classic instances include Marlowe's *Doctor Faustus* where Faustus cries out in despair, 'See, see, where Christ's blood streams in the firmament'; Berlioz's *The Damnation of Faust*; and the career of Tom Rakewell in Stravinsky's *The Rake's Progress*. The chronically indebted 'Christian' lives in two worlds with incompatible frames of reference which cannot be brought together and create a condition which might be described as 'moral osteoporosis'. It is precisely here that the dramas of confession and restoration take place. In many modern versions there is only waste without redemption, a form of tragedy without catharsis anticipated in Shakespeare's *Antony and Cleopatra* and *Troilus and Cressida*.

Let me move on to re-present a crucial turning point in the narrative of the Passion: the kiss of Judas. This cameo is not a statement about relations between entities summed up in the dictum *rerum cognoscere causas*, but an encounter we understand according to the logic of the situation. In sociological terms this is the deployment of the classic Weberian method of *verstehen*, except that 'understanding' is not at all specific to sociology. We understand in precisely the same way when we scrutinise what is involved in dramatic re-presentation, for example Shakespeare and Ibsen, *and* in the re-presentations of religious narrative. We 'understand' whether we consider the data of sociology or the closing scenes of *King Lear* and *Antony and Cleopatra*, or Titian's last painting of the *Pietà* or the final chapters of the Gospels. Sociology is affiliated in a profound way with the humanities, including theology. Some sociologists reject any such affiliation, perhaps for reasons connected with status anxieties about the nature and purity of their scientific intentionality as understood from a natural scientific perspective. This status anxiety complements the reluctance of natural scientists to enter into the problems and practices appropriate to social science.

The kiss of Judas represents an act of treachery consummated through the act of love. It also represents the arrest by night of the non-violent innocent by the corrupt forces of state violence 'with swords and with staves'. The arrest of Jesus is a turning point in the narrative because the range of options available to Jesus is drastically reduced. The exercise of the integrity of the non-violent Christian subject has to accept the likelihood of its own total negation and destruction rather than compromise its integrity and thwart redemption by exercising the will to power and calling on material force. The imperative of non-violence is announced and proclaimed in the Sermon on the Mount and realised in the Passion narrative, which means that Bernard Shaw's distinction between

Christianity and Crosstianity misses the intrinsic connection between word and action, between the Sermon on the Mount and the moral and existential drama of redemption.[3] The drama of redemption is one of descent into limitation without which there can be no ascent into glory: no crucifixion, no resurrection. Both Creed and Scripture agree that 'He that ascended is he that descended.' Humility and glory are as closely related as Sermon and Atonement.

The distinction between different kinds of truth is intimately related to the distinction between different kinds of causation: there are relations of cause and effect belonging to the realm of physical nature; and relations of intention and consequence that belong to the moral causes we embrace, the ends we seek and the means by which we seek them. The chronic confusion between the discourse of cause and effect and the discourse of intentionality reaches back to a more fundamental confusion in the late medieval period associated with Duns Scotus between God understood as a factor within the ensemble of causes and God understood as the transcendent ground of all being which we encountered in the debate between Richard Dawkins and Rowan Williams. The logic of causation is constantly misapplied in the realm of intentionality, and the resulting confusion has distorted the practice of all the humanities in the modern university to the point where the defence of theology is the defence of the humanities, and vice versa. The paradox of sociology, of course, is that it has to take the former into account while needing to understand the latter.

Five key passages in the Passion narrative exemplify the consistency and purity of the purposes of Jesus while at the same time facing quite directly the temptation of an appeal to force. They are the rejection of the option of the two swords in Luke 22:35–8 with the words 'It is enough'; the healing of the wound inflicted by Peter on Malchus, the servant of the high priest; the rejection of an appeal to 'twelve legions of angels' in the exchange with Pilate; the silence of Jesus in the Judgement Hall when confronted by the question 'What is truth?'; and the cry of desolation from the cross, 'My God, my God, why hast thou forsaken me?' The cry of desolation represents the uttermost limit of self-negation freely accepted as the cost of non-violence: the plumb-line of redemption reaches to the very bottom to redeem the full range of human experience, including the absence of God. The significance of the silence of Christ when faced with the question 'What is truth?' lies precisely in the *kind* of truth Jesus represents, which is the truth that sets you free under constraint. It belongs to the category of existence and the freedom of the spirit, as in the saying 'I AM the Truth',

---

    [3]   George Bernard Shaw, *Major Barbara* (Harmondsworth: Penguin, 2005, Preface) (original copyright 1907).

rather than the category of causation where truth is a property inhering in fixed chains of causation.

All our life choices belong to the category of existence and the freedom of the spirit, and are therefore *beyond* empirical truth without contradicting empirical truth. They are subject to costs and benefits that operate according to a moral calculus which includes all the discourses of tragedy, whether historical, literary, psychological or theological. No one can dismiss these discourses as 'superstitious', given that superstition is generated by the category of mistaken causation, whereas tragedy is generated by life choices circumscribed by consequences, dilemmas and limits. Sociology is as much the analysis of limits as is theology. Moreover, existential truths are made urgent and demand resolution under the pressure of shortness of time, which in the Gospel narrative takes the form of eschatology and the imminence of divine judgement, but which in human experience takes the form of the mortal dangers of contingency and the uncertain interval between the present moment and death.

This condensed and paradigmatic narrative, with its dense and impacted signs, above all the sign of the stripped and humiliated body at the hands of state power and corrupt justice, was infiltrated into societies dominated by codes of face and honour such as feudal society at the time of the Crusades. The 'countenance divine' encountered societies where the maintenance of face by the arbitration of violence is written into every social relationship, including negotiations between heralds over the proper occasions of war and the domestic relations of one sex to another. That is why insult is the trip-wire initiating violent operations on the body to the point of castration and extraction of the guts of the offender, and why adultery is the trip-wire activating murder. The tension between these two moral systems is bound to require strategies of negotiation and partial reconciliation.

The prime paradox will be one which provides a major exhibit for those who present Christianity as a key actor in the theatre of war: the Crusades were concerned with taking holy territory by force in the name of a faith whose paradigmatic discourses reject both territory and force. It is entirely correct to note the paradox but mistaken to miss its significance as the fulcrum of a negotiation between a non-violent discourse and the exigencies of a warrior code, between blood given in the course of personal sacrifice to establish a brotherhood of peace and the blood of enemies shed by the blood-brotherhood of arms.

We can trace the negotiation and amelioration of the tension between the non-violent discourse and the patriarchal honour code in the Renaissance realisation of feudal relationships and knightly honour found in Shakespeare's

Henry V and other early modern classics of representation. In *Henry V* the king is represented as choosing between different moral strategies, many of which crucially involve negotiations between the feudal codes of honour and war and the very different imperatives of Christianity, as well as somewhat more compatible moral models in the Old Testament. We find the Old Testament invoked after Henry has triumphed over the French at the Battle of Agincourt when he gives thanks to 'the God of battles' and commands *Non Nobis Domine* be sung attributing victory to God rather than to English valour. Elsewhere, Henry displays a calculating version of Christianity to the citizens of Harfleur by promising them mercy if they submit, but unrestrained violence if they do not. Henry also veers between a utilitarian ethic designed to secure compliance with English rule because it endeavours to pacify by justice and mercy, and an ecstasy of violence against prisoners, stimulated by fear of a French counter-attack.

Perhaps the tension between Christianity and the early modern moral code emerges most starkly when monarchs appropriate different biblical images and exploit analogies between the biblical past and the early modern present. It was, for example, easy enough for Henry VIII to represent himself as King David, or for Edward VI to understand his Protestant reforms as allowing him to assume the role of the biblical reformer King Josiah, or for Oliver Cromwell to be portrayed with politic ambiguity by Andrew Marvell as Gideon and as the bramble who agreed to be king of the forest (Judges 9:8–14) in his poem *The First Anniversary*.

However, it was much less easy for monarchs to imitate Christ. A non-violent preacher condemned and executed by properly constituted authorities had scant appeal to the Renaissance 'Godly Prince', ruling *jure divino*. Richard II as depicted by Shakespeare and Charles I as depicted in contemporary iconography appropriated discrete elements in the narrative of the Passion rather than Christ crucified. In the case of Shakespeare's *Richard II* the king in his last extremity complains melodramatically that he is pursued by more traitors than Christ, and claims each of them is much worse than Judas. (Queen Elizabeth saw Shakespeare's representation of Richard as mimicking her own precarious situation and was far from pleased.) In *Eikon Basilike* Charles I is represented as Christ in Gethsemane, but the martyrdom of Charles is hardly a 'passion narrative' freely accepted.[4] These *exempla* bring out the profound incompatibility

---

[4]   Jessica Martin and Alec Ryrie (eds), *Private and Domestic Devotion in Early Modern England* (Aldershot: Ashgate, 2012). See especially Chapter 3: Erica Longfellow, '"My now solitary prayers": *Eikon Basilike* and Changing Attitudes to Religious Solitude', pp. 53–72. I am very grateful to Jessica Martin for directing my attention to many examples from early modern England.

between the non-violent sacrifice at the centre of the Passion narrative and feudal and early modern discourses of power. The early modern monarch exploited an analogy with Christ crucified only when under duress, and even then only at a tangent. Stuart kings expected and required non-resistance to monarchs by God appointed, but did not for a moment contemplate non-resistance to rebels. They understood the reciprocity of violence as part of the natural order of things, whereas the mutuality of non-violence belonged to a 'kingdom not of this world' represented by Christ under questioning by Pontius Pilate.

The Gospel narrative from the Sermon on the Mount onward pursued the logic of human mutuality in a way indifferent to the logic of power, though it proved sufficiently threatening to the powers that be in 'synagogue and state' to bring about the drama of the Passion. It triumphed over everything implied by the corrupt lust for 'great possessions' depicted in the story of the 'rich young ruler'. The mutuality incarnate in Christ challenged the organisation of society into social hierarchies by demanding its disciples 'call no man father' in order that they might 'all be one' as Christ was at one with his Father in the mutual love animating the Godhead. Christ reversed the natural order of precedence at the Last Supper when he enacted the radical sacrament of washing the feet of the disciples to show that 'the Lord of all' is 'the Servant of all'. This was appropriated by both Church and state through the liturgy of feet-washing on Holy Thursday, though the English monarchy successfully extracted even the residual sting of the implied reversal of roles by turning it into a royal disbursement of money. George Fox well understood the mutuality demanded in the Gospel in defiance of all the demands of settled power, but even his movement was partially appropriated by the imperatives of economic power, for example in the more recent history of a great Quaker foundation, Barclays Bank.

Through all vicissitudes the radical version of Christianity remained embedded in the iconography of power: for example in the Pietà; in the Last Judgement of the Romanesque tympanum; in the Dance of Death that includes high and low, Pope and peasant alike; and in the devotion to Mary Magdalen as the outcast pardoned and accepted on account of an extravagance of love. It also manifested itself in the communitarian movements that planted unexploded bombs within the structure of Christendom that had to await auspicious openings, strains and social fissures to exert their latent power, often outside the confines of the Church. It should surprise no one that even the radical tradition

bred its own pathologies, for example in the long-term consequences of what
Charles Taylor has called 'the turn to the self'.[5]

From time to time, and perhaps increasingly in the course of the eighteenth
century, the appropriation of exemplary figures from the past included classical
mythology as well as biblical figures – though they could be merged, as they
were in Handel's oratorio *Hercules* or in the iconography of ceilings as in the
monastery at Benediktbeuern. A major mutation occurred when the English
Puritans adopted the anti-monarchical strain in the covenant between God
and the people of Israel. The American revolutionaries adopted this covenant
relationship, under the auspices of a moderate and semi-Christianised
Enlightenment, imitating classical models. The gap between classical virtue and
the pragmatic necessities of *realpolitik* is far smaller than the gap between the
Passion narrative and each and every discourse of power. No wonder classical
virtue proved so attractive to the Renaissance prince and the early modern
monarch. An idealised portrait of power to which rulers were subtly encouraged
to conform through techniques of flattery was far less threatening than the
reversals and 'the transvaluation of values' found in Christianity.

The incompatibility between discourses of power and the action of the
Passion can be illustrated from the poem *The Dream of the Rood*, composed in
Anglo-Saxon England (roughly) in a period when Bede first identified Saxon
England as a New Israel. Christ was assimilated to the 'man of mettle' climbing
the tree of redemption with the heroism of a warrior. More than a millennium
later, in the Surrey town of Guildford at the time of the 2012 Olympic Games,
an Evangelical church displayed an image of Christ, 'Champion of all nations', as
a muscle-bound Olympic gymnast in what is technically known as 'the crucifix
position' directly echoing *The Dream of the Rood*. Similar identifications occur
throughout European history and beyond, for example the representation
of Mazzini and Garibaldi, and indeed all the young men who fought for the
Risorgimento, as Christ figures willing to sacrifice themselves for the nation and
their comrades.[6] This theme was pursued globally in representations of figures
as different as the Fascist dictator Mussolini, the bandit-hero Che Guevara and
the hero of non-violence Mahatma Gandhi, though Gandhi also exemplifies a
rather different 'axial' narrative of non-violence. Gandhi equals Garibaldi equals
Christ, and the first two are placed together on account of their role in national

[5]   Charles Taylor, *Sources of the Self: The Making of the Modern Identity* (Cambridge:
Cambridge University Press, 1989).

[6]   Lucy Riall, *Garibaldi: Invention of a Hero* (London: Yale University Press, 2008).

liberation and collective national redemption analogous to the 'salvation history' of the Old Testament and its current Zionist appropriation.

Figures of this kind illustrate the role of non-empirical and non-rational categories like Charisma and Founding Fatherhood in religion, nationalism and revolutionary political ideology *alike*. 'Secular' discourses and 'religious' discourses both appeal to non-empirical categories. At the same time the comparisons of later historical figures with Christ are far more likely to appropriate the aspect of self-sacrifice than the central story of non-violent redemption by the abandonment of the love of possessions in favour of possession by love. The appropriation of that narrative, and/or of the radical critique of possessions and hierarchy in the Gospels, is left to voluntary groups in the 'sectarian' tradition, like the Lollards and the Mennonites. More recently, in the wake of the First and Second World Wars, commemorative iconography turned to the text 'Greater love hath no man than this, that he lay down his life for his friends', but that clearly refers to the blood-brotherhood of arms rather than the peaceable fraternities of early Christianity.

Chapter 5

The Rival Narratives

Why are we so fussed about religion and its relation to war and violence? It is because a particular narrative of the French Enlightenment identifies religion as an irrational mode of belief and goes on to claim, first, that the irrationality of religion is linked systematically to disgraceful practices and to retrogressive political and moral regimes, and second, that these regimes are to a quite special degree implicated in violence. The narrative has anticipations in Montaigne and his comments on the relation between religious faith and a predisposition to conflict fostered by experience of the French 'wars of religion'.

We have been dealing with a banal and empirically unproductive truth which leads nowhere except to a fresh and negative dogmatism about a falsely hypostasised 'entity', religion in general and religion at all times. It leads by a far from obvious extension to the assertion not only that religion is essentially irrational, but to the *dogmatic* claim that there is an intrinsic connection between irrational beliefs and evil behaviour, between, that is, the true and the good. A dogmatic claim of this kind, shorn of the provisional character intrinsic to science, reminds one of similar statements found in certain kinds of Christian discourse: for example, the medieval Catholic notion that *because* the theologically dualist Cathars were doctrinally mistaken and heretical they were bound to be morally deviant and perverse.

We have to ask what historical experiences, interests and perspectives predisposed intellectuals in France to adopt a narrative which identified religion rather than other equally obvious factors as *peculiarly* responsible for bellicose behaviour. The same applies to a narrative constructed in the Anglo-American Enlightenment which estimated religion much more positively. For Thomas Paine much depended on separating natural religion from specific claims to revelation and all religion from entanglement with state power following the model of voluntary religion that provided Paine's own background and found untrammelled expression in America.[1] Protestant thinking pinned most of the blame on Catholicism and priestcraft. Herbert Spencer adopted the same

---

[1] John Keane, *Tom Paine: A Political Life* (London: Bloomsbury, 1995).

approach in the nineteenth century when he identified Protestantism with a commercial liberal pacifism.

There has been a Catholic master narrative locating warlike and imperialist tendencies in the link between Protestantism and capitalism. Contemporary agnostic or atheist identifications of religion with war fuse the French Enlightenment narrative with the Protestant and Catholic narrative, and feed in a revival of a nineteenth-century narrative identifying religion with fundamentalist opposition to science, in particular evolutionary biology. This is reinforced by the construction of the category of a specifically religious terrorism which ignores anti-religious terrorism, for example anarchism.

This is backed up by thought experiments, first about the possible consequences of accepting beliefs that cannot be proved empirically, and second about accepting beliefs on authority: God *told* me to act violently and has promised me an eternal reward. Here one might ask just why 'ignorant and unlearned men', and women, should not feel empowered under the impulse of the Spirit to speak what is in their hearts as well as professional intellectuals. In any case, most of our life choices, religious or otherwise, are unprovable, and that includes atheism, scientism, the human rights discourse and all political ideologies. As I have already indicated in my comments above on nationalism, there is a vast area of non-rational, non-empirical characteristics shared alike by politics and religion.

I make three observations. First, most of our life choices are commitments: no one lives by proof alone. Second, taking opinions on the basis of authority and acting on them is normal, even if it is the opinion of a scientist on matters he knows little about, or public opinion, or Zeitgeist, or nationalist or political fervour. Third, acts of violence are not necessarily irrational or unjustifiable. They may serve the cause of justice. Dietrich Bonhoeffer had to suppress his religious scruples to join the Hitler bomb plot, but the plot was morally justified. We cannot even assume that Islamicist terrorism is pure gratuitous evil. There are oppressive situations that might lead us to redefine religious or irreligious terrorism as legitimate acts of war. At the very moment of writing (August 2012) there is clearly a major body of educated and morally responsible opinion that classifies 'acts of terrorism' by the rebels in Syria as legitimate acts of war in the service of democracy and freedom, though the evidence suggests a context of contestation much more complex and ambiguous than that. We at least need to *consider* the justifiability of violent responses to those largely secular western powers which have propped up corrupt regimes because they cooperate with western economic and political imperialism and have pushed democratic impulses in North Africa and the Middle East in an Islamic, even an Islamist, direction. There are plausible parallels with the oppression of Poland by the militantly secularist regime of Soviet Russia and the strong identification of religion with the movements for democratic and national self-determination that emerged in consequence. Maybe political, cultural and economic imperialism in Britain, France, Soviet Russia and Imperial or Communist China is a geopolitical constant dependent on power and opportunity, *whether religious or not*. Maybe war, irrational fervour, the spread of virus-like enthusiasms and the acceptance of authority are also semi-constants, which we load onto religion rather than face empirical social reality.

We in the West elide such an interpretative move because our sense of an ordered social universe depends on a secular master narrative of progress and elides instances and movements that may contradict it. We are swayed by the Whig interpretation of history, and that includes our estimate of what we call *the* Enlightenment, neglecting its racism, its autocracy, its expansionism and its demand for assimilation to its preferred norms, as incidental to its *real* liberating character.[2] As I shall indicate, the distinction between real and incidental is central to rhetorical moves in this debate: Torquemada was not a *real* Christian; Stalin's atheism was *coincidental* to his monstrous behaviour and his persecution of Christians.

However, contemporary contentions about the *peculiar* capacity of unproved beliefs, including specifically religious beliefs, to issue in violence do not depend on psychological constructs. They are also backed up by simply *pointing* to instances where religion plays a role in conflict, in particular conflicts and wars conventionally grouped under the rubric of '*the* wars of religion' but also in similar instances today in Bosnia, or Israel or Sudan. This tactic of pointing makes an appeal to 'the obvious'. President Assad is an Alawite; his opponents in Syria and other 'combatants by proxy' in the Gulf States are mostly Sunni. His supporters in Iran are Shia, therefore this is a religious war. Syria is in fact an interesting case because western media have (up to the point of writing) largely avoided the terminology of 'sectarian conflict' that skews our perception of the nationalist/loyalist conflict in Northern Ireland. That is because Syria is so far assimilated with Libya, Egypt and Tunisia, to the narrative of increasing progress towards democracy. We have to enquire just when the terminology of *sectarian* conflict is felt appropriate and why.

---

[2]   Colin Kidd, *The Forging of Races: Race and Scripture in the Protestant Atlantic World, 1600–2000* (Cambridge: Cambridge University Press, 2006).

That pushes us to ask those questions that characterise the social sciences and are in addition rather more realistic than implausible psychological experiments as to the consequences of holding unproved and unprovable beliefs of all kinds, like utopian socialism or human rights discourse. These social scientific questions begin with an interrogation of the basic terms of the debate and of their historical genesis, not just the word 'religion' but also science and the rhetorically loaded terminology of warfare, terrorism, civil war, genocide etc. From the seventeenth century on natural science has released itself from an imprecise and historically and culturally embedded vocabulary, whereas social science has rightly and inevitably retained fundamental concepts that are embedded in the semantic auras of subjectively and historically located meanings. In sociology concepts are not bounded thing-like entities, though one might mention in passing that modern natural science is not at all straightforwardly a matter of entities, and involves the use of metaphors (like 'the selfish gene') along the lines discussed by philosophers of science like Mary Hesse. In sociology much depends on the way context inflects meanings, on the determination of the boundaries of usable concepts, and on the way these boundaries are expanded and contracted as part of the rhetoric of public contention over 'religion'.

Rhetorical Manipulation

Let me illustrate this rhetorical manipulation. You can manipulate the reception of arguments over the value or otherwise of religion by expansions and contractions of what you take to count as religion, or science, or terrorism or war. Let us suppose someone points to the oppressive regime in North Korea as an instance of an atheist regime more bellicose than (say) the relatively religious and relatively peaceful Philippines. You can shift this instance from the irreligious column to the religious column by dropping the substantive definition of religion in favour of a functional definition, allowing you to include the mobilising power of mass rituals and the icons of sacred nationalism such as one observes in North Korea under the label of religion. For the purposes of argument you opportunistically sacrifice the contrast between atheism and theism. Christopher Hitchens did precisely this in a lecture given in Tennessee in 2004. Alternatively you play a game of comparative moral statistics over historical time: the regimes of Stalin, Mao and Pol Pot were responsible for so many million deaths, while religious regimes were responsible for many fewer or many more deaths.

One can make the rhetorical move whereby a Christian person or regime that is oppressive and violent, like Torquemada or the Inquisition, was not *truly* Christian; or suggest that a Christian person or regime that is non-violent, for example Martin Luther King and the American civil rights movement, was not *truly* Christian or only *incidentally* Christian; and by the same token argue that an oppressive and violent person or regime, for example Stalin and scientific atheism, was not *truly* atheistic or *properly* scientific or only *incidentally* atheistic. Definitions that might seem crucial to the impact and reception of an argument are routinely expanded or contracted for rhetorical purposes.

Justified War

I return to the possibility that violent acts are justifiable, given that the participants in contemporary debates assume that being peaceable and non-violent is good. They make an ethical (not an empirical) judgement which is not absolute but dependent on circumstances. So, maybe, arguments over these matters are not solely or essentially empirical at all, even when the media celebrities who conduct them, like Richard Dawkins, are implicitly or explicitly dogmatic empiricists. It is all too clear that crucial aspects of debate turn on contradictory ethical and politico-ethical judgements. As I earlier hinted, large parts of the western intelligentsia celebrate guerrilla activities and warlike martyrs like Che Guevara, and condemn Pentecostals in Latin America for supine quietism in the face of injustice. Half-hearted warriors for justice are not preferred to whole-hearted ones, and that includes the Sunni in Syria, and associated Jihadis and Salafists, whose religion helps them endure in the face of oppression. And yet religion is roundly condemned for 'causing war' *irrespective* of the justice of the cause.

The issues are complicated. Christianity has doctrines relating to the criteria for waging just war which were invoked by the papacy and other Christian leaders to condemn the attempt to overthrow Saddam Hussein and his oppressive (and 'secular') Ba'athist regime. That reminds us again that one major critique of Christianity focusses on its *reluctance* to fight and focusses on the opportunities and comfort such reluctance may offer aggressors. As with modern criticism of Pentecostal quietism, so in classical and Renaissance times the monkish virtues of Christianity were contrasted with the citizen virtues, including readiness to fight against external and internal enemies. Humility and turning the other cheek militate against the necessities inherent in political power: Rome cannot forgive Carthage and still hope to secure the dominance on which Pax Romana depends. The same applies to all hegemons, including Britain and the USA. Britain paid very heavily for its inter-war pacifism which had a strong Christian component. Peace depends on power and the ability to respond with force, as the history of the inter-war period illustrates.

I return to difficulties associated with the blanket category of religion. Religion is an essentially contested category and one that has particular historical antecedents, for example the way it partly derives from a Christian binary between the religious and the secular originally expressed in the binary opposition between faith and 'the world', the *saeculum*, and partly, following Talal Asad, from the colonial encounter and the need to characterise the practices of non-Christians.[3]

Religion, Violence and Different Types of Society

The final part of my argument concerns the different relations between religion and violence depending on the *type* of society, in particular the contrast between cosmological religions in large-scale archaic civilisations and the developments of the Axial Age in the first millennium BC. When engaged in argument about what 'religion' is or does one has to specify the type of society in question and not just pluck useful instances from any period and type of society. One has in particular to look at the implications for violence and religion in the Axial Age of the different angles of transcendence emerging in Greece, Israel, Persia, India and China, and at the different degrees of world rejection they imply, including rejection of sacred kingship, sacred sexuality *and* sacred violence. Clearly the proclivity for violence may be a generalised biological constant based on mechanisms of evolutionary survival, but equally clearly, the way that is channelled or *challenged* by religion varies, and enters a new phase in the Axial Age.

In archaic civilisations religion and power are intertwined and the cosmic and the political orders reinforce each other. Sacred violence is executed by rulers to restore cosmic order against the threat of chaos. That is as true of contemporary China as of archaic China. Older configurations are constantly carried forward, so that the Axial Age carries forward formations from the archaic period, including in the Hebrew Scriptures the God of war and moral bargaining with God or the gods, and these are further embedded by the stabilisations made possible by text, as pointed out by Bellah, Assmann and

---

[3]   Talal Asad, *Formations of the Secular*.

others.[4] Thereafter these embedded elements provide a varied repertoire that can be drawn upon according to political necessity or the requirements of different kinds of political order.

Different angles of Transcendence

In different ways these axial civilisations embody angles of transcendence and rejections of 'the world as it is' that generate visions of a new kingdom of peace and righteousness. In the case of Israel these visions are initially embedded in a covenant relation between God and a particular people that is then broadened out into a vision of Jerusalem at the heart of a restored world. A restored world can either be brought into existence by violence or it may lie in wait in God's good time. After the Jews had more than once attempted unsuccessfully to 'restore the kingdom' by violence the rabbis of the second century BC shifted to a pacific stance whereby the faithful were enjoined to wait in patience for the divine restoration. This was a religious expression not of power but of powerlessness. The same was true of Christianity: it emerged on a despised margin and rejected all violence. Of course, when it was adopted as the religion of the Roman Empire it bifurcated into the non-violence of the powerless and the exigencies of power as expressed in a *partially* renewed relation between the cosmos and the political powers: partial because the subversive imagery of the peaceful kingdom is also carried forward 'on the books'.[5] This bifurcation constantly reappeared – for example in pristine monasticism, the Lollard movement and the Radical Reformation – and there is a discernible relation between the political realism of the powerful and territory and the political idealism of the powerless and voluntary association, or alternatively of what some sociologists call 'vicinal segregation' like the territorial enclaves maintained by the Amish. Both synagogue and church were initially non-territorial voluntary associations, and Judaism and Christianity may be jointly credited with the invention of a crucial feature of the modern world, with major premonitions in early modernity.

Christianity explicitly universalised the idea of the coming kingdom, maintaining that it was both already present and to come, and elevating the kingdom and Jerusalem to the realm 'above'. Moreover, the Christian angle of

---

[4] Bellah, *Religion in Human Evolution*; Jan Assmann, *Religion and Cultural Memory* (Stanford: Stanford University Press, 2006).

[5] Thomas R. Yoder Neufeld, *Jesus and the Subversion of Violence: Wrestling with the New Testament Evidence* (London: SPCK, 2011).

transcendence both accepted the world as good and rejected it as ruined and in need of redemption, and this tension between the actual world and the kingdom in waiting, and between the particular role of Israel and the universal message to the Gentiles, created a symbolic logic of themes in tension and paradoxical images: the themes of the particular in tension with the universal and of the genealogical continuity of the fathers in tension with the break of a new birth that released the universal fraternity of the brothers; the disfigured face of man and the transfigured face of man; the paradoxical images of the vulnerable child who also holds the whole world in his hands; the defeated and derided man who also rises triumphant over sin and death. Occasionally it seems possible that the powerless may seize power and inaugurate a new kingdom, but these revolutions always fail and leave a pacific deposit of small radical cells, like the Quakers, and of radical themes that fructify far beyond the borders of institutional religion.

This tension is superimposed on tensions within social reality itself. There is a tension between the solidarity of the group, which generates the category of those with us and those against, thereby giving rise to potential conflict, and between the logic of universality that creates a border between those who accept the universal message and those who do not. These are twin sources of conflict written in from the beginning. Perhaps the solidarity of the group against the 'Other' is rooted in *biological* mechanisms of survival that include cooperation and empathy alongside hierarchy and defence/aggression, but the prerequisites of *cultural* survival are roughly the same. In short, the inevitable cost of solidarity is conflict, and insofar as religion, or some other factor like nationalism, reinforces solidarity, it generates conflict.

However, apart from Us and Them there are *many* sources of conflict, such as face and honour, rivalries in love and war, tensions over territory and resources, and the logic that decrees that you either expand or accept contraction, leading to overstretch and to the formation of alliances against hegemons. This social logic is inimical to primitive Christianity because it lacks an analysis of power and simply contrasts spiritual power with wickedness in high places. Only when it experiences power can it work out a casuistry of the proper use of force and the just war; but by then it is entangled in the exigencies of power, as the history of the medieval papacy illustrates, and becomes a power base in its own right. That entanglement in turn gives rise to the distinction between Church and state, originally embodied in the Dominical distinction between God and Caesar, in the Gelasian doctrine of the Two Swords, with all that implies for the slow enlargement of a free space between religious organisation and political power.

PART II
Religion and Nationalism, Religion and Politics

Chapter 6
The Political Future of Religion

Preliminary Exposition

To look at the political future of religion I set on one side the idea of the separation of the spheres of religion and politics because it is rare in the historical record outside the French and American revolutions, and because it generates an unrealistic account of religion and politics now and in the future. An establishment of religion of *some* sort is normal, and not merely if you include functional equivalents like the panoply of images paraded by the communist regime in North Korea or the sacred icons held up in the western media. There is a persistent relation of society to core values, and the sacred is ceremonially exposed in its 'high places' for obeisance and emulation. This relationship is mediated by a temple which is also a 'template', meaning a significant arrangement of sacred space in (let us say) Tiananmen Square or the Kremlin, lying at the sacred heart of sacred territory. Religion responds to the territorial imperative. You blaspheme or commit sacrilege when you defile established shrines, rituals and icons.

All that is functionalist sociology in the Durkheimian tradition, formulated when France was torn apart by an uncivil political war between two versions of establishment, the Catholic Church and the Republic. The Republic won. The Church was disestablished in 1905 and religion of a kind migrated to the shrines and icons of the Republic. When the Republic exacted blood sacrifice on a vast scale during the First World War the sacred flame of the Unknown Warrior was located under the Arc de Triomphe, not in Notre-Dame. If you want to know whose heraldry occupies the high and holy places and spaces you have to seek out the commemorative icons of blood sacrifice. In Britain, with a different history of relations between Church and state, the monument to the Unknown Warrior lies in the 'royal peculiar' of Westminster Abbey. The graves of the dead in war, whether in defence of the nation, or the revolution, or both, represent sacred territory in miniature, securely maintained against defilement. Russia condemns interference with the monuments to its 20 million dead in World War Two as 'blasphemy', and when Palestinians want to protest against what they see as occupation of their sacred territory their targets include Jewish graveyards.

The relationship of religion to the state, to territory and to a people has a *longue durée* to come. It is not at all a necessary relationship such as might allow one to characterise 'religion' *as such*, even supposing the term 'religion' can be used coherently. But there is a persistent tendency for a link to be forged between what one may call the territorial imperative as that is linked to the dynamic of power and *realpolitik*, and a predominant structure of values characterised by the features I have already indicated.

That is my argument, and it holds even in the United States. The USA celebrates what Thomas Jefferson called 'the wall of separation' between religion and the state, and boasts of being the home of the voluntary and non-territorial principle; yet it celebrates a form of religious establishment, in particular a curious political coinage called Judaeo-Christianity. Conor Cruise O'Brien, in a book entitled *God Land*, recalled a prayer breakfast in Washington which began: 'We are met today in the presence of Almighty God and the President of the United States'[1]. This is the political role of religion in the heartland of the voluntary principle and the separation of Church and state and in the most technologically advanced and rationalised society on the world. The power of the established or territorial principle is also evident in Buddhist societies, which in the West maintain a reputation as non-coercive and pacific: in Sri Lanka and Burma alike the state seeks to extrude, subject or harass Christian, Muslim and (in the case of Sri Lanka) Hindu minorities.

That rather leaves France as the standard-bearer of a *laïque* future, though the invocation of 'the Republic' and of La France amply fulfils a functionalist understanding of religion. But if Church and state are once again in collusion in Russia after 70 years of the Soviet experiment and massive persecution of religion, then the onward march of history anticipated by *L'An Un*, Year One, and a new calendar in France after 1789 includes major retreats. Ankara, Nowa Huta and Wenzhou were envisaged as secular cities. Today their skylines witness to that retreat.

I summarise. The future includes the resilience of establishment, of a holy people in a Holy Land and of the role of sanctuaries, sacred texts and icons in holy places. That holds whether we speak of religion as conventionally understood or in functionalist terms that would identify the worship of the great leader in North Korea as religious. However, I am also looking at, and appealing to, the *future-*

---

[1]   Conor Cruise O'Brien, *God Land: Reflections on Religion and Nationalism* (Cambridge, Mass.: Harvard University Press, 1988).

in-the-past, including the remoter past. We forget just how long the durance of our contemporary religion has really been in our obsession with where we go next. Much of what I have just described goes back millennia to cosmic religions centred in vast temple complexes like Karnak, focussed on the divine status of the ruler, and requiring blood sacrifice to the powers of nature and the emperor. China today modernises at breakneck speed, but also celebrates the ancient ideal of harmony posed against the threat of chaos within a sacred territory. Much blood has been shed, long ago *and* also very recently, to secure China's territorial integrity and to fulfil the territorial imperative.

Yet that is not the whole story. 'Religion' generates alternative scenarios. The Axial Revolution of between two and three millennia ago stored up other possibilities for the future that contemporary sociologists analyse as the advance of religion understood as the exercise of *choice*. The ability to choose (or reject) religious affiliation is associated with an individualised faith pursued *in foro interno*, in sincerity and truth, and with the creation of voluntary communities apart from the state and territory. It also has some less obvious relation to the growth of diasporic religion because a religion geographically on the move attracts a more conscious adherence and may even make critical distance or disaffiliation more likely. The Jews in exile and later dispersed around the globe were one of the earliest manifestations of religion in diaspora. The Church of the Early Christians took off from the Synagogue of Rabbinic Judaism. Early Christianity represented a radical disruption of the sacred based on a sense of continuing crisis before the advent of the kingdom. Both Early Christianity and diasporic Judaism were harbingers of an alternative future relatively free of political and state entanglements, of the territorial imperative and of everything state and territory exact in pyramids of blood sacrifice. Since the innovations of the Axial Age, with its universal visions of alternative futures transcending the present, I envisage a constant dialectic between choice and autonomy (including today a discourse of human rights with major roots in religious conceptions) and automatically conferred belonging.[2] There are, first, the sources and resources of religion established in a place and conferred by birthright; and then there are the options provided by the exhaustive

---

[2] The history of human rights, and the associated concepts of natural law and religious or secular universalism, is complex and tangled. Here it is worth mentioning, within the Anglo-American tradition going back to the seventeenth century, the role of the English Levellers in the 1640s, John Locke, John Wesley (regarding slavery), Thomas Paine (of Quaker stock), William Lloyd Garrison (Unitarian) and Frederick Nolde (American Lutheran and a major influence on the 1948 UN Declaration of Human Rights). Cf. John S. Nurser, *For All Peoples and Nations: The Ecumenical Church and Human Rights* (Washington: Georgetown University, 2005).

repertoire made available in the Axial Age, including religion separated from state or from territory or from ethnicity, or from all three.

The Longer Global Narrative and the Recent European Modernist Narrative

I look back to descry what is likely to be in the future, and I do so leaning on Robert Bellah's *Religion in Human Evolution*, glossing it as I proceed.[3] However, whereas Bellah focusses on everything *up* to what Karl Jaspers called the Axial Age, roughly located in the first millennium BC, I focus on the revolutionary possibilities brought into being by the Axial Age and continuing into our present and any conceivable future. I try to grasp the political future of religion by grasping the specific character of pre- and post-axial religion over the past three or four millennia, its social and even its biological roots, and the influence it continues to exercise on how we envisage the world, whether through the religious lens or the political lens or (preferably) through a bifocal lens.

I need to canvass two narratives. There is, first, a grand narrative on a scale of three or four millennia that enables us to descry the durability of religion into the future. There is, second, a much shorter narrative on a scale of three or four centuries that deals only with the transition from early modernity to modernity proper, and that might lead us to doubt whether religion has much of a political future at all. This shorter narrative dominates European consciousness and has been disseminated globally during the colonial encounter. Europeans tell a tale about themselves that starts in the seventeenth century, when Europe began its great leap forward and its global expansion, and focusses on the scientific, technological, agricultural and industrial revolutions. The tale includes three mutations: the Enlightenment in several versions, in particular the French Enlightenment; the rise of nationalism, sometimes seen as secularised religion; and revolutionary ideology, also sometimes seen as secularised religion.

According to the French version of the Enlightenment, religion is, and moreover ought to be, partially privatised. This version is both descriptive and prescriptive. It has undergirded subsequent revolutionary political ideologies in Turkey, Russia and China that have also sought to privatise religion. Yet Russia has already reverted to a collective form of territorial religiosity; Turkey is moving in the same direction and *maybe* China too. That makes France the great exception. For the rest, including the USA, we observe *some* version of establishment, *some* expression of the territorial imperative manifest in the icons

---

[3]   Bellah, *Religion in Human Evolution*.

of the high and holy place. So even in the course of this shorter tale we observe that collective and territorial expressions of religion are astonishingly resilient. Collective and territorial modes of religion continue to exist in what looks like a semi-permanent dialectic with privatised religion on the French model, with diasporic religion on the original Jewish model and with voluntary religion on the American model. I observe the resilience of collective and territorial religion; I note the mutual reinforcement of religion and ethnicity as groups leave the areas they dominate as majorities to become minorities in diaspora elsewhere; *and* I chart the real but chequered advance of voluntary religiosity. If voluntarism is the wave of the future, it runs up against the rock-like reality of automatic belonging and collective religion.[4]

I now turn to the larger narrative covering the last three or four millennia. I emphasise how its various manifestations persist from the era of the cosmic religions of archaic civilisation that provided the backdrop for the emergence of axial religiosity through the vicissitudes of the intervening centuries up to the present. In *Religion in Human Evolution* Robert Bellah stresses an *enlargement* of capacities, not replacement or supersession. He argues that 'nothing is ever lost', in particular because the existence of narrative remains a permanent resource in culture and still constitutes the primary way we understand our individual and collective selfhood.[5] There is no ratiocination without the telling of a story, including the story of the advance of ratiocination. Europeans construct a narrative that begins in ancient Greece and Israel. In ancient Greece it took two forms: the Homeric myths and the rise of philosophical reflection and science. In Israel it focussed on the centre in Jerusalem and the periphery in Galilee. In contemporary England the national song celebrates England as a potential New Jerusalem in prophetic biblical imagery ambiguous enough to unite across political divides; and in the USA 'The Battle Hymn of the Republic' celebrates the American struggle for freedom alongside the Christian aspiration to holiness. The initial narrative is constantly adapted to new contexts.

The Long-Term Sources and Resources of Religion

When we think about the political future of religion, we need to go back to its origins and consider its relation to the primordial without becoming entangled

---

[4]   Slavica Jakelić, *Collectivistic Religions: Religion, Choice and Identity in Late Modernity* (Aldershot: Ashgate, 2010).

[5]   Bellah, *Religion in Human Evolution*.

in an essentially contested definition of religion or devising a set of sequential stages through which it must pass in the course of its cultural evolution. Religion *itself* is *not* primordial, because there are cultures like East Germany where it is of scant concern to the majority of the population and presumably has a distinctly modest political future, in spite of the fact that churches provided the main symbolic assembly points for the mass protests that overthrew communism. But if religion itself is not primordial it does at least answer to potentials that are permanently built in. These permanent potentials are, for example, the solidarity of Us against Them and the struggle over scarce resources, whether material power and wealth or face and humiliation. These potentials sustain the territorial imperative. They impel the demarcation of *lieux sacrés* and sacred territory, and give rise to violence.

In the beginning, according to a modern version of Genesis, certain highly generalised potentials were built into the human psyche by biological evolution and by the prerequisites of any sustainable sociality so that the biological potentials and social prerequisites are mutually reinforcing, and we do not for current purposes need to consider how to disentangle the biological from the social. These potentials and prerequisites are intention and attention; invocation and donation; empathy and friendship; ritual, play and fair play; parental caring and cooperation; fight and flight in the service of self-preservation; competition, ranking, hierarchy and dominance, including dominance by nurture; and violence, against both individual and collective rivals. Bellah concludes that from foragers to schoolchildren to nation states social solidarity between Us will breed solidarity against Them. To revert to the biblical version of Genesis, Cain will always be prone to murder Abel. There is nothing surprising about the mythic histories that religion relates, or that history relates about religion.

We need only add two developments in the course of human evolution, both of which effected great changes and remain with us today. One relates to the key role of language, the creation of a grammar of past, present and future, of volition, of might be and cannot be, of possibility and frustration, in the emergence of religion. The other is the key role of the external memory bank provided by fully alphabetic writing in the emergence of reflection, including the theoretical reflection that constitutes the initial basis of science. Fully alphabetic writing makes possible a stable text and all that implies for continuity and for constant reference back to a shared and extended narrative of goals and origins, and to shared signs and symbols. The sacred and protected text unites the group in the present and carries it forward from generation to generation. The covenant of

Israel mutates into the modern constitution. Indeed, in the case of South Korea the constitution consciously looks back to the covenant.

The Cosmic and the Axial

Once we identify the main forms of cosmic and axial religion we can see how they persisted throughout the Axial Age and still provide major elements of our contemporary repertoire. The cosmic religiosity of archaic civilisations often appears to arise in river valleys at the heart of large territories. They create major temple complexes and processional ways dominated by images and icons of power and they offer up mass sacrifices to the powers of nature and the state. Vast numbers of people, including conquered peoples permanently subordinated or enslaved, are brought together to construct temples, pyramids and fortifications. The imperial rulers are obsessed with immortality and the empires are governed by temporal cycles reflecting the procession of the seasons and the heavens. Earth is a reflex of heaven and the emperor a semi-divine incarnation of the immortal gods. Emperors are constantly on the look-out for potential rivals, particularly successful generals and ambitious members of the royal house, and empires rise and fall in succession.

In mutated form we find most of these features throughout later history until our own times, including the great cities of the Renaissance and the Enlightenment, St. Petersburg, Rome, Berlin with Potsdam, Paris, Washington and imperial Delhi. They were all built on pyramids of skulls and all periodically demanded blood sacrifice in their defence. Great processional ways are constructed, including waterways, for vast and solemn assemblies, exhibitions of power and the display of images and icons. One of the most extraordinary manifestations of a modern version of cosmic religiosity occurred in Romania under the communist dictator Nicolae Ceausescu when vast swathes of historic Bucharest were torn down to create a processional way that led to a palace built on the scale of Versailles.

At some point, however, the cosmic religions of archaic civilisation begin to break down, starting with periods of prolonged chaos when the powers of the heartland are challenged by the powers of the periphery or defeat by other empires. War, famine, division and disorder foster doubt about the ability of the ruler to mediate and reflect the will of the gods. Incipient questions of theodicy arise concerning the justifications offered for the way things are ordered here on earth. Is the Good Shepherd of his people truly good and, if not, who might the true king be? In Greece the true king might be Socrates; in India the prince renounces his power and his earthly inheritance to achieve dominion over the unruly demands of the flesh; in Israel there might be no king but God as witnessed to by the prophets; and in Christianity a true shepherd might reign from the throne of his cross. In Christianity the blood sacrifice is made by God, the blood brotherhood of the local clan and the warrior band is replaced by the universal fraternity of peace, and the reproduction of the generations mutates into a second birth in the Spirit.

The moment the idea of truth and a true God is contrasted with falsehood and false gods, and genuine faith contrasted with bad faith, a revolutionary dynamic is unleashed that closes temples, reprimands kings, smashes statues and abolishes priesthoods. A new or revised or recovered meta-narrative displaces all the old testaments. In the case of Israel, for example, the great redaction that bought together priestly narratives and revised kingly narratives with the Mosaic narrative of direct covenant of God with the People eventually gave the Jews a stable text that enabled them to survive anywhere. It produced the social innovation of Rabbinic Judaism and the synagogue, which in turn produced the great innovations of vast transnational brotherhoods and sisterhoods: the Church with the universities, and the *Umma* with the *madrasas*. The modern transnational voluntary association which today interacts with and challenges religions of the territorial imperative reaches back to the creation of the synagogue as the central institution of Judaism in diaspora, and to the early Christian Church as an association of the like-minded across all the frontiers of the Roman Empire and beyond.

In the Axial Age we are dealing with more universal and ethically informed perspectives that might involve a tradition of prophetic denunciation as in Israel, or of wisdom and theoretical reflection as in Greece, or of renunciation as in India, or reflection on the Way of Nature and of Heaven as in China. Between them they comprise an exhaustive set. Of course, if you stress theoretical thinking, then Greece is the only sure case; and if you stress transcendence, then China is distinctly dubious. But in all these very different cases you find some intimation of the universal and some critical distance achieved from immemorial givens. Within each new perspective you are enabled to redraw the map of human potential and possibility. You can realise how far you have fallen short, through sin, or weakness, or imprisonment in the shadowy realm of Plato's cave, or through illusion (or Maya), or simply because you are out of tune with Heaven and Nature (or Li).

The life choices coded by this range of responses to the world and the new worlds of human possibility opened up still provide our fundamental repertoire. Particular angles of transcendence either exclude or marginalise the possibilities and perspectives emphasised in civilisations structured according to different angles of transcendence. Law and conforming to statute on the one hand, and faith and inwardness on the other, are accorded quite different weights in Judaism and Christianity. At the same time some forms of Christianity are legalistic and some forms of Judaism elevate inwardness above outward conformity. In our modern situation what had been shadowy intimations of the Other within very different projections of the world, previously largely restricted to educated elites, have now become common property. The main civilisational complexes mingle their resources both through communications and through redistributions of population, but the original templates stay intact and continue to provide the frames within which the majority understands the world. Each country in Europe, for example, understands the various diasporas of Judaism and Islam within its own historic model. We call this multiculturalism, but in fact the main projections of the world from China to Peru stay in place.

Religion is profoundly implicated in all the dramatic transformation scenes of the Axial Age, in the narratives they generate, and in the rituals and icons carrying forward the dramas and the narratives from generation to generation. The dynamic released by the Axial Age ensures that the rituals are challenged by anti-rituals. The mediation of icons and priesthoods is challenged by iconoclasms and by demands for lay access. The incorporation and partial expropriation of hope and truth by power is challenged by heresies and movements of purification, often among the excluded and marginalised, but also among counter-elites. The evolution of religion is punctuated by perpetual revolution and perpetual reformation: *semper reformanda*. These reformations and revolutions themselves hide an enduring will-to-power and to dominance behind a claim to nurture and behind the recitation of genealogies and apparently impeccable credentials, as a religion of love in the case of Christianity or as the party of reason and humanity, as in the Enlightenment. A Christian faith in love, and an Enlightened faith in reason, often both together as in the USA, create platforms in consciousness from which to criticise failures to deliver.

The developments of the Axial Age generate a reserve about things as they are in 'the world' from different vantage points and variable angles of transcendence. In the specific case of Christianity a reserve about the world generated the dialectic of faith and the world and the binaries of God and

Caesar, spirit and flesh, law and grace, the City of God and the City of Man, and the Two Kingdoms, and all their associated imageries. The dialectic of religious and secular is itself another derivative of the Christian reserve about the world. I am saying that the grammars that govern the way we think derive directly from the different perspectives opened up by the Axial Age. When we in the West deploy the vocabulary of the religious and the secular we too easily forget that it derives from a specifically Christian history. It may be that the very notion of becoming secular in which the secularisation thesis is embedded belongs to a specifically Christian history and largely applies elsewhere through the consequences of the colonial encounter.[6] During the last half century I have constantly argued that the varied trajectories of the secular within Christianity, for example in the very different American and French versions, do not provide prototypes for likely changes in the rest of the world. Those who regard politics as primary are reproducing a template forged in the revolutionary fires of French history, and are too prone to forget that the religious and the political are not so easily separated. They share fundamental orientations and different civilisations parse their intertwined relationship very differently. If we think of China as the coming superpower we gain some idea of the range of possibilities by seeing how differently it parses the shared axes of human existence.

Axial Religion in Two Contrasting Modes

I am suggesting that if we are thinking bifocally about religion and politics and the political future of religion, we need to recognise that the different perspectives on the world set up by the religions of the Axial Age continue to shape the repertoire of options routinely entertained by both politics and religion in each major civilisation. That is true not just of 'enchanted' continents like Africa, India and Latin America, but of highly secularised parts of the world like the contemporary European West and contemporary China. Fundamental modes of being, and of relation to time and space, hierarchy and equality, individual and collective, simultaneously undergird the politico-religious taken for granted, and demarcate the boundaries between civilisations. The question is not how we eliminate these boundaries and these differences through some notion of a common global culture, but of understanding the gains and losses severally entailed by living within these boundaries. The repertoire itself is

---

[6]   Martin with Catto, 'The Religious and the Secular'.

exhaustive, but within each boundary a different balance of opportunity and cost can be exploited.

The markedly different angles of transcendence and the radically different degrees of tension with 'the world' between China and western Christianity create different relations between cyclic time and forward looking time; between Being and Becoming; between the Outer and the Inner; between divine dissatisfactions and the pursuit of an ideal Peace and Harmony; between failure as weakness or inadequacy and failure as evil or alienation; between the meditative mode of the wisdom of the sages and prophetic denunciation. At the same time mirror images of the Other appear in disguise and with more or less centrality: the Chinese concern for a right relation with the cosmos and the associated geomantic orientations is shadowed by Renaissance ideas of proportion in music and architecture derived from ancient Greece. Contemporary humanists steeped in the Greek tradition relate easily both to Renaissance ideas of harmony and maybe the life of the courtier, and respond with equal ease to a Chinese aesthetic and the modes of being cultivated by Chinese poets, painters and sages, especially those forms which bring Nature and society into right relations.

This pursuit of right relationships within a scheme of prescribed roles and attendant duties contrasts sharply with the Christian world of strenuous moral self-scrutiny without the secure definition of role offered by the idea of my station and its duties[7]. Christian self-fashioning is both ill-defined and open-ended to allow for the forward pull of time and purpose and the realisation of a kingdom beyond this world. The Christian world is visited by divine discontents and a profound sense of the distance between the fallenness of human nature and the demand to pursue perfection in alignment with the perfect will of God. The Christian sense of the radical nature of evil and of a need to seek a city 'whose builder and maker is God' is endemic to modern culture in the West, both with regard to self-fashioning and the purposes of politics. Secular politics are not concerned so much with the establishment of harmonious order, or what Shakespeare called 'degree', as with the re-creation of society sometimes within the context of a millenarian hope. Contrasts of this kind mean that when elements of the Christian repertoire seep into Chinese society, often through missionaries, the settled order suffers a major inundation. The idea of a great leap forward incorporates the forward impulsion of time and the replacement of the old order by the new.

---

[7] Ryrie, *Being Protestant in Reformation Britain*

The kind of contrast just sketched between the West and China might be made between any two major civilisations. It is too easily assumed that we are confronted with a global smorgasbord of incompatible options understood as mutually contradictory beliefs about the world, and that these beliefs are internally incoherent. On the contrary, we live within civilisations that between them provide an exhaustive repertoire of life choices and ways of being and becoming. Each of these ways is both internally coherent in terms of a logic of signs *and* set at an angle which cannot cover all possibilities. Coverage in one area creates gaps and lacks in others. For example, the Christian pilgrimage from the City of Destruction to the City of God includes periods of sojourn in the Delectable Mountains for refreshment of spirit but the journey forward must be resumed, whereas a Chinese adept wends a peaceful way through a carefully tended landscape punctuated by shrines to a temple at its heart that provides the focal point of the journey. For the Chinese adept rituals and codes of behaviour offer settled and satisfying models of being in the world, whereas within Christianity rituals and codes may well be suspect and subordinate to the inward quest for grace and for salvation driven by shortness of time.

This suspicion of codes and rituals as providing cover for overt power and inner corruption is now endemic in western society irrespective of its religious roots. The desire to maintain outward composure and secure respect without loss of face is very widespread in all kinds of human society, and yet Christianity lacks an honour code and provides no rules to compensate for loss of face. It is a gap that has to be filled from other sources, in particular from the inheritance of the ancient classical world. A care for the continuity of the generations is another very widespread human characteristic, and in China the care for continuity is expressed in forms of veneration that mount perpetual guard over the honour of the family so that the individual is inserted within a chain of being. Judaism also exhibits a care for genealogy expressed in the invocation of the patriarchs as founding fathers. Yet Christianity has trouble with the venerations of ancestors and founding fathers, and even with a primary loyalty to the family: it is a religion of the Son and the charismatic gifts of the Spirit breaking into the continuity of the generations and falling on whom it will. 'Let the dead bury their dead' represents a demand to go forward and not look back and it runs contrary to what most of humankind regards as natural human instincts.

Whatever concessions Christianity has to make to the imperatives of territory and to the continuity of the fathers from generation to generation, it deals in a world that is passing away and giving place to the new. Once you have a faith that breaks with the continuity of the generations and invokes a Spirit that falls on whom it will as part of a new birth that sets aside the tradition of the fathers, you have the beginnings of a voluntary religiosity. This voluntary religiosity challenges the territorial imperative and undermines automatic incorporation within the territorial group in union with others who acknowledge the ties of blood, even if these are purely fictive. If the reserve towards the world in Christianity creates a hiatus with regard to loyalty to the family from the Chinese perspective, the Christian reserve towards wealth creates a hiatus with regard to the commendation of honestly achieved prosperity in Judaism. The Christian exaltation of 'the poor', of charity towards the poor and of the embrace of poverty, was from the beginning in tension with the particular rights and duties of citizenship as understood in the Roman Empire.[8]

Diasporic Religion

Diasporic religion was initiated by a break with territory where the Jewish people under covenant wandered across frontiers and sometimes found themselves a source of chronic contention, partly on account of different perspectives on the world, for example, attitudes to prosperity; partly on account of the social niche they occupied, especially where it involved greater wealth and lower socio-religious status; partly on account of the dynamic of relations between majorities and minorities; and partly on account of difficult but intertwined histories. Membership remained an ascribed status acquired at birth, but the link with a homeland was cut and the synagogue became the local focus of an ethnic group wandering across frontiers. The Jews were pioneers of religion in diaspora; and in more recent times various ethno-religious peoples like the Armenians, the Greeks and the Christian Lebanese have scattered to the far corners of the world, often fulfilling particular occupational roles and living in ghettos. The relationships experienced by the Jews in diaspora, though they have their own specific problems, provide a paradigm for contemporary flows all over the world, from Muslims in Europe to the Chinese in South-East Asia. In general the minority status of an ethnic group in diaspora will reinforce religious identifications that distinguish the minority from the majority in the host country. All over the world religion is reinforced and made more explicit by the mere fact of intensified contact, especially where there are serious differences of power and status between one civilisation and another and by the dynamic of relationships between minorities and majorities. These dynamics are reinforced

---

[8]   Brown, *Through the Eye of a Needle*, Chapter 4.

where ethno-religious groups lie at the edge of major boundaries or across them: for example in Northern Ireland, the Caucasus, South-Eastern Europe, the Levant, the countries on the Islamic-Christian frontier from Ghana to the Sudan, western China and South-Eastern Asia.

Contemporary Voluntarism

Diasporic religion breaks the tie with the territorial imperative, but at the same time it reinforces the nexus of religion with ethnicity. Classical voluntarism represents a much more dramatic break because it releases religion from the ethnic tie as well as from the territorial imperative. This release from territory and ethnicity was dramatically present in Early Christianity, even though Christians often drew their converts from diasporic Judaism. Apart from sectarian groups that revived the radical spirit of the Gospels, voluntarism lay dormant for many centuries once Christianity itself became an established faith. Then at some time in the post-Reformation period, small groups emerged within established Christianity that pursued a more intense individual piety, beginning in Germany and England.[9] Today classical voluntarism presents the major challenge to established majority faiths everywhere, with different balances of power in each case: voluntary religion in the form of Evangelical Christianity in Latin America forges ahead, whereas in Afghanistan it is violently extruded and in China watched with a suspicious and vigilant eye.

Classical voluntarism began within established Protestant churches, often at a quite high social level, and then created large communities further down the social scale as these subordinate communities came to self-consciousness. Classical voluntarism took increasingly populist forms up to the emergence of Pentecostalism in several parts of the world, but most dramatically and influentially in the United States. Pentecostalism brings together black and white revivalism and the charismatic 'gifts of the Spirit' with layers of inspirited religiosity all over the globe, and is able to cross any number of cultural frontiers and adapt to local culture without ceasing to be recognisable as a populist form of Christianity. It provides platforms for the disciplined pursuit of moral and material betterment, including a reconstitution of the family where the male renounces macho irresponsibility to embrace the domestic virtues. Everywhere it is poised against the emplacements of territorial religion, although insofar as it enters into local cultures it may take on their specific colouring, for example

---

[9]   Gregory, *The Unintended Reformation*.

among the peoples of the Andes or in relation to the shamanistic traditions of South Korea, or as it converts large numbers among the Roma of Southern and Eastern Europe. If these ethnic groups themselves move across frontiers to North America or Europe their local Pentecostal churches, whether in Boston or Amsterdam, take on some of the characteristics of diaspora. Ghanaian Pentecostals in the cities of Northern Europe or North America constitute a people in diaspora.

If Pentecostalism represents a voluntarism where the religious community holds individualism in check and inculcates the disciplines of betterment and survival, modern spirituality of the self sees no needs for such communal disciplines. It shifts from dramatic new birth in order to live a new life and finally banish chaos, to a therapeutic mode that concentrates on the flowering of the true self. The lack of a strong communal bond means that there is relatively little by way of moral demand and only a barely discernible moral structure. That is because morality is generated by living together over time in a particular place, and people who embrace free-floating spirituality are usually on the move. Spirituality picks up fragments of cosmic religiosity, for example where individuals on the move come together in a temporary communitarian celebration of the procession of the seasons and a reverence for the amoral forces of Nature. Neo-paganism of this kind flourishes in countries where the established churches have been seriously weakened and intelligentsias look back to pre-Christian cults as sources of authentic and unfettered Being, for example in the Balkan States, in parts of Russia and the Caucasus, as well as in many parts of sub-Saharan Africa where elites strive to create new forms of indigenous cultural bond.

I have been arguing for the resilience of established religion and the recurrence within established religion of elements of the repertoire of archaic religiosity. If we take established religion and archaic religiosity together the thematic repertoire includes festivals of nature and the life cycle and the demand for blood sacrifice from the warrior hero; the maintenance of peace and order against chaos; the celebration of sacred territory for a sacred people; a myth of origins, recurrent crises and eventual destiny which includes a special status within the order of the world; Founding Fathers and a succession of iconic leaders; the principle of securing sacred boundaries, often in relation to natural features such as the sea, rivers and mountains; sacred centres dominated by major monuments and icons of identity. There are also forms of collective religion in diaspora which are both pulled towards the sacred centres of major civilisations and are liable to be either subordinated or extruded by the host civilisation, as the Jews in ancient Egypt were subordinated by their hosts, at least according to their founding myth in the Hebrew Bible. Diaspora groups will strive hard to maintain collective solidarity. They carry with them a carefully tended memory of their original homeland and its sacred sites.

I have also argued that the expansion of the voluntary principle constantly interacts with the resilience of establishment and the persistent repertoire of archaic religiosity. Voluntary religion is most likely to emerge where the axial angle of transcendence encourages direct access of the individual to the divine and creates an individual conscience that transforms the images of cosmic religiosity into a spiritual landscape of inward progress from destruction to redemption or spiritual fulfilment. The optimum conditions for the expansion of voluntary religion occur where Protestantism mingles with the Enlightenment to produce what in the West would be regarded as the 'modern subject' and everything Charles Taylor has discussed in his *Sources of the Self*.[10] Voluntary religion provides fertile soil for a concept of human rights in persistent tension with the necessities of collective survival in all the modes of established religion and of religions in diaspora. Diasporic religions both seek to protect their integrity against the disintegrative potential of human rights discourse and to deploy that discourse in their own collective defence.

It would be possible to devise a global map of the distribution of these three types of religiosity – established, diasporic and voluntary – perhaps beginning with Islam, which, after all, accounts for over one-fifth of humankind. From Dakar in West Africa to Jakarta in Indonesia, Islam achieves some kind of establishment, perhaps most obviously in the central belt of the Arabic states, Iran and Pakistan, but also in somewhat lighter forms in Indonesia and parts of West Africa. Islam also exists in diasporic forms in areas from China to Western Europe. At the same time individualisation, self-conscious commitment and the separation of religion from the primordial collective and 'immemorial' tradition occur within Islam to some extent just as they do in Christianity, and can even involve conversion to Christianity in places as unlikely and diverse as Iran, Morocco and Algeria. Faith can separate itself from identity. That at least is the argument of Olivier Roy which I take up in a further treatment of the tension between the voluntary and the collectivistic (or traditional) forms of religion in Chapter 7.[11] Here I rather conclude by sketching what a global map of established and voluntary religion would look like in America and China as the

10   Taylor, *Sources of the Self*.
11   Olivier Roy, 'The Transformation of the Arab World', *Journal of Democracy* (July 2012, 23: 3, pp. 5–18).

two contemporary superpowers, in India as a future superpower and in Russia as perhaps a superpower of the past.

I would contrast America and India on the one hand as pre-eminent examples of the separation of religion and the state; and China and Russia as pre-eminent examples of what in the West would be called caesaro-papism. I would want to show that even where religion and the state are clearly separated religion is still in some important sense established. The Indian sub-continent presents an interesting case because its partition in 1947 proceeded entirely along religious lines with very large Muslim majorities in Pakistan and Bangladesh, where minorities experience serious pressure from the majority, and India, where there is a large Hindu majority and two significant minorities, one Muslim and one Christian, both concentrated in particular areas and both under pressure in spite of the separation of religion and the state and the secular credentials of the founding political dynasties. One of the great parties of the Indian state promotes the ideology of the essentially Hindu character of Indian society through the concept of Hindutva.

Likewise in the United States – in spite of the First Amendment and the secular credentials of the Founding Fathers, and a massive pluralism characterised by constant switching between denominations – the nation is defined in Judeo-Christian terms which reflect the religious range of its European origins. There are shadow establishments of religion area by area, especially in the South, and local forms of religious hegemony, for example Methodists and Catholics in Kansas. America is defined as an imperium stretching 'from sea to shining sea', its boundaries are celebrated as demarcating 'the last best hope of mankind' and its leaders are accorded iconic status.

In the case of Russia, it has throughout its history regarded itself as a third Rome on the Byzantine model of the virtual fusion of Church and empire, and it has now returned to a modified form of this model after just 70 years of undisputed communist hegemony. The breakup of the Soviet Union in 1989–90 occurred entirely along ethno-religious lines, above all in the Muslim states of Central Asia; and the remaining points of tension are found in Muslim majority areas within the Caucasus.

Finally, in the case of China we have the most impressive example of the continuity of establishment over more than two millennia based on a dualism where religious needs have been provided by Buddhism and Daoism, and the hierarchical structure of the state has been maintained by a tradition of Confucian wisdom still intact today and undergoing revival. The centre encounters problems in its eastern and southern peripheries where the majorities are both religiously and ethnically distinct. Christianity arrived in a collectivistic Catholic form, first at the elite level with the Jesuit missions and then through Catholic missions with a strong communitarian character; Christianity also seeped in through the syncretism of the Taiping movement which resulted in chaos and the re-establishment of order only after the loss of millions of lives; most characteristically Christianity has come through versions of Protestant voluntarism that have expanded considerably over recent decades, but only up to the level of, say, 3–4 per cent. As in the case of Soviet Russia, China experienced strong nationalist and communist movements, each with some Christian elements in the background, that led to the establishment of a communist hegemony 'with a Chinese face', and massive manifestations that recouped features from the repertoire of archaic civilisation, including sacred leaders and sacred texts, the execration of the foreigner and the invocation of the sacred land. The contemporary interest, particularly among academics, in some revival of Confucianism, represents a desire to recuperate in modernised dress and as a matter of conscious choice rather than immemorial tradition an ethos of social respect, dedication and harmony, combined with a wisdom tradition with deep roots in Chinese history.

In all four cases the human rights discourse has cut across the interests of an established collectivity and the *realpolitik* of survival. Although many commentators might regard the United States as an exception, its political behaviour, particularly after its symbolic heartland was attacked on 9/11, suggests that collective survival and the interests of the sacred nation override adherence to human rights. The same is true of India, while in the case of Russia and China there is an explicit commitment to the necessities of political order against chaos and to collective survival.

Even if one were to extend this global map to Western Europe it would be obvious that the majoritarian principle in alliance with some form of establishment extends from Britain at one end of the continent to Greece, Romania and Poland at the other. Much sociological writing, including my own, has been devoted to tracing the advance of a voluntary principle often derived in its several origins, though not necessarily in its development, from Protestantism in alliance with the Enlightenment. The voluntary principle in its pietistic and ecstatic form has made its most spectacular advances in the spread of Pentecostalism over the last half century. But one may doubt whether *active* voluntarism is likely to include significantly more than 10–20 per cent of any given society, though its underlying ethos may seep through society as a whole with an increase in personal choice and individual commitment.

Establishment and the territorial imperative taken together remain stubbornly resilient. As I argued at the outset, if voluntarism is regarded as the wave of the future it beats against an obstinate core of territorial religion exhibiting characteristics recurrent over the last four millennia and most unlikely to disappear any time soon.

Chapter 7
Nationalism and Religion: Collective Identity and Choice

In common with Anthony Smith and Adrian Hastings I regard national self-awareness as having a longer history than the strictly modernist approach might allow. Unlike the modernist school in studies of nationalism, associated in particular with Ernest Gellner, I see the English nation, including the political nation, as long pre-dating industrialisation.[1] From the outset I need to make my position clear on this controversial issue in the study of nationalism.

My interest in nationalism began with my work on pacifism, given that Christian and secular pacifists alike blamed nationalism for encouraging violence. Nationalism played a crucial role in my general theory of secularisation. To devise a theory of secularisation I had to place the role of nationalism alongside the role of the Enlightenment and the role of revolutionary political ideology. In the general theory I integrated broadly accepted empirical tendencies in belief and practice in modern societies with wide variations due to different historical experiences and types of Christianity, especially the difference between Protestantism and Catholicism. The vitality of religion in industrialised modernity depended to an important degree on whether it acted as a benign midwife at the birth of the nation, as in Poland and Ireland, or a malign fairy, as in France and Italy. The same was true of the Enlightenment. Religious vitality depended in part on whether Christianity and the different versions of the Enlightenment were partially aligned – as in England, Scotland, the USA, Canada, Switzerland and Germany – or at war, as in France and Italy. The same was true of revolutionary political ideology. A great deal depended on whether there were non-revolutionary potentials for change – as in England, North America and Germany – or whether there was outright war between clerical reaction and revolutionary change, as in much of southern Catholic Europe.

---

[1] Anthony Smith, *Nationalism* (Cambridge: Polity, 2001); *The Antiquity of Nations* (Cambridge: Polity, 2004). Adrian Hastings, *The Construction of Nationhood: Ethnicity, Religion and Nationalism* (Cambridge: Cambridge University Press, 1997). Ernest Gellner, *Nations and Nationalism* (Ithaca: Cornell University Press, 1983).

I focussed in particular on the morphological similarities between Christianity and nationalism, Christianity and Enlightenment, Christianity and revolutionary ideology. I canvassed the Romantic messianism analysed by Jacob Talmon and (latterly) charismatic leadership and Founding Fatherhood.[2] I was interested in the clash between the children of darkness and the children of light, and a shared inheritance of forerunners, martyrs and heroes, vanguards and avant-gardes, ages and stages, rituals and icons, holy lands and universal cities, realised eschatology and canonical texts. Above all I was interested in the different *outcomes* in the relationship of religion with nationalism, religion with Enlightenment, religion with revolutionary political ideology.

What were these different outcomes? Nationalism has remained pervasive in the USA, in non-revolutionary England, in secularist France, in Soviet Russia and now in post-communist Russia; but the outcomes for religion turned out to be strikingly different. In the USA the secularisation of the state and pluralism, taken together, secured the autonomy and vitality of religion. In England and Northern Protestant Europe religious establishment has resulted in a passive religiosity that in practice could easily succumb to passive secularity. In France a revolutionary secularism tried to confine religion to the private sphere; and in Russia, China, Ethiopia and Turkey revolutionary secularism launched major assaults on religion, mostly unsuccessful.

If secularisation had triumphed unequivocally my argument here would be otiose. If the Enlightenment had triumphed then we would already be safely lodged in an Age of Reason. If religion had morphed into nationalism without significant remainder I would only be discussing a transition. If religion could be comprehensively understood as an alienated sign of the human aspiration for a new earth and a new man then religion would have emptied out into ever-glorious political revolution: 1989 said 'Goodbye to All That'. The revolutions my Marxist colleagues expected did not happen, while those none of us expected did; hence a little book I wrote entitled *Forbidden Revolutions* comparing the forbidden Evangelical revolution in the Global South, notably Latin America, with the forbidden revolutions of 1989.[3]

For my part I was, first of all, dubious about secularisation as a homogeneous process leading inexorably to a future presaged by France or Sweden, and much

---

[2]   Jacob Talmon, *Political Messianism: The Romantic Phase* (London: Secker and Warburg, 1960); Chapter 8 in this book, published originally as David Martin, 'Charisma and Founding Fatherhood', in Vivian Ibrahim and Margit Wunsch (eds), *Political Leadership, Nations and Charisma* (New York: Routledge, 2012, pp. 40–51).

[3]   David Martin, *Forbidden Revolutions: Pentecostalism in Latin America and Catholicism in Eastern Europe* (London: SPCK, 1996).

later I have been equally dubious about claims that 'God is back' merely because religion is back as a social problem.[4] Religion never went away and it was never privatised. Only the historically exceptional French model of privatisation led us to think religion excluded from the public square. Throughout the post-war period the major force in European politics was Christian Democracy. What *has* occurred is the triumph of personal choice in Western Europe, Canada and the USA. In Western Europe and Canada that means passive dissociation from religion, whereas in the USA it means active association with religion, except where social capital had been eroded in the way identified by David Putnam in *Bowling Alone*.[5]

I come now to my promised contrast between collective identity and individual choice. For the West at least that is a crucial dialectic and one that reaches back, as Adam Seligman maintained in *Modernity's Wager*, to the emergence of religion as choice and inwardness in a sequence running from Jeremiah to Jesus, Paul and Augustine, and to Early Christianity as a voluntary association in its three formative centuries.[6] My task now is to trace how that dialectic has worked out between the two autonomous powers of religion and nationalism in three revolutionary transformations. The revolutions of 1989 look like evidence for the resilience of ethno-religion as a vehicle of collective identity. Evangelical Christianity in the Global South looks like a primary expression of personal choice in collision with nationalism, including nationalist religion, in Latin America, Africa and Asia. As for the revolutions in the Arab World, some see them as nationalism in another guise, while others regard them as Islam taking over from nationalism as a primary vehicle of collective identity.

This problematic pushes me to trace the mingling of motifs in Christianity and nascent nationalism over the last half millennium *without* Christianity being straightforwardly taken over and secularised by nationalism. That requires some engagement with the role of elites in promoting nationalism, and it has particular relevance to the ethno-religious transformations beginning in 1989. Then I have to trace the emergence of the voluntary principle of personal choice and lay participation in Evangelicalism. That requires some engagement with cultural revolution *from the bottom up* and it has particular relevance to Latin American transformations that have now spread to sub-Saharan Africa and Asia.

---

4   Micklethwait and Wooldridge, *God is Back*.
5   David Putnam, *Bowling Alone: The Collapse and Revival of American Community* (New York: Simon and Shuster, 2000).
6   Adam Seligman, *Modernity's Wager: Authority, the Self, and Transcendence* (Princeton: Princeton University Press, 2000).

Finally: how far have these shifts occurred in Islam? I have to draw out the difference between ethno-religion after 1989 in post-Soviet Eurasia as it struggled against a foreign secular ideology and Islamic movements in the Arab world struggling against oppressive nationalist movements that imposed western secularism and colluded with western interests. Cairo is not Prague. I have to draw out the difference between the chosen religious faith of Christians in the two-thirds world and what may be the emerging element of choice in the Arab world. That includes the very *conscious* embrace of some form of Islamism *and* of a semi-secular self-determination among the vast swathes of alienated young people. Olivier Roy even suggests that Islam might follow Christianity in gradually hiving off from the broader culture and becoming a highly personal faith, leaving passive secularity to occupy the space of the sacred.[7]

The Transformations of 1989

As a prelude to thinking about the events of 1989 I emphasise the *mutuality* of religion and nationalism over several centuries, not the nineteenth-century mutation of religion into nationalism. Consider John Wycliffe. Wycliffe was a progenitor of the Reformation who sought in 1384 to put an English Bible before the English people so that they might hear the Word and judge for themselves. The choice was between Edward of England and Urban of Rome. Consider John Milton. In his *Areopagitica* published in 1644 Milton envisaged a noble and puissant English nation, and he understood the role of print in creating the unified cultural construct of the nation. He also lived at a time when Protestant faith in the perspicuity of Scripture led to any number of jostling interpretations of Scripture. An open Bible meant pluralism and faith as personal choice.

Consider George Friedrich Handel, also discussed by Linda Colley in relation to English nationalism.[8] Handel's Italian operas were attacked because Italy was associated with the foppish world of Baroque and Catholic autocracy, and admired because Protestant England was a New Rome where Ciceronian civic humanism celebrated the triumph of duty over love. Handel's English oratorios

---

[7]   Roy, 'The Transformation of the Arab World'.

[8]   Linda Colley, *Britons: Forging the Nation 1701–1837* (London: Pimlico, 1992, pp. 31–3): David Martin, 'The Sociology of Religion and Handel's Reception', in Elisabeth Arweck and William Keenan (eds), *Materializing Religion: Expression, Performance and Ritual* (Aldershot: Ashgate, 2006, pp. 161–74); and David Martin, 'The Handel Revolution', *Books and Culture* (March/April 2011). Those interested in Handel's reception should consult the scholarly work of Thomas McGeary and Ilias Chrissochoidis.

celebrated a collective religiosity on the Judaic model where England played the typical Protestant role of a New Israel following a tradition exemplified by Milton in *Samson Agonistes*. Yet through *Messiah* Handel became central to the voluntary faith of Evangelicalism as that provided the collective identity of Victorian England. According to John Osborne he gave England its lay religiosity.[9]

This dialectic of the collective (whether religious or nationalist or ethno-religious) and personal religious inwardness can be traced throughout European history. In the fifteenth century there was an association between the proto-Protestant Hussite movement and incipient Czech nationalism which still survives in the mythology of Czech nationalism. In Hungary, a country that fits very well Ernest Gellner's model of linguistic homogenisation as a criterion for membership in the nation, the national myth was associated with Protestantism.[10] In Germany Luther is celebrated both as an icon of the individual standing up to Pope and emperor and as an icon of the Germanic nation and language. In Norway the Pietist preacher Hauge and the Haugean movement were instrumental in tending Norwegian consciousness (as well as industrialisation). In Denmark Grundtvig played a similar role, which is one reason he was targeted by Kierkegaard in the name of existential choice.

The events of 1989 did not straightforwardly herald the arrival of democracy, as recent trends in Hungary, Romania, Moldova and Ukraine indicate. As communism and the Soviet Empire broke up, the roles played by religious nationalism and cultural nationalism varied considerably from country to country, though there was clearly a moment from Lithuania to Ukraine where the movement for national liberation processed into the public arena behind the banners of religion. After that, religion was partly compromised by entering into politics or seeking old positions of power and wealth, as in Russia.

The power of ethno-religion was particularly clear in Serbia, Poland and Romania. In Poland the influence of the Pope and of Solidarity was obviously significant, and it was also significant far beyond the borders of Poland. In Serbia the Church adopted a hyper-nationalistic attitude based on the role of Serbia as a victim nation and the threat to the sacred pilgrimage sites of Kosovo. In Romania the initial thrust of revolt was led by a Hungarian Protestant pastor. But religion was also influential in Ukraine, Slovakia, Croatia, East Germany and Lithuania. In Ukraine Uniate Catholics and Ukrainian Orthodox looked

---

[9]   John Osborne, *God Rot Tunbridge Wells* (DVD for the third centenary of Handel's birth in 1985).

[10]   Daniele Conversi, 'Homogenisation, Nationalism and War: Should we Still Read Ernest Gellner?' *Nations and Nationalism* (2007, 13: 3, pp. 371–94).

to the West and provided the core of the movement for national independence, while the Orthodox of the Moscow Patriarchate looked more to Russia. East Germany is especially interesting because the old association of Lutheranism with nationalism had been discredited by the Nazi period and the Lutheran Church severely weakened by planned secularisation. Nevertheless it provided the sacred space out of which vast crowds of people sallied forth to confront and overthrow the regime. Religion also assisted in the mobilisation of minority groups and submerged nations: Bulgarians and Germans inside Russia as well Georgia and Armenia; and the various Muslim nationalities of the Caucasus, and Muslims in Bosnia and Bulgaria. Pentecostalism even found a response among the Roma as part of a revision of their despised identity, though Pentecostalism more generally transcended frontiers and in Ukraine encouraged migration.

But in Estonia and Czech Lands religion had associations with German cultural superiority which meant that religion could be severely weakened under communist pressure and the potential for change carried therefore by culture, liberalism and nationalism. In Slovenia language was more important than religion, and in Bulgaria religion took the form of attachment to the land as well as Orthodoxy.[11] In Hungary there were various foci of revolt: some more nationalist, historical and linguistic; some more associated with Catholicism. The revival of paganism by intellectuals in the Baltic as the authentic pre-Christian religion of the folk has as much to do with cultural nationalism as religion; and cultural nationalism lies behind the deposition of Lenin in favour of Tamerlane (Timur the Lame) in Uzbekistan and Genghis Khan in Mongolia.[12]

Yet there was also much evidence for the transnational status and autonomy of religion in, for example, foci of protest at both a compromised official Church and the state: for instance, Father Alexander Men in Moscow, and Tomas Halik and other associates of Vaclav Havel in Prague. There were transnational charismatic movements of many different kinds to be found among the Transylvanian Calvinists and Baptists, the Lord's Army in Romania, the monasteries of the Ukrainian Uniates and a remarkably successful Pentecostal mega-church in Kiev led by a Nigerian. Ecumenical agencies sought to offer a ministry of reconciliation as they did in Europe after the Second World War.

---

[11]   Chris Hann and Hermann Goetz (eds), *Eastern Christians in Anthropological Perspective* (Berkeley: University of California Press, 2010); Jakelić, *Collectivistic Religions*. This excellent volume by Jakelić stresses the resilience of automatic and collective belonging.
[12]   Ališauskienė and Schröder, *Religious Diversity in Post-Soviet Society*.

The Global Evangelical/Pentecostal Transformation

Turning to the global expansion of Evangelical Christianity, I need to outline how choice was fostered under the aegis of Evangelicalism, even though temporarily checked after the Reformation by the creation of the Church-state, and then the Church-nation, and the capacity of Evangelicalism to become the accepted faith of the majority. Earlier I outlined the reciprocal relation between religion and nationalism in English and European history in figures like Wycliffe and Hus, Luther and Milton. There is a complicated dance here between Protestantism as a faith based on choice and nationalism as an ideology based on birthright identity because once a religion based on choice becomes the faith of a majority – as it did in Pietist Scandinavia, New England, Northern Ireland and Victorian Britain – it confers birthright identity.[13] Nevertheless a faith which expects a crisis of conversion to be resolved by mature commitment is in a profound sense a 'religion of choice'; and its astonishing expansion all over the two-thirds world represents the global expansion of an egalitarianism of the spirit lighting on whom it will, vigorous popular leadership, lay organisation, self-education, personal commitment, individualisation and interiority.

History so far has been a story of birthright identities, so the dramatic global expansion of options, inwardness and active commitment over the last half century represents a major revolutionary transformation. Arguably the popularity of spirituality in the contemporary West at the expense of institutional forms and external formulae further extends the inwardness of the spirit anticipated by Troeltsch as the modern form of Christianity.[14] There is a major difference between western spirituality and religions of the spirit elsewhere because western spirituality often dispenses with any long-term denominational commitment, whereas in the developing world conversion and change of life entail corporate discipline and mutual support. Of course, one should never forget that the Church-state order remains a presence throughout many of the sometime imperial territories of the developing world, above all in the massive

---

[13]   Pentecostalism is a sung creed and owes much to the spontaneous 'singing in the spirit' characteristic of the Welsh Revival of 1904–05. The hymns of the revival were mainly sung in Welsh and were part of an implicit revival of Welsh consciousness, according to James Deaville and Katherine Stopa in a chapter on the Welsh Revival contributed to Martin Clarke (ed.), *Music and Theology in Nineteenth-Century Britain* (Farnham: Ashgate, 2012, pp. 117–32).

[14]   Ernst Troeltsch, *Kritische Gesamtausgabe Band 17* (Berlin: De Gruyter, 2006, pp. 176–87).

emplacements of the Catholic Church in Latin America but also within the ex-territories of the British and French empires.

The subversion of the state churches of the Reformation began with the inwardness of Pietism associated with places like Herrnhut and Halle. It continued apace when Evangelical Revivals and Awakenings, notably Methodism, broke away from the state Church in Britain and eventually contributed mightily to the universal voluntarism of the United State. This meant that for Americans voluntary religion became just as much an inheritance by birth as it was in Victorian England, and that American Evangelicalism forged a strong tie with American nationalism. This historical process whereby voluntarism stepped westward from Germany to England and then from England to America came to fruition in Los Angeles in 1906 when white and black revivalism fused in Pentecostalism to create a faith capable of crossing any number of cultural species barriers, from Brazil to the Philippines and from Ghana to South Korea.[15] Of course, nothing prevents Evangelicalism from forging intermittent alliances with nationalism virtually anywhere in the developing world, from South Korea to Tanzania.

Nationalism, like Enlightenment and like radical political revolution, was fostered by elites. The Evangelical transformation comes from below and is so peaceful most people have no idea how fast it moves. In Brazil, for example, there are now some 40 million Protestants, a three-fold increase in 30 years. By comparison, the parallel movement of the Catholic base communities was under the aegis of a hegemonic Church, and was therefore both more sophisticated and less popular. Pentecostalism was propagated by buccaneering religious entrepreneurs like Aimee McPherson, drawn from what I call a 'buried intelligentsia'. Its leaders trained on the job and spoke the language of the people to the people. At the same time versions of Pentecostal and charismatic Christianity also appealed to large sectors of the rapidly expanding middle classes all over South and Central America, many of them organised in mega-churches and inclined to prosperity theology. In Guatemala, for example, Pentecostal and Evangelical Christianity together number over 25 per cent of the population and appeal equally to the large Mayan minority and to the middle classes of Guatemala City.

Popular Pentecostalism is often dismissed as inauthentic by cultural elites when compared with spiritist movements like Candomblé or revivals of pre-Columbian practices.[16] That fits very well with a long tradition among

---

[15]   David Martin, *Pentecostalism: The World Their Parish* (Oxford: Blackwell, 2006).

[16]   David Lehmann, *Struggle for the Spirit: Religious Transformation and Popular Culture in Brazil and Latin America* (Cambridge: Polity, 1996).

intellectuals of romantically idealising the culture of the folk. Béla Bartók would not have been interested in collecting Evangelical choruses and turning them into quartets: Gypsies yes, Pentecostals no; and definitely not today's Pentecostal gypsies. Pentecostals can be derided as American imports, but in their own eyes they had gone over the head of contemptuous local hierarchies to enjoy a transnational modernity for which America often acts as a universal lode-star, especially though modern communications. Pentecostals are as much a consequence of the communications revolution as the young protesters of Tahrir Square, and they are conspicuous virtuosi in the use of contemporary media. They are global and local, rapidly indigenising and easily linking up with global modernisation. They represent a clash between a global voluntarism and various forms of cultural nationalism, including the kind of established Catholicism that understands itself as part of the national tradition. It is too often forgotten how much of the Catholic Church maintains its alliance with social paternalism and with the social elite, in particular through the role played by the newer religious orders in elite education.[17]

Pentecostals are not only criticised for pre-empting the natural constituency of the base communities but for helping to erode the authentic cultural integrity of indigenous peoples like the Maya and the Aymara. For their part Pentecostals believed they had given up semi-paganism for the authentic world of the New Testament: speaking in tongues, exorcism and divine healing. From a rather different viewpoint Pentecostals in Latin America are criticised as reviving ancient spirit cults in modern guise. And the argument is not without force because Pentecostalism is both very ancient and very modern. That is as true of Africa and Asia as of Latin America. There are many contexts in Africa, for example Uganda and Zimbabwe, and in Asia, for example South Korea, where the Pentecostal fusion of ancient and modern spiritism seems more attractively authentic than the sober worship of the mainstream churches. The Catholic Church and the other mainstream churches in Africa act as non-governmental organisations (NGOs) and as major agents of modernisation and cultural modification. They have challenged the corrupt political elites. Pentecostalism resonates with the enchanted spirituality of Africa. It reinforces and incorporates tradition as well as creating a rupture with the past through conversion.[18] No wonder it succeeded. Indeed its success was so great from Accra to Manila that it

---

[17]   María Angélica Thumala, *Riqueza y Piedad: el Catolicismo de la Elite Económica Chilena* (Santiago: Debate, 2007).

[18]   Birgit Meyer, *Translating the Devil: Religion and Modernity among the Ewe in Ghana* (Edinburgh: Edinburgh University Press, 1999).

helped stimulate major charismatic manifestations in nearly all the mainstream churches. An expanded definition of the charismatic phenomenon even allows some sources to claim a global constituency of over half a billion people.

When Pentecostalism spread to sub-Saharan Africa it became part of a very rapidly expanding post-colonial Christianity reaching some 400 million people. Sub-Saharan Africa mostly lacks anything like the established majority church of Latin America, apart from the ancient churches in Ethiopia and Eritrea. Instead there is the shadowy presence of what were once established churches as in Europe, like the Catholics, Anglicans and Lutherans, alongside numerous Protestant denominations and African Initiated Churches or AICs. Choice is the norm. Pentecostals are very competitive and face vigorous competitors, including revivals of traditional religion actively constructed by nationalist post-colonial elites.

Post-colonial nationalism is a powerful force and the mainstream churches attempt to accommodate it with a conscious acculturation. In the immediate post-colonial period attention was focussed on the AICs as authentic expressions of African culture rather than on Pentecostal churches. At the same time Pentecostal churches share cultural genes with AICs, and can emerge in parallel with African nationalism and deploy the rhetoric of black power: Ezekiel Guti's transnational Pentecostal Church, the Zimbabwe Assemblies of God Africa, had its origins in the same part of Harare as Zimbabwean nationalism and has formed intermittent alliances both with Mugabe and the Movement for Democratic Change (MDC).[19]

Pentecostal churches adapted as rapidly to Africa as they had done to Latin America. Sometimes Evangelical and charismatic churches saw themselves as the authentic carriers of the national tradition so that in Tanzania, for example, political leaders went so far as to declare it a Christian country, in spite of a considerable Muslim minority. For some observers Pentecostals adapted all too well to an African interest in the goods associated with the gods and developed a neo-Pentecostal prosperity gospel that drew more on the Hebrew Scriptures than the New Testament. They were Afro-Jewish. The prosperity gospel was often promoted in transnational mega-churches appealing to the middle class and providing a complete alternative social environment, complete with banks, educational and medical facilities.

When Pentecostalism and the charismatic revival arrived in Asia it faced non-Christian establishments fortified in their resistance by nationalist movements that had fought for independence and against colonialism.

---

[19]   David Maxwell, *African Gifts of the Spirit: Pentecostalism and the Rise of a Transnational Religious Movement* (Oxford: Currey, 2006).

Pentecostalism and charismatic Christianity found three social niches very like those in Latin America and Africa: the minority ethnic group, for example groups in the interior of the Philippines and Borneo and the Chinese diaspora in Malaysia, Singapore and Indonesia; the poor, for example semi-literate women in China during the Cultural Revolution; and the new middle class of business people and specialists in communications technology in China and the Chinese diaspora alike. There seems to be an elective affinity between Protestant Christianity and Chinese culture.

How fast Pentecostalism and Christianity more generally spread has depended on whether the local nationalism was receptive or hostile. In mainland China, Taiwan and Japan nationalism defined Christianity as a foreign import and tried to inhibit its growth, so that Christianity has only affected some 4 per cent in China and Taiwan, and 2 per cent in Japan. Nevertheless there has been rapid growth recently in China so that the Evangelical community in Wenzhou, a coastal city in a geographical enclave, numbers some 15 per cent of a population of 6 million.[20] It ought to come as no surprise that these Chinese Evangelicals listen to Handel's *Messiah*. In South Korea, by contrast, Christianity affects some 25 per cent of the population, while in Singapore it affects some 15 per cent; and in both contexts there are large numbers of neo-Pentecostals attached to modern mega-churches. Mega-churches like New Creation and City Harvest in Singapore boast over 20,000 members, while some mega-churches in South Korea claim memberships in six figures.

Pentecostalism expands in India and even in Burma, but it encounters a strong current of ethno-religious nationalism directed at both Muslims and Christians, and at religious difference in ethnic minorities. The Philippines is a special case because there is a majority Catholic Church together with American cultural influence and the use of English. English is a major carrier of Pentecostal faith, and charismatic movements have expanded as much inside the Catholic Church, especially in the middle class, as outside it.[21] Nationalist feeling throughout Asia encourages a revival of indigenous religious traditions such as Confucianism, Buddhism and Daoism. Confucianism experiences a revival among the Chinese intelligentsia, and there are major Buddhist revivals in mainland China, South Korea, Singapore and Taiwan. Moreover, there are major sectors of people who

---

[20]   Nanlai Cao, *Constructing China's Jerusalem: Christians, Power and Place in Contemporary Wenzhou* (Stanford: Stanford University Press, 2010).

[21]   Kathleen Wiegele, *Investing in Miracles: El Shaddai and the Transformation of Popular Catholic Culture in the Philippines* (Honolulu: University of Hawai'i Press, 2005).

are merely secular in South Korea and Singapore; and in China itself, of course, the ruling Communist Party and its cadres are ideologically secularist.

Religion and Nationalism, Choice and Collective Identity in the Arab Spring

When we come to the Arab Spring we can dismiss western media approaches featuring good guys struggling with bad guys to establish democracy. Cairo is not Prague, and is not likely to be in the future. Instead I turn to some theses of Olivier Roy that bear on collective identity and choice.[22] Roy insists that the initial demonstrators in Tahrir Square were neither nationalists nor Islamists, but members of a demographically multitudinous new generation of sceptical and individualistic young people in the big cities with access to the internet. This generation disdains charismatic leaders and the patriarchal and clientelistic model of political relations. The Arab–Israeli conflict is not central, and they are not fanatical partisans of a supranational cause.

Yet in the Tunisian and Egyptian elections Islamist parties expressing religious values shared by the popular majority triumphed as the only 'credible parties of government'. Islamist parties have no more affection for democracy than the Egyptian army, and they deplore western values, pluralism, secularism and individualism. They affirm religion as central to national identity, and reject the kind of secularism promoted by earlier Arab nationalists.

These parties will succumb to internal individualisation and to demands for democratic debate, which means we are deluded in imagining democracy has to be associated with secularisation. The Islamists of Tunisia or even the Salafists of Egypt could become reluctant agents of a *political* secularisation, *not* the secularisation of society. For Roy, collective identity and faith are very different. Islam cannot be reconstructed as political ideology, and any attempt to restore Islamic norms by legal regulation is doomed. In part this is because Salafists declare that only a strict personal return to faith could serve as the basis of an Islamic society.

So, even among 'fundamentalists' we find personal choice, conviction and increasing diversity, separated from inherited tradition, traditional authorities and culture. Religious institutions hive off from the state, and there is scant agreement as to what in Islam is non-negotiable. Maybe in time the individual right to choose in religious matters will be accepted, though the response to the emergence of Evangelical churches in Morocco and Algeria does not suggest the transition will be easy. One major option is the Turkish model of a modern

---

[22]   Roy, 'The Transformation of the Arab World'.

political party trying to attract voters beyond the faithful, and adopting vaguely conservative causes like the family, property, honesty and the work ethic. As for uprooted global jihadists dreaming of a supra-national *umma*, they are now confined to the peripheries of the Arab world in Somalia, Yemen and the Sahel. The conflict that matters is not between the West and Islamic terror, but between the conservative Sunni world and the 'Shia Crescent', between Saudi Arabia and Iran. If Yoel Guzansky and Benedetta Berti are right, the initial thrust to democratisation has deepened old religious differences in a way dramatised for the whole region by unrest among the Shiite minority of Saudi Arabia and the Shiite majority of Bahrain.[23] At the same time, parliaments are not mosques. Religion turns into an horizon of meaning rather than specific norms, and Muslim conservatives resemble conservative Evangelicals in their defence of shared *values*. For Roy the separation of religion as personal faith from culture involves the embrace of 'holy ignorance', and this he sees as analogous to the spread of Pentecostalism within Christianity.[24]

The emergence of numerous individualistic young people sceptical of both the older kind of Arab nationalism and contemporary Islamism, but accepting Islam as their collective identity, raises interesting questions. According to Tarik Ahmed Elseewi there has been a transition from the 'imagined community' of Arab nationalism to a subjective imagination derived from innumerable nodes of transnational contact, including migrant bodies and migrating messages.[25] Of course, there are also those who point to polls of Egyptian opinion showing that whatever the electoral success of Islamists, in practice nationalism trumps religion. But if Elseewi is right these are the same developments that fostered the imagined transnational community of Pentecostalism. They are like and unlike, and the new subjective imagination should not be identified with the deepened religious consciousness illustrated by François Burgat in his *The Islamic Movement in North Africa* through numerous personal biographies.[26]

In several contemporary Muslim contexts, for example Turkey, Malaysia and Indonesia, religion and associated parties articulate broad values in the public square that may be widely shared outside the faithful. In its most benign

---

[23] Yoel Guzansky and Benedetta Berti, 'Is the New Middle East Stuck in its Sectarian Past? The Unspoken Dimension of the "Arab Spring"', *Orbis* (Winter 2013, 57: 1, pp. 135–51).

[24] Olivier Roy, *Holy Ignorance: When Religion and Culture Part Ways* (New York: Columbia University Press, 2010).

[25] Tariq Ahmed Elseewi, 'A Revolution of the Imagination', *International Journal of Communication* (2011, Feature 1197–206).

[26] François Burgat, *The Islamic Movement in North Africa* (Austin: University of Texas Press, 1997).

version the public sphere could become passively secular according to Lily Rahim. It could even echo constitutional arrangements in Northern Europe where the sacred is accepted as a public presence, subject to negotiation, provided society is not subject to religious regulation.[27] This suits a faith like Christianity, especially Pentecostalism, based on the spirit rather than the letter of the law, but can be made compatible with Islam. Whatever the distinctly alarming portents of the moment, perhaps in the longer perspective we might recollect José Casanova's comparison between nineteenth-century discourse about Catholicism as inherently illiberal and disloyal to the nation state and contemporary discourse about Islam.[28]

Conclusion

In conclusion, religion in the Arab world has not morphed into nationalism; nor has culture been secularised. Instead we may have some differentiation of politics and religion, though the omens in Egypt at the time of writing in December 2012 were dubious, and some embrace of choice in matters of faith, with Islam as the primary marker of collective identity. In Eastern Europe by comparison ethno-religion played a crucial role in the demise of a foreign secularist political ideology, for example in Poland. Where religion had failed to play a positive role in the emergence of the nation, as in Slovenia, Estonia and the Czech Republic, culture and language took its place. Yet even where religion succumbed to planned secularisation, as in East Germany, the churches provided symbolic space for political mobilisation.

In Eastern Europe and post-Soviet Eurasia collective religious belonging reflects history and ethnicity. As ever, the appeal to authenticity is a potent weapon in the hands of intellectual and political elites. In post-Soviet Eurasia the religion of the majority is recognised by the state and majority religions often collude with political power. Though relatively few may be regularly involved in religious practice or pilgrimage, as in Russia, the majority accept religion as a marker and personal choice is exercised in the interstices, often in Evangelical and Pentecostal denominations. Religion carries national identity under

---

27   Lily Rahim, 'Towards a Post-Islamist Secular Democracy in the Muslim World' (www. Sidney.edu.au/arts/government_international_relations/downloads/documents/1_3_Rahim_papers), a paper for the Contemporary Challenge of Politics Research Workshop, 31 October 2011 (University of Sydney, NSW, Australia).

28   José Casanova, 'The Politics of Nativism: Islam in Europe, Catholicism in the United States', *Philosophy and Social Criticism* (May/June 2012, 38, pp. 485–95).

threat: after all, religion almost always fulfils other roles than what we today label purely religious. The Muslim Brotherhood earns social credit and loyalty through its role in providing services in the voluntary sector, just as Protestant denominations earn social credit in Anglo-American societies and the Catholic and other mainstream churches earn credit throughout sub-Saharan Africa.

When we come to the developing world things vary across the continents. In Latin America much of the Catholic Church remains aligned with national elites, and the expansive voluntary sector of Evangelical Protestants is attacked as an inauthentic import inimical to historic national traditions. In Africa shadow establishments perform a vital role as NGOs in failed states and in a context of vigorous religious competition, in particular Pentecostalism. As in Latin America, Pentecostalism encounters nationalist criticism as an intrusion of transnational modernity. In Asia all forms of Christianity, including Pentecostalism, face pressure from religious establishments associated with nationalism, anti-colonialism and independence. Success depends on their ability to pick up sources of disaffection among the excluded or among marginal ethnicities: South Korea is a marginal nation whose nationalism has been carried by Christianity. The extraordinary expansion of Evangelical and charismatic Christianity throughout the Global South not only represents religion as choice but as modernisation, notwithstanding evident recourse to magical thinking. Magical thinking is both self-delusion and a way of imagining what is possible.[29] Assisted by modern communications, it reinforces confidence and the will to act. As for revolutionary political ideology, it has collapsed nearly everywhere outside North Korea, overtaken by a corrupt nationalist state capitalism in China and a corrupt nationalist state–Church alliance in Russia.

I have traced the incursions of personal choice into the powerful bastions of collective identity in three transformations and their implications for nationalism. There remains the question of the advance of personal choice understood as the embrace of mere secularity, not the kind of assertive secularism confining religion to the private sphere still influential in France, Turkey and China. From Sweden to the Congo the strength of religion is negatively correlated with existential security, according to Norris and Inglehart, and with individualisation according to Bruce.[30] All the Americas remain believing, apart from planned secularisation in Uruguay and Cuba. In Brazil 97 per cent believe

---

[29]   Paul Gifford, personal communication regarding a forthcoming book contrasting Catholicism and Pentecostalism in Africa.

[30]   Norris and Inglehart, *Sacred and Secular*; Bruce, *Secularization*.

in God, and even in Canada 80 per cent believe. Africa, India and Central Asia are throughout religious.

The billion or more secular people are found above all in Protestant Northern Europe, plus France, and in the Protestant British Commonwealth – all places where educational and media elites have sponsored secularisation – and in Israel. There are also countries like South Korea and Singapore where Protestantism has established a serious presence and there has also been a palpable secularisation. Japan is a special case. It is a secular country, resistant to Protestantism on nationalist grounds as a foreign import, though much influenced by it, and otherwise inclined to Buddhist new religions and rites performed simply as folk practice. Finally, there are those parts of Eastern Europe, China and Vietnam where planned secularisation has been successfully imposed. Wherever secularity advances the rate of reproduction declines, with obvious consequences.

Maybe those thinkers (Ernest Gellner, for example) are right who regard Protestantism, particularly its opening onto individual religious choice, as *the* modern religion. If so we can ask whether the vast contemporary expansion of Evangelical Christianity presages the advent of choice as fragmentation and secularisation. We can enquire whether the inundation of Catholic monopoly in Brazil by enthusiastic Protestantism prefigures the expansion of a passive secularity. In 1904 Wales experienced an Evangelical revival that with other global movements fed into the Pentecostal explosion in Los Angeles in 1906. It was part of the modernisation of Wales, and its spread was greatly assisted by reports in the newspapers. The splendid Baptist chapel in Bethesda was a centre of the revival and has recently been turned into flats. The area is Welsh-speaking and is now represented by a Welsh Nationalist MP. As elsewhere in Western Europe, and Québec, religion in Wales has been displaced by cultural nationalism, leaving a deposit of passive secularity and a love of singing. When I was in the Yucatan I noticed that the new Protestant chapels often looked like replicas of chapels in Wales. Perhaps Bethesda is a harbinger of things to come elsewhere. If so, then maybe Durkheim was right to link religion so closely with totems and the expression of a collective consciousness rather than with individual experience.

Any serious sociological imagination needs to take such views into account. I take a more dialectic view of the tension between religion as collective manifestation and religion as individual experience, and do not see the advent of Evangelical Protestantism and individual choice as presaging the end of socially significant faith.

Chapter 8
Charisma and Founding Fatherhood

Fundamental Distinctions and Alignments

In this chapter I argue for the conceptual unity of religion and politics. I suggest that Founding Fatherhood and charisma belong indifferently to religion and to the politics of nation and of party because these three seemingly distinct sectors of human activity share characteristics that belong to the nature and dynamics of the social as such, including resort to violence. I take off from an extended version of the conceptual apparatus of Weber's sociology of religion not simply because the original habitat of concepts like charisma and Founding Fatherhood was religion, but because all the binary oppositions I intend to deal with inhere in the nature of sociality itself. At least that has been the case since the rise of cities, along with writing, texts and the religious changes of the Axial Age, including the embodiment of the spirit in a charismatic narrative. The spirit takes up its abode in the letter, and the letter, meaning by that the charismatic narrative and the mythic text, is to be found throughout the unified field of religion, nationalism and politics along with charisma, Founding Fatherhood and violence. In the Bible, as the main governing narrative of the so-called West, the name Abraham means Father of many nations, and he set out from the very early city of Ur of the Chaldeans to start the story off. It was, of course, through his biblical studies that Weber quarried the notion of charisma.

The assumption of a conceptual unity is bound up with another assumption. It is that the numerous binary oppositions informing the unified conceptual frame of religion, nationalism and political ideology can be set more or less in alignment with each other, and that we learn a great deal from alignments that are out of true. I am thinking of the oppositions between personal and institutional (or manufactured) charisma; the spontaneous and the routinised, the prophetic and the priestly, the marginal and the established, the core message and the extended dogma, the solidary and the conflictful, the remembered and the forgotten, the victim, the victor (and the victorious victim), the TriumphLied, the grief song (and the triumphant grief song). These binaries, these oppositions, these distinctions perform a dance with each other and with all the other binaries as part of the unified conceptual field. This unity is more basic than the simple fact that a figure like Abraham has historically been assigned a role as Father of a faith and Father of a people, or the kind of linkage we imply when we speak of 'political religion' and 'political messianism'.

Starting with an extended version of Weber's sociology of religion, my initial focus is on the binary oppositions between charisma and routinisation, change and continuity, crisis and stability (or peace), the unpredictable wind of the spirit and stable legitimation. Then there is the important distinction between the prophetic and the priestly, which ought to include a third element, the preacherly. There is also the distinction between overcoming the world and withdrawing from it, which includes intense striving within it, as well working within it pragmatically or just keeping the ship afloat. This distinction is bound up with the difference between the prophetic tradition of the righteous rebel and the wisdom tradition in which the sapient ruler keeps the show on the road. Then there is the difference between the little flock of the fully committed, meaning the sect, and the universal communion, or Church, which remains in 'the world' but with monastic enclaves for those virtuosi who aspire to perfection. That binary opposition ought to include a third element, 'the denomination': a voluntary religious organisation (like Congregationalism) emerging in the early modern period which can modify the claims of Church and sect and can be pragmatic in its organisation, including the adoption of representative religious democracy and separation from the state. These 'third elements' or intermediate positions, exemplified by the preacherly and the denominational, remind us that all the oppositions we deploy – like those between personal and institutional charisma or between prophet and priest – define the extremities of a spectrum as well as being interdependent.

Charisma originally referred to the special quality attending the one on whom God's grace and favour rests. The grace may inhere in the office (say) the kingship of Solomon, or in the person (say) the prophetic mission of Amos, or in some combination of office and person. Such a combination is normal because the mission of a prophet or a messiah is an understood role awaiting an expected incumbent, and because the one who holds an office may have the kind of personal charisma attributed to Pope John Paul II.

I say 'attributed' because charisma requires a willing audience in a favourable situation, perhaps a crisis. Adolf Hitler, Winston Churchill, Giuseppe Mazzini, Mahatma Gandhi, Nelson Mandela, King David and King Alfred the Great were all major figures marked by an aura of potent grace – or disgrace, since I do not see how we can avoid distinguishing between malignant and benign charisma. They were all dependent on a situation and empowered by a crisis. However, you can be a Founding Father and not all that charismatic. Bismarck was not charismatic; and Nelson Mandela, though a potent icon with many facets, was not charismatic in his own person or in his rhetoric.[1] There is usually some creative management of charisma in the background when it comes to religion and politics. Creative management can include praise for qualities of solidity, steadfastness and 'granite', by way of contrast with merely superficial forms of charismatic appeal. Some kinds of anti-charisma can be quite effective when rightly presented with an emphasis on the sterling virtues of 'steady as she goes'. It helps, of course, if manufactured charisma can fan a genuine charismatic spark. At the same time, the spark can be put out and the treasury of charismatic grace or credit forfeited by a 'fall from grace'. Some genuinely charismatic figures – like Winnie Mandela, the Founding Mother of South Africa – can be quietly expunged from the record and their accumulated 'treasury of grace' and moral credit expropriated. Not only is Founding Fatherhood or Motherhood often attributed retrospectively, but it can be lost retrospectively too. Charisma is not stable.

Only some of the figures just cited – Mazzini, Gandhi, Mandela, Bismarck, King David and King Alfred – are candidates for the role of Founding Father of the nation, and it is a role that can be contested. There are different, even rival, political lineages descending from them and referring back to them, since Founding Fatherhood is often attributed retrospectively and from a particular political perspective. I see King Alfred as a Founding Father of England because he created schools and translated the founding text of the Bible. Like Luther, Alfred put down foundations for a cultural nation. The Victorians thought that way too, putting up a rather Wagnerian statue to him in the old Anglo-Saxon capital of Winchester.

You see rival lineages very clearly in the rival iconographies generated by the English Civil War. Those who attribute Founding Fatherhood to the republican Oliver Cromwell do not agree with those who see themselves in the lineage of Charles I. There are also different kinds of Founding Father. David established Jerusalem as his capital, but Moses was the lawgiver who led the people through the wilderness to the Promised Land, and Abraham was the one who first left Ur of the Chaldeans to seek a country and scatter a seed. These Founding Fathers are different in kind from Herzl and Ben-Gurion, the modern Founding Fathers of Israel.[2] As Moses and Aaron and Moses and Joshua come in pairs, so too do Herzl

---

[1]   Elleke Boehmer, *Nelson Mandela: A Very Short Introduction* (Oxford: Oxford University Press, 2008).

[2]   Allon Gal, *David Ben-Gurion and the American Alignment for a Jewish State* (Bloomington: Indiana University Press, 1991).

and Ben-Gurion, Morelos and Miguel Hidalgo, Gandhi and Nehru, Mandela and Tutu, Masaryk and Beneš, and Washington and Jefferson. I suppose Ataturk and Bismarck come singly, and maybe Italy has three – Cavour, Mazzini and Garibaldi – so you cannot rely on the emergence of just two Founding Fathers. I am underlining the translatability of charisma, crisis, prophecy, priesthood and Founding Fatherhood across the permeable borders of religion and the politics of nation and of party. This translatability goes way beyond the kind of metaphorical usages we encounter when the British Labour Party is described as a 'Broad Church' or the factions of hard right and left as 'sectarian'.

The borders between religion and politics are there, of course, especially given the process of social differentiation, whereby since the early modern period religion and politics are assigned to separate spheres. That differentiation came early and explicitly in the First Amendment of the Constitution of the United States. Yet every student of modern American history knows it is suffused with a civil religiosity and rapid recourse to religious rhetoric: what the elder Bush called 'the vision thing'. The Pilgrim Fathers, the Revolutionary Fathers, as well as Lincoln and Obama share a common language and rhetoric rooted in the story of Moses and liberation from Egypt. I could make out a case in favour of Moses and Cromwell as the Founding Fathers of the United States.

The idea of the one on whom God's favour rests, embedded in the vocabulary of faith, requires only a modest conversion across a permeable border to become Napoleon, the national 'man of destiny', or Spartacus, the revolutionary 'man of the people'. Mazzini was at one and the same time a national man of destiny, a revolutionary man of the people, and consciously prophetic in a religious vein. Religious faith in a providential dénouement of history can be translated into Winston Churchill's faith that the British would survive the crisis of 1940 into the 'sunlit uplands', or into the belief of students at 'Red Oxford' in the 1930s, like Iris Murdoch, that the proletariat was destined by the forces of history to triumph. Religion and all forms of politics participate in the common structure, the dynamics and the vocabulary of the social as such, and charisma and Founding Fatherhood are deposited many fathoms deep in that unified vocabulary.

At the heart of that vocabulary is myth as used by Georges Sorel in his *Reflections on Violence*.[3] Charisma requires a charismatic and authoritative narrative. Myth is not a fairy tale but a story that mobilises a group for action, whether a faith, a nation or a party, and which promises triumph after tribulation. Sorel was ready to cross-reference religion and politics, as well as ancient and

---

[3]   Georges Sorel, *Reflections on Violence*, Introduction by Edward Shils (Glencoe: Free Press, 1950).

modern, in his comparison of martyrdom in the Early Church with the trials of the workers in the throes of a General Strike.

Modern spin doctors mobilise the electorate by devising a narrative, and the editors of the Hebrew Bible did likewise for the elect people of God in the crises of the middle centuries of the first millennium BC. They provided a template for long-term survival and continued mobilisation. A template offers a more durable focus for the people than a physical temple because the physical temple can be, and was, destroyed. T.S. Eliot said we must 'for ever rebuild the temple', but it is even more vital to maintain the narrative template and its special language.[4] Even today a Zionist speaking the revived language of Hebrew wants to live in peace under his own fig tree, as Isaiah promised to his forefathers. He remembers the faithful remnant that endures and the tribulation that has been undergone, and that stimulates him to mobilise for contemporary trials. The remnant might be the saving remnant spoken of by Deutero-Isaiah against the foreground of yet another ancient Exodus, or the remnant left by the holocaust after exodus from Europe.

Of course, the same narrative or template is available for other nations as well as Israel, and these nations may devise new variants on the narrative that challenge Israel for its possession, such as the Qur'an and the Book of Mormon. They may create new sacred cities with new holy temples, while perhaps still laying claim to the original city of the people of the Jews. This is where rival narratives are integrated with political drives and tensions. Joseph Smith led marginal people out into a remote geographical margin, and the Islamic narrative powered a vast geopolitical drive in favour of a relatively marginal area against the contemporary centres of world power, such as Ctesiphon, Rome and Byzantium. Luckily for Israel the narrative of the American Zion is relatively well disposed to the Jewish narrative, while the Islamic narrative is in competition, especially when it comes to the possession of the physical Zion itself. Immediately after the mass slaughter of 11 September 2001 the American ambassador to Britain, as the representative of the most powerful contemporary Zion, went to St. Paul's Cathedral in London and read aloud from the prophetic narrative in Isaiah: 'They shall build up the waste places'. Israel has no monopoly of Zionism. Rebuilding the waste places is a generic social imperative for a nation, a faith and a political movement.

In such examples I have linked ancient and modern, religious and political in order again to underline the permeability of the borders between religion and politics. I take my examples from ancient times, like Abraham and Moses, as well

---

4   T.S. Eliot, 'Choruses from The Rock', in *Collected Poems 1909–1935* (London: Faber and Faber, 1936, p. 164).

as from modern times, like Napoleon and Mandela; and I move from more or less mythic time to the clearly historical, even though the historical is also in part a mythic construction under constant reconstruction. After all, we regularly refer to the 'almost mythic status' of national Founding Fathers, like Martin Luther and Martin Luther King, or fathers of their people, like Abraham and Abraham Lincoln or Benjamin Franklin and Franklin Roosevelt. The continuity of the names across the centuries is not an accident. *Nomen est omen.*

Among major theorists of nationalism I differ from Ernest Gellner and agree with Anthony Smith. It is not so much a question of how modern or ancient nationalism is, since that in part depends on how you narrow or expand your definition of nation. Ernest Gellner believed in a genuine chasm between ancient and modern, which I think implies a strong border between religion and politics.[5] I believe the reverse. My differences with Ernest Gellner are closely linked to differences between weak and strong theories of secularisation. That is because the way you articulate secularisation theory bears very closely on how you understand religion, nationalism and party politics. The controversies in the sociology of religion intersect with controversies in the study of nationalism. Gellner objected to my critique of strong theories of secularisation. Of course, a 'middle range' theory of secularisation fully recognises there was a genuine transition in the early modern period, heralding the emergence of the nation and the political party, even though that transition has religious roots far back in what Karl Jaspers, drawing on Max Weber, called the Axial Age, including roots in the binary distinction Christianity itself proposes between 'the world' and 'the kingdom'. A historically conditional theory, such as I originally put forward, emphasises the continued *coexistence* of Church, nation and party, either in partnership as in the USA or in conflict as in France, as well as bringing out their structural similarities and unified vocabulary. That has crucial implications for the future of religion and of Christianity.

A historically conditional theory allows for the continued presence of religion in modern society. There are indeed general secularising tendencies, such as the working out of the differentiating logic of secular 'world' and divine kingdom; but there are also contingent historical factors tipping the balance of power in different directions, which in Europe can mean extensive secularisation. According to strong theories of secularisation the Western European situation presages the wider global future. That implies there is an absolutely crucial transition from pre-modern to modern, from religious to secular, from religious to political, from Church to nation and party, and from

---

[5]   Ernest Gellner, *Thought and Change* (London: Weidenfeld and Nicolson, 1964).

the traditional or charismatic to the rationalised and bureaucratic. That is why the way you articulate secularisation theory interlocks closely with your view of the permeability or otherwise of the borders between pre-modern and modern, and between religion and the politics of nation and party.

This last transition from the charismatic to the rationalised is one of the areas where I most disagree with strong theories of secularisation, but not necessarily with Max Weber. Although Weber anticipated a mode of secularisation through the incarceration of charisma in the iron cage of rationalised bureaucracy, he also thought charisma might once more break out in prophetic form. He further complicated matters by regarding the Hebrew prophets as rationalising the spirit-infested and magico-religious world of their time. Of course, Weber died before Germany – one of the most advanced, rationalised and bureaucratic societies in the world – was bedevilled by the malignant charisma of Adolf Hitler. Weber also died before Soviet Russia, celebrated in 1935 by Beatrice and Sidney Webb as a 'New Civilisation', was terrorised by Stalin, a tyrant whose charismatic presence can still be successfully invoked and whose statue still stands in Tbilisi as a Georgian national hero. President Mugabe has been the Founding Father of Zimbabwe, and he has strengthened the hold of his tyranny by a combination of personal charisma and the charisma of his office. Once again, seeming oppositions are closely conjoined. Charisma has not lost its power for good or ill, in religion, or in the nation or in politics. At the same time the charismatic leader needs to be able to claim a role embedded in the myth. He has to be a plausible Joshua, Moses or Cromwell. The Founding Fathers of modern Italy, Mazzini and Garibaldi, cast themselves in a contemporary version of religious martyrdom. The Ceausescus made an all-too-plausible claim to the mantle of Vlad the Impaler, and President Islam Karimov in Uzbekistan now lays claim to the civilising inheritance of Timur the Lame. The example of the Ceausescus resonates with the kind of revolutionary politics designed to release the potential of the Superman or the communist New Man, but in practice only confirming the presence of the Old Adam.

There is one other implication of a unified structure and conceptual vocabulary which I can only mention in passing. It is that the attribution of a special capacity for violence to religion is dubious. Vast swathes of rhetoric since the Enlightenment, and since the rise of the nation state and the revolutionary political party, may be misdirected. The very phrase 'the wars of religion' could be part of a hostile narrative motivated by the same will to power and violence Voltaire stigmatised as the special prerogative of priests and kings. Very similar dynamics drove the resort to violence after 1648 as operated in the so-called 'wars of religion'.

Obviously the presence of a charismatic and authoritative myth is central to my argument. That myth specifies where 'we' came from, whoever we think 'we' are as distinct from 'them', and points to our present role and promised future. It is in the nexus between us and them, between our story and theirs, between our sacred city and theirs that violence most obviously resides. That means I am talking about the sacred city of Jerusalem, then and now, as well as the other capital cities of permanent recollection and aspiration, Athens, Rome and perhaps Paris too, since Paris has challenged Rome for European and Christian pre-eminence for most of a millennium. I take it that Mecca represents too big a variant on the Abrahamic story to be dealt with here, even if I knew how, and that Benares is a different story.

In our so-called western history Athens and Jerusalem are often supposed to be at odds, as Tertullian claimed they were in a famous aphorism, but in practice they have a great deal to do with each other. All the same, my centre of attention is Jerusalem. I focus on the Founding Fatherhood of David in creating Jerusalem as a capital, and on the Founding Fatherhood of Moses, the lawgiver, because the Bible is the people's book. The supplementary national anthem of England sings of building *'Jerusalem* in England's green and pleasant land' – not Rome or Athens, let alone Paris. The elites who founded or re-founded new nations had usually read the *Iliad* and the *Odyssey*, the *Aeneid* and the *Georgics*, Ovid's *Metamorphoses*, Herodotus, Tacitus and Julius Caesar. More than that, the founding kings of modern nationhood like Frederick the Great, Joseph II, Peter and Catherine, Louis XIV and even the Hanoverian Georges of Britain – as well as the revolutionaries of France and the United States like Robespierre and Thomas Jefferson – reverted to the classical in their monumental creations and their new cities, like Washington and St. Petersburg. They imagined themselves as grave senators in the agora.

Yet even these elites cross-referenced the Bible and Virgil, particularly in Protestant England and the United States. Henry VIII is a serious candidate for the Founding Fatherhood of an independent Protestant England, and his extraordinarily rich iconography depicts him as a Jupiter who is also a Solomon and an Abraham. Linda Colley in her *Britons* relates the nascent myth of Britain somewhat later to what became the large-scale singing of the oratorios of Handel, and in those great works Handel used typological identifications, lineages if you like, which cross-reference the classical and the biblical: for example, the link between the suffering of Hercules, Samson and Christ. Handel's oratorios also implicitly identified the rival lineages of the Stuart and Hanoverian kings with the prototypical kings David and Saul, and associated George II equally with judicious Solomon and amorous Jupiter. Any early modern tapestry tells the same intertwined typological story of Founding Fatherhood, sometimes reaching back to Adam. In the poetry of James Thomson in the first half of the eighteenth century England plays the role of a modern Israel, as well as Greece and Rome.[6]

Today we find it difficult to read these typological lineages, particularly when they cross-reference the classical and the biblical, but they bear a strong resemblance to the procedures of structural anthropology. They also fit very well with Schütz's concept of a lineage of precursors and successors so central to the discernment of a charismatic advent or incursion. But if cross-referencing the classical and the biblical characterised the elites, it was the mass printing of the Bible in the vernacular in the sixteenth century, and the extension of reading, that fed the imaginations of the people. The Bible informed their vocabulary and provided a potent analogue of their history, as Adrian Hastings has argued, and not just in Europe and North America but in Africa too.[7] In 1985 John Osborne wrote in a play, *God Rot Tunbridge Wells*, that Handel's *Messiah*, based on the vernacular English translation of the Bible, 'gave the English their religion', and it was Blake's 'Jerusalem', set to music at the direst moment of national crisis in 1917, that gave them their supplementary national anthem.

I am pointing to a significant divide between Catholic and Protestant historical trajectories leading to a major difference in the degree to which different Enlightenments, with interacting Jewish, Catholic and Protestant contributions from Spinoza onward, either conflicted with religion in the formation of nations, as happened in Catholic France, or more or less cooperated with religion, as in the United States, England, Ulster, Scotland, Holland, Switzerland and Germany. I am also saying that the charisma or the 'presence' of Founding Fatherhood depends on the supporting presence of a mythic narrative reflecting the contemporary situation, and that the Bible, very much the narrative of a marginal people throughout, performed this role, particularly in Bible-reading Protestant countries. Sometimes that had philo-Semitic consequences, though philo-Semitism is another instance of divergence as well as convergence because the Jewish narrative is sometimes transferred to a rival lineage. France also claimed the role of New Israel, but France was different because it was Catholic and experienced a militant and secularist Enlightenment

---

6   John Chalker, *The English Georgic: A Study in the Development of a Form* (London: Routledge and Kegan Paul, 1969).
7   Hastings, *The Construction of Nationhood*.

rooted in the classical world, which was then globally exported. That introduces one other crucial consideration. In the two-thirds world the weight of influence has shifted from the French to the American model, and that means there has been a further shift in favour of the biblical narrative, and with that an expansion of the long tradition of Christian Zionism.[8]

The Dance of Binary Distinctions

I have set out Weber's basic distinction between personal charisma based on the disruptive power of the spirit and charisma of office based on law and routinised legitimation. As I have already hinted, in the context of roots which go back to the Axial Age, this binary distinction, like the differentiation of secular and religious, is built into the foundation documents of Christianity. That goes back, as Talal Asad has rightly commented, to its long apprenticeship as a voluntary and sometimes persecuted minority. It is the biblical text itself that opposes faith and the world, and it is again the biblical text that opposes the letter that kills to the spirit that gives life. The Spirit authorises the narrative in each of its three basic parts: it broods over the origin or creation; it emerges at the annunciation of a crux or crisis; and it falls upon the prophets of the end-time or of the re-creation and the arrival of a New Jerusalem, as John attests in the first chapter of the Book of Revelation. And it is the letter that confirms the authority of the Spirit and prevents it disappearing like the invisible wind.

I am now going to set out the other binary distinctions inhering in what I see as the common structure of religion and politics. I want to ask just how far these distinctions can be stacked up in mutual alignment and how far they are aligned with the binary distinction between charisma of office and personal charisma. One might treat charisma of office and personal charisma as heading up and implicated in all the other binaries. How far is charisma of office aligned with continuity, peaceful stability, routinisation, legitimation, world acceptance and inclusivity; and how far is personal charisma linked with crisis, disruption, rejection of the present world order and – maybe – violent conflict? We can learn a great deal by enquiring to what extent these alignments are either persuasive or problematic.

Supposing we now select the opposition between the heart of the message which in the New Testament word-book is *kerygma* and the intellectualised and

---

[8]   Stephen Spector, *Evangelicals and Israel: The Story of American Christian Zionism* (Oxford: Oxford University Press, 2009).

stabilised teaching, or dogma. This seems to be closely aligned with personal and official charisma, with grace (in every sense) and the law. But how far is it aligned with the opposition between centre and periphery, margin and established order? How far does charismatic grace emerge from the margin, and how far does law emanate from the centre? This is where matters become genuinely revealing, so I will throw in some more examples taken in turn from religion, nation and political party.

Amos came out of the mountainous margins to descend like a tide of judgement on the cities of the plain which, like Babylon the Great, stood simultaneously for corruption and civilisation. John the Baptist came out of the wilderness to Jordan just like Joshua. Jesus came 'full of grace' from the unconsidered margin of Nazareth to enter into the wilderness like Moses, before he offered a new law from the mountaintop, and confronted Jerusalem, David's dangerous capital. Perhaps these eruptions from the margin strike us as very understandable because those on the margin – the half-breeds, the 'poor' in New Testament terms and the stutterers according to the Hebrew Scriptures – hear God's call more easily than those who are at their ease in palaces. My examples taken from nationalism and political ideology may seem more strained and accidental.

Napoleon came out of the Corsican periphery to save France, and De Gaulle and Joan of Arc lurked in Lorraine till they received the call. The Thracian-born Spartacus was sold into slavery to emerge and challenge Rome, and Trotsky emerged from the second-class citizenship of the Jewish Pale to oust the Tsar of the All the Russias. Perhaps uncertainties will increase as I offer some other examples, like the founding of modern English Conservatism by the Anglo-Irishman Edmund Burke, and of 'One Nation' Conservatism by the assimilated Jew Benjamin Disraeli. Nevertheless I remain inclined to believe that a special role is often taken up by the marginal and by the minorities: for example the role of Arab Christians in the initial creation of Arab nationalism; or the role of an Anglo-Irish poet like Yeats in Irish nationalism; or the role of Pierre Nora, a Sephardic Jew, in recollecting the patrimony of France; or the role of the Hungarian Protestant leader Lazlo Tokes in the Romanian revolution of 1989.

I come now to some more oppositions taking us close to the divisive and reconciling heart of the dynamic of the social as such, that is to the mutual implication of conflict and solidarity. Consider the dance between solemn remembrance and forgetting, and between anamnesis (the constant recollection of the narrative of deliverance) and amnesia. We can ask how far that dance is aligned with the dance between victim and victor as realised in the mobilising power of the experience of *defeat*: at Mohács, Kosovo, Armenia in 1915, Tbilisi,

Katyn, 'Bloody Sunday' in Ireland, the bloody suppression of protest in Russia in 1905 and at Novocherkassk in 1962, Tiananmen Square, Sharpeville and Tehran in 2009, as well as the triumphant Victim at Calvary.

The dance between anamnesis and amnesia can be aligned with the dance between the legacy of disgrace from generation to generation that follows on primal corruption and the treasury of grace created for all generations by sacrificial or exemplary death. That death might be of the marginal innocent individual at Calvary or the collective death of the marginal collective innocents at Auschwitz. That puts Calvary and Auschwitz in apposition. Moreover, in speaking of Hitler and Auschwitz we are once again dealing with the opposition of charisma for good and charisma for ill. We are talking about grace and disgrace, innocence and a *damnosa hereditas*. The interwoven opposition of good and evil cannot be omitted from our account, especially when you recollect that in the text of the *Exsultet* for Easter Eve the Christian narrative of death and resurrection includes the famous '*O felix culpa*', 'O blessed sin that merited so great a redemption'. In the Holy Week liturgy of *Tenebrae*, death is aligned with a descent into chaos as all the lights are slowly extinguished, leaving only the paschal candle hidden behind the altar, followed by resurrection aligned with the new creation of the new man as the candle is retrieved. New Creation and the new man are, of course, profoundly political as well as religious concepts, especially when you remember that resurrection, Risorgimento and renaissance are linked with the restoration of the nation. In the same way the creation of a new calendar, *l'an un*, is linked with political revolution.

But the cosmic reference is also one that reaches back beyond lineages rooted in Adam, the paradigmatic man, to the Fatherhood of God in all its varied manifestations. Here we are following through the complicated implications of the binary between Father and Son, together with a third element which may be the Spirit or the Mother. Notoriously, all kinds of political inferences have been drawn from the 'superiority' of the Father to the Son and of the effective replacement of the Father by the Son. Whereas Adam 'named' the animals, as pictured in William Blake's mystical representation, God 'named' all human fatherhood. A theological *Doppelgänger* shadows the sociological, and vice versa. *Theologically* all fatherhood is 'named under' the Fatherhood of God, and *sociologically* this works itself out in the iconography of power and care for 'the people' ascribed to kings, popes and political leaders alike, from Holbein's representations of Henry VIII where Henry replaces the Holy Father as the supreme father-figure of England, to Ingres' representation of Napoleon. Cromwell was exceptional in requiring at least two portraits of him to show an ordinary human, 'warts and all', but the more usual kind of representation has leaned towards divinisation and idealisation, for example the Founding Fatherhood and Motherhood attributed to, and claimed by, the Ceausescus in Communist Romania. The early Labour Party in Britain in the tradition of its Founding Father, Keir Hardie, spoke of the Fatherhood of God in relation to the Brotherhood of Man, and one of the supreme examples of that linkage is found in Beethoven's setting of Schiller's 'Ode to Joy', now the international anthem of the European Union. That brotherhood 'under God', reflecting the American motto '*e pluribus unum*', is in constant tension with a nationalism that interprets *Gott mit uns* as a divine legitimation for the exclusive demands of the Fatherland or the Motherland. God with us can be understood as an expression of the presence of God, Emmanuel, in human form as the 'express image of God', or in all humanity as the 'image of God' implanted from our very genesis. The ancient 'image of God' idea provides a foundation for the contemporary concept of human rights.

What cannot properly be followed up here are the cultural and political implications of Founding Sonship and the way the New Testament initiates a new spiritual genealogy through new birth in the Spirit, and through the identification of the believer with the incarnate Son. The body of the Son is realised and made present wherever the spiritual 'brothers' and 'sisters' of Christ come together 'in Him' and share a common meal. What we have here is nothing less than the invention of a new template whereby 'the Church', understood as those who are 'members one of another', becomes a moveable feast always available to the 'People of God' as they set out on pilgrimage to the spiritual Jerusalem. This invention complements the earlier invention of the portable God carried around by and with the people in the Ark of the Covenant. Christianity humanises God by 'taking up' humanity into Godhead, and that enables the life and presence of God to be realised in brotherhoods and sisterhoods. It is also realised by the raising up of the Mother alongside the Risen Son, in part as an expression of the radicalism of the *Magnificat*, but also because the Virgin Mother can be assimilated to the powers of sacred monarchy and portrayed as a courtly lady. There is even radical potential in the idea of virginity itself because the natural and particular relationships generated by sexuality are disciplined in the service of concern for all humanity, especially the poor. Christian sermons in the late Roman Empire combined praise of the virgin state and of celibacy with praise for love of the poor and the excluded. As Peter Brown puts it, the preachers of the fourth and early fifth centuries, drawing on the Hebrew Scriptures, adopted 'a view that saw the poor not only as beggars but also as persons in search of justice', with social consequences far beyond the practice of charity towards the destitute.[9]

The partial displacement of the solitary and authoritative Father by the Son and his Mother has radical implications, so that churches are never dedicated just to the Father; but these implications are controlled by the reinstitution of a priesthood made up of spiritual Fathers-in-God. The anarchic implications of brothers and sisters without fathers are kept under control in the monastic tradition but they often leak out in radical and antinomian forms of Christianity, like the Brethren of the Free Spirit. The variable range of implication arising from Founding Sonship is realised in the extraordinary range of iconographic representation as it runs all the way from the abject horror of Grünewald's crucifixion and depictions of the vulnerable child, to the portrayal of the Son as the Resurrected Lamb with emblazoned flag and as the all-powerful Pantocrator. The power of the Resurrection was recruited by romantic nationalists in Orthodox Europe to the restoration of the nation, for example in Greece.

The same variable range of implication lies latent in the exaltation of a humble Jewish mother as Queen of Heaven. This allows the Mother in particular to become the patroness of the city and the nation, and also to be the Founding Mother of a nation, as in Poland and in Mexico, or to emerge to protect the nation in time of danger. In Mexico the banners of the initial insurrections against Spain by the two Mexican Founding Fathers, Miguel Hidalgo and Morelos, were inscribed with the image of Our Lady of Guadalupe, representing the union of the diverse ethnic groups in the formation of a new nation. The Virgin Mother is guardian of Mexico and Queen of Poland and Brazil, and her dowry is England. This role of the Mother can be generalised, for example, in the memorials of the two world wars in France and in the memorial in Berlin to all the dead in the Second World War. The Unknown Warrior in Westminster Abbey and in other countries symbolises the way ceremonies of remembrance can be transferred to the collective body of a whole people, as they were in the prophetic tradition of the Hebrew Scriptures. At the same time these ceremonies of remembrance also place collective sacrifice for the nation (and/or for Humanity) in the context of the voluntary sacrifice of Christ, for example by the use of the quotation 'Greater love hath no man than this, that he lay down his life for his friends.'

The core narrative of a faith, or of a national movement or of a revolutionary political programme turns on a poetic axis of loss and retrieval, the grief song which is also a TriumphLied. The paradigmatic TriumphLied is the Song of Moses, recapitulated in the Easter liturgy. In modern times the recollection of

---

[9]   Brown, *Through the Eye of a Needle*, p. 80.

the two world wars unites lament with retrieval, for example the sounding of the 'last post' and 'reveille' on Remembrance Day in Britain. Remembrance Day is a religious, national and political moment of solemn anamnesis, as it is in Russia whenever and wherever the 'Great Patriotic War' is solemnly remembered. In Britain the core ceremony turns around the laying of wreaths at the Cenotaph (an empty tomb), the singing of a loose paraphrase of Psalm 90 by Isaac Watts and the saying of the Lord's Prayer. At Obama's first inauguration ceremony, a moment of the retrieval of promise if ever there was one, the Lord's Prayer, a purely Jewish prayer of course, was extended to include all the children of Abraham by being introduced as the prayer of Isa, Jeshua and Jesus. The Founding Fatherhood of Abraham, like the Founding Fatherhood of God, can be used inclusively or exclusively as the politics and sentiments of a situation dictate.

Exercises in the Sociological Imagination

I now use my sociological imagination to pursue some of the complexities stimulated by the dance of oppositions by selecting three oppositions which may have important alignments with personal charisma and charisma office, as well as with each other. These are the oppositions between flesh (*sarx*) and spirit; between outward observance and inner sincerity as discussed by Adam Seligman; and between the tangible expression and the intangible mental or spiritual conception as discussed by the anthropologist Webb Keane.[10] All of these are core concepts in the Bible and fundamental to our contemporary world. The working out of the dance of this opposition is very intricate, but I suggest it has an important relation to the dance of personal and official charisma. Suppose we take the opposition between the tangible and the intangible. The physical Ark of the Covenant with its scroll is a tangible expression, and we can regard the covenant *idea* as its spiritual or mental analogue. However, the idea of the moveable Ark of the Covenant is, as Régis Debray has pointed out, an extraordinarily powerful idea on its own account because it enabled the people of Israel to take their portable and invisible God with them, whereas tangible temples have a fixed location in material territory, often at the established centre of that territory, as in the case of the temple in Jerusalem.[11] That suggests one can

---

[10]   Webb Keane, *Christian Moderns: Freedom and Fetish in the Mission Encounter* (Berkeley: University of California Press, 2007).

[11]   Régis Debray, *God: An Itinerary* (London and New York: Verso, 2000).

at least say that the tangible temple has some relation to the priest rather than to the prophet, and therefore to charisma of office rather than personal charisma.

But the idea of the Ark of the Covenant can float free of the tangible Ark in the form of the covenant idea binding a people and their God together, and by extension it can include the idea of binding commitments embodied (say) in the closely related English Bill of Rights and the American Declaration of Independence and Constitution. The lawyers who act as keepers and interpreters of the Constitution are a secular priesthood ensconced in their classical temple the Supreme Court. Lay hands on the Ark of that Covenant, even to steady it, as recounted in the Bible, and you are already as good as politically dead. At this point the distinction between the inward spirit of the laws and outward conformity to the letter re-emerges in disputes over how the Constitution is to be interpreted. You need a very great fund of personal charisma and grace to lay impious hands on the letter in favour of a free interpretation of its inner spirit carried in out in sincerity and truth. You may become a sacrificial victim at the hands of the guardians in Church and state, which in turn brings us back to the arrival of a charismatic prophet from the margins who declared in words quoted by Weber: 'You have heard that it was said of old time, but I say unto you'. The charismatic prophet also picks up the potent strand in the Hebraic tradition that declares it is better to circumcise your inward heart rather than ritually to rend your external garments. That particular pronouncement made so long ago has become the effective creed of the modern United States, and it informs all contemporary education in learning to express yourself rather than obey the rules. Yet public comment is also saturated in righteous judgement, so the ancient distinction between grace and the law remains at the heart of modern culture.

We can now relate the dance of this opposition to the amnesia of forgetting and the anamnesis of perpetual remembrance that constantly recurs in the recitation of the Torah, in the Passover or in the Christian Eucharist with its invocation of a continuing Presence. Charisma is potent presence. This is the intellectual territory of René Girard and, as the religious narrative has it, the placing of the accumulated inheritance of disgrace on the head of the sacrificial and innocent Lamb cancels it all by an act of gratuitous forgiveness. It creates a treasury of grace to be drawn on that cannot be exhausted. That example apparently belongs to the sphere of religion, but analogues occur everywhere in national and party political narratives. Notoriously the Reformation, with all its consequences for nationhood in Northern Europe, was sparked off by raids on the treasury of grace for financial profit and to feed papal ambitions to build magnificent temples in Rome in Southern Europe. Prior to that, the treasury of grace was dispensed at pilgrimage centres. In Germany the treasury was dispensed by actual flows of Christ's blood, and in the city of Naples by the liquefaction of the blood of its patron saint.[12] The liquefaction of the Holy Blood in Bruges is closely linked to local nationalism and it used to be ceremonially attended by the king.

I return now to the charismatic power of the victim in defeat in the mobilisation of a nascent national consciousness, for example at Sharpeville or at Memphis, both of which are celebrated in works and acts of perpetual anamnesis. For my main example I take the relatively unknown massacre at Novocherkassk in 1962 because its recollection in samizdat form to counter the very successful cover-up undermined the faith of the elite and helped hollow out the Soviet system. In the same way, the massacre at Amritsar and the massacres following the Easter Rising in Dublin in 1916 hollowed out the legitimacy of British rule and created a national treasury of grace to be drawn on for generations. At the same time, as Francis Spufford has pointed out, the vast sacrifices of the Red Army at Stalingrad and Kursk, and the sufferings of the Russian people, were drawn upon by the elites of the communist system in ritual acts and parades of perpetual recollection as though they constituted a treasury of grace available indefinitely.[13] The crunch came when a new charismatic leader, Khrushchev, repudiated the terrible excesses of the system in order to steady the Ark of the Covenant. After that Russians assumed such acts of repression were confined to the past. As the protesters gathered at Novocherkassk they comforted themselves with the thought that whereas the Tsar as father of his people had massacred protesters in 1905, and Uncle Joe Stalin likewise, this was a new era. As a result their blood flowed, and slowly the treasury of grace overflowed until the regime fell and the victims were victorious.

Or so it seemed, because the cycle of sacrifice is never finally abrogated and closure rendered complete. The beneficiaries of sacrifices continue to expropriate them for their own purposes. As I already have suggested, Mugabe is a perfect exemplar of the confiscation of sacrifice for the purposes of renewed tyranny. Beneficiaries, whether immediate or remote, regularly draw on the treasury of grace filled up by paradigmatic suffering to inflict suffering on minorities or protesters, and to expel those they want out of their way. That is what was disgracefully symbolised in the reference to the recalcitrance of the Jews in the Holy Week liturgy. Often oppressors deny that the suffering of the victim ever

---

[12]   Caroline Bynum, *Wonderful Blood* (Philadelphia: University of Pennsylvania Press, 2007).

[13]   Francis Spufford, *Red Plenty* (London: Faber and Faber, 2010).

happened, or cite what they regard as their own equivalent or greater suffering. That leads to a competition over who has the moral high ground on account of being the most conspicuous victim. This competition is played out in the minority politics of the West all the time, aided by the effective censorship exercised over critical ripostes from the majority, but I am not certain it works in quite the same way in (say) Turkey. In Turkey it is reference to the suffering of minorities that is censored, and it is the protesters, like Orhan Pamuk, who are arrested or molested. The moral high ground is always a field of battle; and the baring of present wounds or of remote wounds, like the loss of Granada or Constantinople, is part of the rhetorical and ceremonial skirmishing.

Modern Examples and their Paradoxes

Here I want to offer some more extended examples to probe the paradoxes of charisma and Founding Fatherhood as that gives rise to narratives of liberation and victory, which may lead in turn to an ambiguous narrative of dispossession. I use these narratives to introduce the charismatic preacher, as a third kind of figure alongside priest and prophet. The preacher ascends a real or a metaphorical pulpit to expound, exhort and criticise. The tradition is deeply entrenched in the Anglosphere, and I was first introduced to it by Tony Benn, the Labour politician, who told me he used his government department as a pulpit for lay sermons. I am pointing here to a tradition of lay preaching with a particular kind of righteous rhetoric rooted in the Bible, either implicitly in its style or explicitly in its content. Tony Benn came from a devout family with a lay preaching tradition, and his rhetoric rendered the pragmatism of temporisers and trimmers, and of 'normal' pragmatic government, mere treachery. Pragmatic temporisers could easily find themselves lacerated by him as in the bastard lineage of such traitors to Labour and its principles as Ramsay MacDonald.

Michael Foot, who was briefly and disastrously the Labour leader, came from the same tradition of lay preaching as Tony Benn. He possessed an eloquent rhetorical style, and the lineage to which he explicitly looked back was that of the Tolpuddle Martyrs, West Country Methodist agricultural labourers who anticipated the birth of trade unions, the Scottish Labour leader Keir Hardie and the massacre of Welsh miners at Tonypandy. Gordon Brown, as a son of the preaching tradition of the Scottish manse, used this rhetoric in his early years very effectively, before it was inhibited by facts and events, after which it had in part to be manufactured on his behalf. That political and religious lineage has been populist rather than Marxist, and today it is a virtually extinct style either as sermon or political speech. The immediate precursors of this populist rhetorical style are the early nineteenth-century radical journalist and Unitarian William Hazlitt and the sometime Quaker Thomas Paine.[14] With the onset of political and national amnesia, a tradition of political principle rooted in sophisticated historical recollection, has disappeared to be replaced by straightforward calculations of interest and power.

However, the radical tradition of passionate lay preaching goes back much further than Hazlitt to Latimer's famous 'Sermon of the Plough' at the beginning of English Reformation, and beyond that to the friars preaching in the open air or in large hall churches to mass congregations, and to Savonarola. Whether Foot and Benn saw themselves as destroyers of the vanities I doubt, but both placed themselves in a lineage going back to Cromwell. That link allows me to move to the United States and the early preachers of a new city set on a hill, like the Massachusetts Puritan John Winthrop. It is through the Puritan revolution and its direct revolutionary successor in America in 1776, as well as through the mass preaching of people like the Calvinistic Methodist George Whitefield, a fervent patriot in the revolutionary war whose tomb became a pilgrimage centre, that I would defend the idea that Moses and Cromwell were the Founding Fathers of the United States. Jesus may be, indeed is, the 'personal Saviour' of Americans; but the lawgiver is Moses, and there is plenty of evidence for his formative and continuing role. The American lineage I propose runs from the charismatic figure of Moses to the charismatic figures of the Rev. Martin Luther King, the Rev. Jesse Jackson and President Obama. Space forbids a sidelong glance at an alternative black lineage including the new 'Nation of Islam'. The appropriately named Rev. Jeremiah Wright, who embarrassed Obama with his message of 'God damn America', represents the Christian variant of this rival lineage.

I go back now via Boston to the early modern Reformation and the period of nation building. That means I go back to the Founding Fathers, Luther and Calvin. Both of them sought a return *ad fontes*: one to Paul, the apostle of the gift of grace; and the other to Moses, the giver of the law and therefore the Founding Father of Geneva as a New Jerusalem set on a hill before that vision moved on to Boston . I have to leave out the Radical Reformation, even though that third lineage lay behind the founding of Rhode Island, with its tradition of the separation of Church and state, and the creation of Pennsylvania. The radical Baptist Roger Williams, from the English dissenting University of Cambridge, was thrust out of Boston to become Founding Father of Providence,

---

[14]   Keane, *Tom Paine*.

Rhode Island, and has now been added to the Founding Fathers of the United States. So have several others, like the black woman Sojourner Truth, selected to represent lineages not so far accorded adequate honour. In Britain Mary Seacole was briefly promoted alongside Florence Nightingale as a Founding Mother for her exemplary courage in the Crimean War. Sarah and Rachel are now matriarchs in a revised Jewish liturgy. There is a close and visible relation between the promotion of new figures to the role of a Founding Father or a Founding Mother and rebranding. The construction of Founding Fatherhood and Founding Motherhood are continuing and retrospective mythic enterprises as well as prospective ones.

I take Luther first. He is the Founding Father of the German cultural nation and of its language through his translation of the Bible and the setting up of schools, long before Bismarck created the political nation, and he is at the same time the Founding Father of the Reformation. In the mythology of the Counter-Reformation he was the wolf that descended on the Catholic fold. Through a genealogy which passed through German Pietism and Anglo-American Evangelicalism Martin Luther spiritually begat Martin Luther King. King founded or re-founded the new nation of African-Americans as Martin Luther founded or re-founded the German nation centuries earlier, and Luther King begat Obama, King's conscious heir as he is also Abraham Lincoln's conscious heir.

But Obama is heir to Calvin, to Geneva as well as Wittenberg, because that trail leads back to the freedom trail in Boston, and from there to Jerusalem. This trail also leads back to Moses the lawgiver, and the liberator who first rang the Liberty Bell, so it is no wonder Obama instituted the first *seder* in the White House in 2009. The story of the Exodus from Egypt to the Promised Land through the wilderness was consciously recapitulated by the Pilgrim Fathers, and then again in the Revolutionary War and once again in the peaceable slave revolt of the African-Americans. Moses had Pisgah gleams from Mount Nebo of the Promised Land; Luther King also had sight of the Promised Land of full citizenship according to the promise of the American covenant before his exemplary death; and Obama entered into that inheritance, like a veritable Joshua.

However, the figure of Joshua reminds us that those who have been liberated according to a covenant promise may also expropriate 'the people of the land', as the early Americans expropriated the Native Americans and some of the heirs of the Revolutionary War, like Jefferson, kept slaves. The task of African-Americans was to wrest the promise from the exclusive grasp of white Americans, which is why one of their most eloquent historians referred to the Bible as the poison book as well as the book of the Exodus. Who exactly are the peoples who play the roles of the children of Ham and of Ishmael? There are always disputed and rewritten lineages and ferocious disputes, political and religious, about who occupies the super-ordinate or subordinate roles. There is nearly always a cold war as well as a hot war about who is loyalist or rebel, patriot or traitor, and therefore about who should be expelled from the land or well advised to make a rapid Exodus from it. That is what many of the luckless American loyalists had to do, some of them ending up in Sierra Leone, as well as the Akkadians expelled by the British and often ending up in Louisiana. This is a poignant illustration of the fundamental dynamic of the social, in that exodus and liberation are linked to episodes of people cleansing, which may be religious, or ethnic or part of the perceived necessities of revolutionary politics. The contemporary examples are legion. Bulgakov's *The White Guard* (1926) tells how terrible it was in Kiev during the post-1918 civil wars in conflicts involving the Germans and the various factions of nationalist or revolutionary Russians and Ukrainians.

Of course, before the mobilisation of the African-American new nation, marginal white Americans had made their exodus under Joseph Smith, eventually to found another white new nation with a temple at Salt Lake City in Utah, where they drew the wrath of the USA on their heads, in part by reinstituting the marital arrangements of patriarchs like Abraham. As usual an angel dictated the new version of the narrative in the Book of Mormon especially for the benefit of North America, hitherto left out of the story. With enough personal charisma borrowed from an angelic presence you can rewrite the narrative of liberation to power a new national drive, as in the case of Joseph Smith, or a new geopolitical drive, as in the case of Mohammed.

Of course, these are not the only lineages in the United States. The Irish were massacred by Cromwell at Drogheda, and dominated by the British; and they made their own exodus to Boston and elsewhere. Their Founding Father, celebrated in parades of 'the Green' in Boston and elsewhere, is the semi-mythic figure of St. Patrick, who, as a matter of more or less fact, originated in Wales. Once again we run into the rivalry of lineages because the Protestants of Ulster, who became defined by the Orange against the Green, also made their exodus to America under the auspices of Calvin and Moses, in accord with the original founding story of America, and they mostly fought on the revolutionary side against the British. They also contributed an astonishing proportion of incumbents to the American presidency.

A similar problem to that faced by Martin Luther King was faced by Nelson Mandela in South Africa because the Dutch white settlers had already appropriated the Exodus story in their Long Trek from domination by the

British to the Orange Free State. The Voortrekker memorial remains to this day. There was an analogy available for polemical deployment between apartheid South Africa and 'the settler society' of contemporary Israel face to face with the Palestinians. At the same time millions of black Christians in South Africa embraced the longing for Zion, creating their own Jerusalem, and some black Christians linked their release from apartheid to the Israeli recovery of the original Zion. Stories are subject to multiple and contradictory appropriations.

The brief examples I now offer are of the interchange and partial expropriation of iconographies and narratives by religion, or by nationalism or by revolutionary politics. In the cases of Mazzini and Garibaldi discussed by the historian Lucy Riall, Mazzini adopted an ascetic lifestyle and a passionate if generalised religious rhetoric. Mazzini drew on the charismatic 'prophetic' tradition and identified himself with the Italian people. At the same time he both promoted Garibaldi in the romantic garb of guerrilla hero and genius and deployed a highly authoritarian style of leadership. Both Mazzini and Garibaldi used heroic failure to present themselves as icons of martyrdom and even of crucifixion in the Catholic tradition.[15] That struggle for possession of traditional religious symbolism was all part of an intense struggle between the Church and the nationalists.

This struggle for possession can take many forms, including a reversion to religion, such as we observe in Islam, Judaism, Russia and parts of Eastern Europe. After the events of 1989, the monuments of the nationalist revolutionaries of 1848 in Romania were marked by crosses and became traditional religious shrines. In Timisoara the liberation and the massacre of 1989 is solemnly remembered on the Feast of the Assumption, even though the prime mover at the time was a nationalist pastor (later bishop) serving the Hungarian Calvinist minority. Religion and nation were once more fused together.

I come now to a narrative that links the pre-Reformation New Jerusalem of Hussite Prague to the communist attempt in Eastern Europe to assimilate the narrative of Czech nationalism to the communist version of 'salvation history'. I also look at the communist attempt to assimilate elements in the cultural history of the German nation to what became the German Democratic Republic. On the whole it is the preferred strategy of conquerors and oppressors, especially when presenting themselves as liberators, to absorb and reuse the iconography of an earlier nationalism and a previous revolutionary movement to stabilise their own legitimacy. In Czech Lands they took over the iconography of the Hussite Revolution in the fifteenth century, including its aspiration to build a

---

[15]   Riall, *Garibaldi*.

New Jerusalem in Prague, and appropriated the charisma of such figures as the leader of the Taborite left wing, General Ziska. Czech nationalism under Beneš and Masaryk had been very successful in recruiting Hus and his martyrdom, and in representing the Czechs as innocent and democratic victims, which was a something of an exaggeration.[16] This role of innocent victim so governed the self-image of Beneš that it informed the decision not to resist the German invasion. At the same time it was also useful in justifying the expulsion of the Sudeten Germans after the war in revenge for the German takeover in 1938. As so often, liberation is linked to the expulsion of the people of the land as well as to the recovery of the land promised to the forefathers.

In Germany itself after the Second World War and the division of the country the national icon of Luther was initially assimilated by the communists to the earlier and superseded bourgeois revolution; but then it was decided to take over his image, shorn of the intermediate lineage of Bismarck (let alone Hitler), along with Bach and Handel and others, as forerunners of the people's state. To give one example, the Handel Festival was launched in Halle in 1952, attended by vast crowds and representatives of the Soviet Union, and the words of the 'Hallelujah Chorus' were rewritten to celebrate the triumph of the people, just as the Nazis rewrote *Judas Maccabaeus* as *Wilhelm von Nassau*. In the case of Handel this shows how a major figure can feature in several competing lineages. Historically Handel was the Founding Father of the musical canon at the same time as the putative rise of nationalism, and in due course he was introduced into the lineage of 'genius' and Founding Fatherhood in the British, the German, the Nazi and the German communist narratives. Since 1990 he has figured as the great cosmopolitan composer symbolising the restored unity of Europe. Contemporary Europe needs its Founding Fathers, beginning with Charlemagne, crowned close to the Franco-German border at Aachen/Aix-la-Chapelle.

A final narrative with some poignant paradoxes is found in the charismatic figure of a Founding Mother of Britain, Boudicca, who unsuccessfully fought the Romans and was crushed in 61 AD only a few years before the Jews were crushed at Masada at the other end of the empire. By contrast, Arminius in Germany earlier in the same century successfully overwhelmed the Romans, and has taken up his mythic place in the Founding Fatherhood of Germany. In Boudicca and the Zealots at Masada we again encounter the link between Victim, Victor and Victorious Victim. Queen Boudicca was probably client sovereign of the Iceni in what is now the east of England, but she may also have been a Roman citizen.

[16] Mary Heimann, *Czechoslovakia: The State that Failed* (New Haven and London: Yale University Press, 2009).

That made her lashing by the Romans and the rape of her daughters heinous even in Roman eyes, and helps explain the violence of her revolt when she burnt down the cities of Camulodunum, Verulamium (now St. Albans, in honour of England's founding saint and martyr) and Londinium. After a millennium and a half had passed, her defeat led to her apotheosis as a Founding Mother of Britain alongside the purely mythic Britannia. She was invoked in the iconography of the Virgin Queen Elizabeth as England first sought a place in the sun against the power of Roman Catholicism and the might of imperial Spain. She was once more invoked as a wronged queen prior to the divorce of Queen Caroline, and then again deployed in the iconography of Queen Victoria, Regina Imperatrix, as she ruled over yet another empire on which the sun never sets. Boudicca's nineteenth-century memorial – rampant and defiant in her war chariot, with her name Latinised as Boadicea – is on the Thames Embankment opposite Big Ben.

The paradox is that Boudicca, the original colonial victim, who raged like a lioness against imperial Rome, as Tippu Sultan raged like a tiger against the imperial British in India, re-emerged a mere 18 centuries later as a Founding Mother of a world empire consciously emulating imperial Rome. Britain has been as prolific in stimulating the emergence of Founding Fathers for new nations all over the world as Napoleon was in Europe; and some of these Founding Fathers used the democratic literature and rhetoric of British politics, of the British self-image and of the educational institutions they attended – such as Oxford, Cambridge, the London School of Economics and the Inns of Court of the legal profession – to gain their independence. Maybe this form of moral suasion based on the proclaimed values of the British Empire was not available to those struggling against Ottoman imperialism.

Conclusion

In contemporary usage charisma has broken free from its specific theological and social scientific meanings to become a floating signifier, and that immediately implies the central relevance of charisma to all kinds of power – whether malign or benign, whether religious, national or political. Charisma indicates the presence of power and the power of presence, and the two are often one.

If I were to pursue the issue of Founding Fathers and their relationship to charisma and narrative, I would look at rival claims to succession and alternative genealogies: for example in Hungary, where one genealogy goes back to St. Stephen and St. Stephen's crown; one to Louis Kossuth, nationalist hero drawn from the marginal religion of Lutheranism; and one to Béla Kun, the Jewish communist. I would also look at the revival of semi-mythic Founding Fathers, as part of a nationalist move to displace more recent genealogies, defined as alien and oppressive, whether religious or political. This move is congruent with neo-primitivism in modern art and iconography. I am thinking of the quasi-worship of figures like Genghis Khan and Timur the Lame in the Central Asian republics; the reference back to folk narratives in Europe, such as the *Kalevala*; and the revival of pre-Columbian figures in Central and South America. The revival of the *Kalevala* in Finland reminds us that a Founding Father of a nascent nationalism can be a musician, as was Sibelius, the writer of the national hymn, *Finlandia*. Curiously enough, one recognised Founding Father of Finland was actually the Tsar Alexander II, who, on taking Finland into his empire and building its capital on the model of St. Petersburg, declared Finland should be a nation like other nations, which is why his statue still stands in Senate Square in Helsinki.

Finally, I would look at the varying constellations of national Founding Fathers: some with military heroes, like General Mannerheim; some with political leaders; and some with saints, monks and poets. As a sociologist of religion I might find the monks, saints and poets particularly interesting. The semi-mythic saints are assigned to the origins as Founding Fathers; the monks salvage the history and the language; and the poets write or rewrite the national script. But 'ill fares the land' where saints, monks and poets take on these roles. It is all too likely that they have been long under foreign domination, and have achieved independence very late in the day.

Chapter 9

Religion and Politics

The Sequence of Discussion

My theme is once again the crossover between religion and politics. Rather than face the issue head on I approach it sideways through the contemporary debate about the proper role and the actual role of religion in the political sphere. Some influential thinkers place religion in a sphere of the irrational, whereas politics is a sphere of the rational. For them politics makes ordinary common sense and serious, informed and intellectually conscientious persons do not have to subscribe to strange and unusual beliefs to engage in it. They think that if religious actors want to contribute to political debate they had better adhere to the agreed rules of reasonable argument.

This is an area where the analytic, the descriptive and the normative are entangled, and the tangle only grows worse when the participants in the debate have incompatible understandings of religion. Given this awkward entanglement, I ought to show my own hand, and say I have some sympathy with a modest version of the secular approach. When it comes to the legal and institutional forms of the state, with regard (say) to what people shall wear or the role of women, I do not want these institutional forms influenced by some fundamentalist lobby reading off the answers from revelation. On the other hand, I think that religion involves matters much more profound than detailed regulations about how people should comport themselves. At least in its origins Christianity is not a legalistic faith based on regulations promulgated by religious experts. That is how I read the New Testament strictures on the letter that kills and embrace of the spirit that gives life, and on the relation between the law and Christian liberty. So much, then, for the problem posed by what some influential voices take to be the irrationality of religious actors in public debate, and so much for my own position. My interest here is solely in using the debate to question the supposed rationality of politics and to look at common features characterising politics and religion alike.

One way of confronting the notion that religion brings irrationality into public debate is to deny the premise, and to claim that religious actors, or at any rate *some* religious actors, engage in a rational mode of debate. Instead I ask just how rational politics really is by bringing out the non-rational aspects of religion and politics alike. I am not for one moment denying that politics is driven by interest and versions of reasons of state, but that is also true of religion insofar as religion is a system of power as well as a system of meaning. In that respect the politics of religion are on all fours with politics in general. What the Russian Orthodox Church does in Russia and the Near Abroad of the Russian Federation obeys the usual imperatives of power. All that I take for granted. My object here is simply to draw out and illustrate the way politics is governed to a remarkable degree by images and narratives that have much in common with religious images and narratives.

For example, politicians engage in ritual anathemas in a modern version of Greek public theatre where the antagonists and protagonists strive for rhetorical victory as well as devising sensible means to deliver desired consequences. There are times when politics takes on the shape of a phantasmagoric drama. Its ritual performances are a form of stylised role-play requiring a willing suspension of disbelief in order to keep the show on the road. No doubt technical rationality plays a major role when it comes to concrete measures, and we can take it as given that a politician had better be competent (say) in market economics, as well as accounted politically righteous and doctrinally correct. Nevertheless, correctness construed as doctrinal rectitude and manifested in what I call political righteousness – especially in the deployment of the language of condemnation and commendation, blessing and cursing – is hugely important. We are quite literally governed by broad swathes of sentiment, many of them with a borrowed religious resonance. One can easily suppose that politicians are relativistic pragmatists shifting position as political opportunism requires, and Pope Benedict in particular expressed anxiety about the philosophical relativism all around us. But pragmatic relativism is only half the story. In the articulation of our sentiments we have become relativists in one mode only in order to be dogmatic in other modes. Some of the more obvious examples might be sentiment centring on the natural world and the animal kingdom, or un-negotiable affirmations about the dignity of man and of woman.

I need to make clear the assumptions that underlie my argument. The first is obvious. When I refer to the similar structure of both religious and political myths I am bracketing the issue of truth. Myths are governing ideas that propel movements forward and mobilise people to achieve social and political ends, and maybe it helps if they have at least some plausibility – but that is not the issue here. Myths may even incorporate well-established facts. For example, history as taught in schools is infiltrated by potent myths, but no sane person outside France doubts that between them the British and the Germans won the Battle of Waterloo.

My other assumptions are rather different. Whatever the structural similarities between the mobilising ideas and images of religion and politics, I do not believe they are the same enterprise pursued in different modes. Moreover, it must already be clear I do not believe religion is a kind of cloudy poetry which has eventually to be translated into rational and empirical prose. It may well be that religion more often exhibits the poetry of the transcendent while politics often has a more prosaic, immediate and mundane focus, but that does not mean the religious mode is just waiting to be collapsed into the political. There is no once-for-all secularisation of religious poetry into political prose, and that includes any once-for-all translation of religion into the poetics and the rhetoric of nationalism. I put a fundamental question against the idea that modernity is defined by such once-for-all secular translations.

Let me put it in another way that is directly relevant to current debates over the secularisation thesis. Secularity is not built a priori into the definition of what we mean by modernity. Religion, political ideology and nationalism flood into each other, even though they are different. For sure, there are major mutations in the way they relate to each other. Very important mutations have occurred, particularly in the eighteenth and nineteenth centuries with the different Enlightenments and the varied forms of Romanticism; but religion does not empty itself into nationalism and it is not waiting to be collapsed into political ideology.

I need to extend that. There is a poetry of the transcendent that resists translation and engenders its own distinctive and irreducible language, even though it has manifestations in the here and now. You find it, for example, in the beckoning image of a future New Jerusalem or shining city above. Ronald Reagan was fond of invoking the 'shining city', and I refer to Reagan here because we are talking about raw politics, not about airy-fairy notions. The word 'above' is crucial because though the New Jerusalem is thought of in Scripture as 'coming down' from heaven, its plenitude is not emptied out in mundane reality. It achieves momentary and partial realisations in our sublunary world, for example the heavenly city of the eighteenth-century philosophers.

But there is always a surplus of what I have to call 'glory' in language of religion which never becomes fully present in an imperfect reality. Beckoning images of this kind hover over the mundane world and are earthed and birthed within our everyday existence – but as glimpses, intimations, markings. Above all they are realised in dramatic liturgical enactments of celebration and inclusion,

of sharing and nurture though the distribution of our daily bread; through the offer and reception of signs of peace; through recognition of breakage of fellowship followed by reconciliation and forgiveness; through love tempered by judgement; through acknowledgement of profound loss edged with the hope of glory. Perhaps it appears surprising that a sociologist invokes the action of the Eucharist so directly, but it was a very distinguished anthropologist, Mary Douglas, who pointed to the profound concentration of meanings and signs in the short span of liturgical space.

What St. Paul calls 'the perfect' does not come down in spite of the ability of an anticipated advent to move the hearts of people and to become 'a movement'. In part that is because the arrival of the perfect ends history, just as the arrival of what in musical theory is known as the perfect chord ends the music. The music of time only moves at the behest of imperfection and under the impetus of jarring notes that imply the possibility of resolution. Take but disharmony away and nothing follows. If that sounds much more like theology than sociology, I am suggesting that our fundamental assumptions – for example about whether religion is or is not poetic fantasy destined to be emptied out into prosaic political reality – are beyond the reach of any straightforward empirical and historical adjudication.

All the elements I invoked as found in liturgical enactment are also hinted at in the Gospel story of the banquet to which everyone is invited. And yet, as I have also indicated, they are also half realised or overheard in everyday manifestations of what the anthropologist Victor Turner calls liminality and communitas. The spirit of communal sharing takes over in a temporary epiphany, as it took over in the Orange Revolution or in the events in Tahrir Square, Cairo, before corruption in some form or other resumes its usual reign. Revolutions, including the initial and paradigmatic Christian revolution we see unfolding in the New Testament, are always being confiscated and then renewed in first, second and third awakenings. Once the cycle has been started and a tradition of revolution established, fresh revolutions become necessary to restore the pristine vision of the first. They all require a narrative; they need immediate and long-term objectives; and they are likely to find an emotional focus around an icon, like the innocent young woman killed in Tbilisi in 1990 when the Russian soldiers occupied the central square, or the innocent young woman shot down in the Green Revolution of 2009. Revolution requires a designated malign other, a sacred history of suffering and an assurance of victory after tribulation.

Maybe I am not really talking about religion as such. For much contemporary scholarship religion as such is a dubious catch-all category. I am mostly talking about Christianity understood as a distinctive repertoire of related motifs selected from according to social and historical context. I am talking about Christianity understood as a distinctive articulation of the relation of the transcendent to earthing and birthing, and of faith to the quotidian world. No doubt that repertoire and that relation of faith to the world overlap the repertoires of other religions, but the grammar of Christian motifs is distinctive. If Christianity is a particular inflection of an even deeper mythic structure, I am not obliged to pursue that question here.

Islam, Christianity and nationalism all share the concept of martyrdom, but the understanding of martyrdom differs. In Christianity there is a singular emphasis on humility and a lack of code of honour which results in odd compromises once a Christian veneer is adopted and forcefully propagated by elites for whom honour is all. There was very little non-violent humility in Capetian France, eleventh-century England or Norway, or Renaissance Italy. Yet an insidious seed of doubt about honour and the feud had been sown in Christian preaching about the innocent man enduring shame and buffeting at the hands of men who were nevertheless forgiven because they 'knew not' what they did. That revolution could hardly be more fundamental because it trans-values the normal hierarchy of values and reverses the 'instincts' of the natural man.

Given what I have just argued with respect to modernity and the specificity of Christianity, I shall be taking my initial examples from the USA, which is a society profoundly infiltrated by the Christian repertoire and a society at the forefront of modernity. I am not here concerned with the well-trodden paths of voting behaviour, religion and party affiliation, or analyses of how religious pressure groups operate in Washington. Instead I want to canvass broad governing narratives, images and frames of reference that I see as flooding across the conventional boundaries of the religious and political.

I shall begin at the highest level of generality because that level infiltrates all the more specific, lower levels, whether we are dealing with religion or politics. It is also the least immediately obvious because these are the assumptions we take for granted. This is the frame of reference that hides itself as we focus on the action of the central figures in the picture. The obvious is virtually invisible.

Both the religious and the political realms share a sense of forward movement or telos. I have already pointed to the importance of a narrative, and revolution in particular needs a forward-looking narrative of eventual triumph after trial. Once there was a time of original and authentic being which then suffered degeneration and oppression until there came a time of redemptive suffering and eventually a longed-for liberation when original authentic being shall be restored. There is therefore a backward and a forward look in both the religious and the political realm and it is peopled by exemplary figures, both prophetic and redemptive. In practice it may well be that at the religious end of the spectrum reference is made to a larger and more universal story, whereas at the political end of the spectrum reference is made to a more particular story, even though the more particular story may still carry religious resonances and exhibit structural similarities. For example, religion is replete with precursors of revelation, and politics replete with advance guards of revolution. To give another example, politics and religion, revolution and revelation alike engage in the construction of sainthood. In both exemplary suffering plays a redemptive role. John Paul II exercised power in part because he, and Poland with him, had suffered; likewise Nelson Mandela.

Images and Narratives: The USA and Related Examples

I now turn directly to the images and narratives as they are found in the USA, such as the idea of providence, the ideal retrospect and prospect, and the construction of icons of sainthood. When I lived in Dallas, Texas, I encountered a remarkable illustration of the intersection of the larger religious narrative with the more immediate political narrative. An American told me he was engaged in a programme to educate inmates of American prisons, for which purpose he was using Renaissance techniques of memorisation. When I asked about the content of his programme he said it covered 'all the events of world history from the Resurrection to George Washington'.

In case that illustration should seem slightly lunatic, I back it up with two further illustrations: one provided by a respected political figure who was an American ambassador, and the other by an influential American theologian. Both of them were Catholics and therefore people one might expect to be immune to messianic expressions of nationalism, let alone manifest destiny. The ambassador asked me why my belief in God did not entail belief in the United States. To me these were very different kinds of belief, as well as utterly disconnected; but they were not that different to him.

We were jointly celebrating and commenting on the 200th anniversary of the American Constitution in Williamsburg, Virginia. The sometime American ambassador was unhappy that in my presentation of the social preconditions of the American political epiphany I had offered so many contingent and accidental reasons. For him the ideas were primary, but for me there were all kinds of circumstantial factors why the ideas of the American patriots had the opportunity to mature and eventually to triumph in the promulgation of the Constitution. His concern about the role I assigned to luck and contingency was entirely on all fours with the way the American Enlightenment, like the British Enlightenment, maintained a belief in Providence and a secularised telos. America was the happy recipient of the special favour of Providence. End of story.

The comments of the Catholic theologian were equally obvious to him and startling to me. He explained that in the contemporary USA you found migrants from all over the world seeking a promised land of freedom. This mixing of 'all nations, tribes and tongues', to quote the New Testament, presaged the universal realm of God's coming kingdom on earth.

This Catholic theologian also believed that legalised abortion in the USA amounted to murder on such a scale that it arguably released him from loyalty to any state that permitted it. One might think the two positions contradictory, but that is exactly how such high-level background assumptions work. You appeal to one assumption in one context and to another assumption in another context. As the American poet and celebrant of the American dream Walt Whitman put it, 'I contradict myself. So I contradict myself. I contain multitudes.'

We are dealing in metaphors and imprecise images capable of absorbing whatever people may project upon them. Our references back to the mythic past or forward to the mythic future – whether in the larger religious frame or the more immediate political frame – relate to resonant images, not to clear and distinct ideas. The Tea Party movement in contemporary America simultaneously refers back to God's own country and to a mythic tale of its liberation from British oppression, now reapplied to the aim of getting God's country 'back' on its rightful track. Huge swathes of political emotion are mobilised by potent images and mythic histories relating the dream time of the birth of the nation to its present perils. When Ronald Reagan appealed to manifest destiny in the form of images of the shining city set on a hill, he held up an icon which religious people in the States filled in with their own interpretations, and he promised a future where America and the world could begin again *de novo*. Beginning *de novo* through revolution is important since, like conversion, it enables one to slough off the accumulated moral burden of the past and to transfer it to the scapegoat. Revolution is first cousin to the Christian idea of New Creation, in the world around us and the world within us.

The American myth embraces most parts of the political spectrum and was vividly illustrated in the course of the election of Barack Obama. During the 2008 election Obama acquired messianic stature as the one who would fulfil and redeem the delayed promises of the 'American dream'. Obama clearly realised he now carried a religious freight dangerous to his long-term credibility, as he clearly indicated by explaining he did not walk on water and by the deliberately modest tone of his inauguration speech. Expectations infiltrated by religious resonances are built into the rhetoric of American culture, which means that icons are set up for deconstruction, apart from Washington and Lincoln. These are Founding Fathers needing to be placed on pedestals beyond reach, else the foundations of the republic are themselves endangered.

That brings us to the construction of secular sainthood. Washington and Lincoln are as God the Father and God the Son in the salvation history of American liberty. Washington was the Father of the nation, while Lincoln the Beloved Son fulfilled part of the American promise in his role as the Liberator of the slaves. He died after several hours of agony caused by the assassin's bullet on Good Friday 1865, and was immediately translated to a higher realm. Of course, the script is accidental, but it could have been taken from Scripture, in particular the halo of the holy that surrounds the innocent person martyred for a cause. Lincoln, the murdered secular saint, now has his temple at one end of the sacred field in the centre of Washington.

Honest Abe was a typical Protestant saint, without strong institutional attachments but alone with the Book and speaking in a manner saturated in biblical rhetoric. He was also the quintessential American in his rise from log cabin to White House, thereby consolidating and propagating the dream of American social mobility. Yet there was a darker side to Lincoln that only intrepid blasphemers care or dare bring out, because it reveals him not only as a very pragmatic politician but someone who believed in the superiority of whites. To be pragmatic and to obfuscate the issues is part of any politics aiming at modest real achievements rather than at fulfilling righteousness. But the explicit embrace of white superiority and of a plan to expel blacks to some colony elsewhere than America was not a necessary part of political subterfuge, even then. Early on, Lincoln's aim was to safeguard the westward settlement of white farmers from the competition of the slave system, and that objective was a crucial factor in the events leading up to Civil War. It was a war on an industrial scale and pursued by Lincoln to the point of destroying much of the South. None of this means that Lincoln was other than a very great man, but the need I feel to reassure you on that point suggests this is territory where you tread delicately.

Of course, most revolutionary anticipations end in disillusion, just as the vast majority of political careers end in failure. That is because politics is not an arena where you triumph because you have successfully completed a sensible and limited programme; nor is it a matter of realistic assessments carried out by designated experts. Politics calls up and calls upon imagined scenarios invested with a transcendent surplus. It invokes and it evokes. People cherish a hope of the one who will maintain personal and doctrinal purity to the end, and who will not sell the soul of the country or the soul of the revolution for a bowl of pottage.

I give examples. One after another politicians have emerged in British politics carrying the burden of such hopes. One after another they have been crushed by the burden of the expectations that brought them to power. They have been cast out with political anathemas as betrayers, at best self-deluded, at worst self-serving hypocrites. Tony Blair is only the latest in a long genealogy of saviours turned traitor. His election victory in 1997 was treated in some parts of the media as an epiphany, especially as the epiphany of a new generation. Ten years later his name was ritually cursed and his icon spat upon. The election of Kennedy in the USA, though very much a matter of money and political rough trade, was also treated as an epiphany of the new, though the ritual curses were delayed and still remain muted on account of his assassination. In all these instances there is a hint of corruption by 'the world'; and corruption is one of those words that straddle the spectrum of religion and politics, referring to our generic sin in Adam and the dissolutions of physical and spiritual death, but also to specific practices of political malfeasance and taking your 'cut'.

Not only is politics invested with providential hopes and brief epiphanies, but one also finds discernible traces of the Elect Nation defined, in the words of Abraham Lincoln, as the 'last, best hope of mankind'. We find such language acceptable and even normal because the idea of a nation which carries a hope for the good of others is written in to our civilisation. Perhaps it is just as well such a notion inhabits our subconscious because it spurs at least some people to embrace historical privilege as including moral responsibility. Patriotism does not necessarily mean 'My country, right or wrong', and the original Jewish paradigm of election in the Hebrew Scriptures makes it clear in at least some of the prophetic books that divine goodwill depends on fulfilling that will.

The historical genealogy of America's election to a glorious destiny was received from the original Scottish, Scots-Irish and English Puritan settlers, and election becomes particularly seductive when the 'last best hope of mankind' is cast in universal terms. In that most acceptable and therefore most dangerous form it can easily be translated into a responsibility to pass on your own special gifts to others less enlightened even if initially they are too backward to appreciate them. The British were deluded in this way in India and it needed the Indian Mutiny in 1857, now known as the first war of national liberation, to apprise them of the condign costs of such cultural interference; though it did not inhibit them from building railways, even across the sacred Ganges, to unify the subcontinent and ensure more effective control. British beliefs in an imperial mission were perhaps tempered by the way subject peoples objected to being simultaneously improved and exploited. All the same, British delusions are not quite as undiluted as American ones, because the national myth is divided between the seventeenth-century English Republicans, who passed it on to British North America in the form of resistance to monarchical tyranny, and the figure of the martyred king, virtually sainted because he died nobly on the scaffold outside his own banqueting hall in Whitehall in January 1649.

The trouble with election to historical responsibility is not merely the existence of alternative authorised versions within a nation, but the geopolitical consequences of rival versions between nations – for example between the USA, France and Russia, and their rival exemplary revolutions. Providence decreed that an American leader, Ronald Reagan, would anathematise Russia as 'an evil empire' and that a Russian leader, Nikita Khrushchev, heir to a long tradition of religious messianism as well as secular historical metaphysics, would tell the Americans 'We will bury you first.' Faith in the triumph of Russia as the spearhead of the last and best hope of revolution was maintained against all the evidence by a large section of the intellectual representatives of political rationality in Europe.

The most dangerous moment of historical hubris arrived when the Americans won the contest with Russia, and some Americans concluded that the rest of history was little more than a cleaning up operation. Hope was on the dizzying verge of realisation. The problem here is that the universal mission – in its American, French, British or Russian forms – rapidly confuses or fuses national interest with doing good to benighted others, either by forcibly helping them on their way or else misunderstanding their hopes as a local version of one's own. When the Statue of Liberty was raised as a sacred icon in Tiananmen Square it was easy to suppose the authors of these events were replaying western revolutions rather than demanding that communism should live up to its promises.

The American experience of global hostility has not generated a coalition of all potential rivals; but it does show how rapidly the universal liberator can be identified as a universal oppressor responsible for all the ills afflicting the planet. That is not simply an observation within the remit of political science: rather, it is about a moral dynamic in which the polyvalent notion of corruption plays a key role. There is a binary opposition of Liberator and Oppressor, and an elect nation can very rapidly lose the role of Liberator to acquire the role of Oppressor precisely because of the eschatological surplus that has built up around the idea of liberation. The case of modern Israel is rather special because the age-old status of suffering nation was briefly exchanged for the status of liberated nation before a series of victories over enemies created the spectacle of the oppressor nation.

The Jews are a people empowered and even granted a limited moral franchise by their terrible suffering; but that franchise has also become a moral burden because they are now a people whose use of power is judged by a higher standard than we ask of others. We suppose that they above all should be equipped with moral imagination and able to go beyond the exchange of anathemas based on who is to be identified as the real and original culprit blocking the way of lasting peace. Victories like that achieved by the Israelis in 1967 entail long-term moral costs in terms of the loss of honour imposed on a defeated enemy. Only the Egyptian successes in the war of 1973 made possible the peace accord with Israel.

Who wields the power bears the blame, and the expensive role of moral policeman to the world exposes one to blackmail, for example the constant assistance demanded from the Americans by the corrupt regime in Pakistan. It also leads to resentment at your importunate interference with other people's corrupt and tyrannical business. Your flattering self-portrait leads to any number of disappointments and delusions: you are disappointed by people's lack of gratitude, which can be particularly glaring when the debt is real; and you are deluded about the motives and consequences of your own actions, as when George Bush declared that America had only ever intervened in the cause of liberty.

The USA illustrates two basic versions of the notion that there was once a golden time of original and authentic being. One version is found in the Jeffersonian ideal of the sturdy independent farmer retaining the right to bear arms. The other is located in the wisdom of the Native American understood as the incarnation of the noble savage and bearer of an uncorrupted wisdom from the primeval dream-time.

The American case is not at all unique. Most countries provide local illustrations of these two basic versions. The English Revolution of 1642–49 was in part empowered by the mythic invocation of Saxon liberties wrongfully abridged and annulled by the Norman yoke. Up to this day the Magna Carta, or Great Charter of 1215, is the marker symbolising the restraint of monarchical power, and the Kennedy Memorial is placed in close juxtaposition to the meadow of Runnymede where it was sealed. In England there is both the notion of the sturdy yeoman defending his native fields and the idea of a pre-Christian relationship of Man to Nature which involved mutual respect between hunter and animal, and a harmony without exploitation.

In Germany too future glories were prefigured by the idealised retrospect. There was the guildsman of the medieval city. Then there was the man of the primeval forest who, like Arminius when faced with the Roman imperial intrusion, resisted the slavery of incorporation in a sophisticated but alien regime. No country, however small today, is without this kind of retrospective glance to a past glory. In Lithuania the intelligentsia invokes the unfettered paganism of the Grand Duchy before Teutonic knights forcibly included the country in Christendom. It is nearly always the intelligentsia, the self-appointed guardians of reason, who create these potent myths; and it is the people who are elected in poetic imagination to carry them and bring them to fruition. Few nations are without a poet to frame the burden of its historic destiny: Walt Whitman in the US, Taras Shevchenko in Ukraine.

Luther is the quintessential instance of a religious figure who is also a political icon borne aloft for various purposes for very different ends. Before the First World War Luther was often presented as the fearless Reformer who freed the German people from Roman domination and the country from the control of the Church, as well as consolidating the language through his classic translation of the Bible into the vernacular. With defeat in 1918 Luther's reputation as the greatest German suffered, but it could be rehabilitated in part by political conservatives who regarded Weimar as dominated by Catholics and Socialists, and sought to restore the glory of the Protestant Reich. But there are other points of symbolic reference apart from historical icons like Luther. There is the idea of the medieval guildsman celebrated in Wagner's *Mastersingers of Nuremberg*. This can be linked to the great period of the Holy Roman Empire, centred on Germany and by extension to the promotion of the modern German nation. Then there is the idea of the Forest in Germany which can easily intersect both with the idea of blood and soil and with the idea of 'Wanderbirds' free to wander wherever they wish. Such images are ubiquitous.

Appeals to Nature

The idea of nature and the natural as it passes through all kinds of mutations up to its apotheosis in the Romantic period rarely loses its political potency. It might seem such large-scale and generalised myths rarely interact with immediate questions of political decision-making, or indeed questions of great political moment. But one only needs to think of issues like the industrial 'rape' of Mother Nature designed to exploit resources to feed the inordinate greed of oil-guzzling societies to grasp the emotive resonances. This is where modern politics have become more sentimental, in the strict sense of governed by sentiment, than was once the case. There are rational arguments, at least in the short term, for the exploitation of the earth, and there are sentimental objections calling on primordial imagery. A least since the Romantic period politics has been thoroughly infiltrated by sentiment about Nature, and were I to extend the analysis I would also argue that politics has been infiltrated by religious sentiment about Human Nature and Dignity.

Sometimes there are paradoxical consequences of our sentiment about Nature. Hunters in the pristine Far North are close to Nature and are believed to regard it with the appropriate respect required by the holistic vision; but maybe they also profit by the fur trade, which depends on a slaughter of the natural denizens of the untouched wilderness. The abolition of the fur trade might then drive the sometime human inhabitants of the wilderness to work for companies exploiting natural resources for profit. They might themselves become greedy consumers seduced by refrigerators and modern medicine. In this type of scenario it is traditional ways of life going back to the times beyond human memory and embodying accumulated wisdom and experience of the texture of living according to Nature that triumph over modern enlightenment and progress. Enlightenment triumphs in one context and accumulated Tradition in another.

The Beatles, notably John Lennon, were religio-political myth-makers in just the primordial vein just canvassed. One the one hand they expressed their contempt for the corrupt religious and political institutions of the past and tradition, and claimed that their fame was such they had even eclipsed Jesus. On the other they invoked a more 'natural' state of being where there was nothing to fight for and nothing to die for. All you needed was love. That means they looked forward to a time when love conquers all and naked humanity is at one from pole to pole, except that the entrenched forces and interests of 'the world', including the hypocritical powers of institutional religion, stand in the way. Lennon looked down on the struggle from his rich apartment block in Central Park, but few accused him of hypocrisy; and when he was murdered candles blew in the wind from New York to Liverpool, and beyond.

So the unifying vision of Humanity at last at one with itself, present in the Beatles, creates a binary opposition between those who possess authentic knowledge of the truth and those who are entangled in the regime of the Lie and of lies. The agents of that regime infiltrate everywhere. In the image of the world fostered by the Beatles, the partisans of love engage in a paranoid identification of the sources of malignancy that combines the myths of left and right. From a right-wing perspective it may be the New World Order or backward ethnic intruders and aliens, while from a left-wing perspective it may be the political frontmen of the capitalist world and their inordinate greed. Few notions carry a more obvious religious weight than the notion of the inordinate. The antithesis of the ordinate is the daemonic. The corrupt, the inordinate, the daemonic: these are at the heart of the political as well as the religious lexicon. When we contemplate what happened in Bosnia, the only shorthand we have available is the daemonic.

Of course, this is not to say that all the myths are straightforward untruths. The issue of truth has to be put in brackets in any discussion of the mobilising power of myth. Rather, it is to say that religion and politics alike, whether we speak of the politics of nation or of ideology, have a pervasive mythic structure marked by retrospective and prospective visions, and by ways of identifying the prime suspects standing in the way of recovering the idyllic past and reaching forward to the promised world of authentic being.

There is also a pervasive recourse to common metaphors. The rhetoric of Enlightenment appropriated the Christian metaphor of light and the Christian contrast between the light of the world and the powers of darkness that prowl around, full of menace. The light was first anticipated in unrecognised or martyred torchbearers. It then overwhelmed the entrenched powers of tradition which have had their bright brief day and are now for the dark. These metaphors of occluded and then universally recognised light, and of resistant darkness and sinister forces, are unselfconsciously built into religious and political rhetoric alike. The myths of dawning light and resistant darkness, of golden retrospect and ideal prospect, of precursor and incarnation, of interim and realisation, of suffering and liberation, and finally of exaltation have not been banished from discourse or deprived of power by the myths of the triumph of technical reason or of enlightened rationality. The realms of the political and the religious are different; but the capacity of the religious to flood across the different borders with the political we erect to indicate that difference remains undiminished in our contemporary modernity.

Chapter 10
Religion, Politics and Secularisation

Comparisons between Western and Eastern Europe

This is an exercise in free-ranging sociological comparison designed to show how socio-logic works and to index the most relevant themes. It links different relationships between politics and religion with different patterns of secularisation in Western and in Eastern Europe, using Britain and Spain as polar cases in Western Europe and the interlinked histories and cultures of Ukraine, Poland and Lithuania in Eastern Europe.

I deal first with Britain because it is a key instance of what has happened in the world's first industrial nation in a relatively sheltered geopolitical environment. Britain is a very distinctive case but nevertheless illustrates themes that play out very differently elsewhere. It offers a major contrast to Spain, and both countries have transmitted their cultural templates to North America and Latin America. The pattern of religion and politics and of secularisation is perhaps even more different in Eastern Europe. Whereas Britain and Spain are ex-imperial countries with fairly well-defined borders (even though they have major peripheries, like Scotland or Catalonia), countries like Ukraine, Poland and Lithuania have alternately expanded their frontiers and been subjugated by neighbouring empires. They have existed in exposed geopolitical environments. Their borders have shifted and their populations have been decimated or forcibly transferred elsewhere, with the tides of war, the decisions of dictators and the consequences of alliances and treaties.

Britain

We now turn to Britain, in particular England. Henry the Eighth nationalised the Catholic Church and centralised the country in the 1530s, and England became officially Protestant under his son Edward, and effectively Protestant about 1570 under his daughter Elizabeth. Between 1642 and 1660 England was ravaged by revolutionary civil war that disestablished the Church and set up a religiously Puritan republic, with some developments anticipating democratic, anarchist and communist elements in later revolutions but mostly in Christian language. After all, a devout reading of the Bible easily leads to politically radical conclusions. Those conclusions included eschatological expectations, and led the Republic to invite Jews back into England, even though the major influx of Jews came in the late nineteenth century.

The memory of the civil war lives on today, and the republican leader, Oliver Cromwell, is commemorated as a hero of radical politics and reviled as a regicide. Moreover, the seeds of Cromwell's revolution, and the principles of the English Bill of Rights promulgated in the 'Glorious Revolution' of 1688–89, were exported to British North America and came to maturity in the American Revolution of 1776. In Britain there were further revolutionary possibilities in the 1790s, 1830s and 1840s, but violent revolution was avoided by combinations of reform and repression. Moreover, historians have argued about how far Evangelical Revivals from the 1730s on absorbed and redirected revolutionary energies. So much for a broader background: it shows that Britain differs not only from France and Spain but from almost anywhere in Europe, West or East.

The comprehensive coverage claimed by the Established Protestant Church was further undermined in the course of the Industrial Revolution from (say) 1760 on. During this period the dissident religious groups previously involved in the Puritan Revolution were affected by a major Evangelical Revival and they rapidly expanded *alongside* Methodism, a new movement *initially* part of Evangelical Revival inside the Established Church. Religion in nineteenth-century England became divided between a much more active Establishment and a very lively voluntary or Free Church sector. Between 1840 and 1950 England, like North America, became more religious than it had been in the long eighteenth century from 1690 to 1830.

The Established Church of England and the Free Churches created lively subcultures linked with the two main parties, Conservative and Liberal; and the Liberal Party drew energy at its local grass roots from the support of members of the Free Churches, who suffered civil disabilities and felt hostile towards the Conservatives and a largely Anglican elite. Thus the slow extension of the vote was associated with the emergence of mass parties that were far from anti-clerical, let alone antireligious, but associated either with an established Church largely dominant in the south and most rural areas, or with Free Churches mainly strong in the northern industrial areas and the west, above all Wales. This is very different from Spain and Latin America where liberalism was associated with anti-clericalism. The British Liberal Party was a lay party and against religious establishment but was often animated, as were parts of the Conservative Party, by Evangelical and other efforts to ameliorate the condition of the masses. The masses included increasing numbers of migrant Irish Catholics whose aspirations were on occasion supported by the Catholic Church. After 1918 the Irish Catholic working class and some in the Free Churches moved over to support the recently formed Labour Party, hitherto in alliance with the Liberals.

Here we need to look back to signs of secularisation beginning in the 1880s, and to the social and intellectual radicalism emerging between 1880 and 1914 – some of it secularist, some even Marxist. All the same, the churches were numerically at their height in 1905 just before the Liberal victory of 1906; and that victory led to the first instalments of the welfare state as Liberalism finally abandoned laisser-faire economics. The Free Churches greatly increased their representation in the 1906 Parliament and this period broadly saw an end to their major grievances. The 1914–18 war did not undermine the churches, but the Irish Rebellion and the creation of the Irish Free State ended Irish nationalist representation in the Westminster Parliament. As Simon Green has argued, that change, together with the decline of a Liberal Party identified with the Free Churches, broke the link between rival political parties and rival religious bodies, so that both Labour and Conservative parties became multi-denominational.[1] The Labour Party had a Marxist wing, but its main roots were in Scottish and Welsh Protestantism as well as in English Methodism, and in some industrial areas it relied on Irish Catholic votes. The Anglican Church could now resume its representative national role, and some of its leaders, including some in its more Catholic-minded wing, drew on earlier traditions of Christian Socialism to support an emerging *consensus* in favour of welfare. In the 1920s welfare was further extended from the Conservative side under the Unitarian Neville Chamberlain, as well as supported by the Labour and Liberal parties.

From the mid-1920s on most of the indicators of religious vitality moved downward, except those for the Roman Catholic Church, which only experienced decline once the Irish migrants became mobile and more integrated in British society. Eventually Ireland itself – including the strongly Protestant North and the Republic – as well as the other national peripheries of Scotland and Wales moved closer to the lower English levels of practice and even of belief. Simon Green concludes that by the end of the Second World War it made little difference whether politicians claimed membership of a

---

[1]   Simon Green, *The Passing of Protestant England: Secularisation and Social Change c.1920–1960* (Cambridge: Cambridge University Press, 2011).

religious body or exercised a modicum of moral prudence.[2] Looking further ahead to the end of the century, he suggests that politics had as much difficulty in fostering long-term commitment as religion, so maybe religion and politics suffered from a common situation.

This does not mean that the churches, whether Roman Catholic or Protestant, became privatised. Indeed they spoke on the condition of the inner cities, ecological sustainability, the moral hazards of commercial greed, the integrity of the family, the just war and nuclear war. They maintained an informal alliance with the politics of welfare and criticised the neo-conservative policies of the Thatcher governments between 1979 and 1991. The Established Church also offered a protective umbrella for minorities, including a Muslim minority today numbering about 5 per cent. When it came to the legal regulation of the intimate life of citizens, the Established Church either recognised that it was powerless or positively supported changes, for example those proposed by the Wolfenden Report of 1957 in favour of decriminalising homosexual behaviour and made into law in 1967. Though religious people, particularly devout Catholics, were conservative on the issues of abortion and euthanasia, many Christians shared in a broad utilitarian consensus based on minimising harm and increasingly on issues like homosexuality and contraception, official Catholic teaching did not even convince Catholics.

But what were the causes of the diminution in religious commitment, and maybe commitment more generally? Some of the causes are long term: the alienation of many in the working classes, especially men, from the culture of the churches; the ethos of large cities and the relativism stimulated by mixing in a pluralist environment. Then there is the emergence of distinct spheres (social differentiation), each with its own ethos and professional dynamic partly supplanting the clergy, for example in education or social work. Finally, there are the intellectual changes of the last two centuries. One such change was the Romantic movement, with its pursuit of self-expression and individual autonomy, its worship of nature and the natural, as well as its propagation of nationalism through a mutation of religious themes.

All these causes have *varied* consequences in *different* countries. Much depends on whether the nation emerges in defiance of religion as in France, or in alliance with it as in much of Eastern Europe, or on whether Church and state are separated as in the USA or closely linked as in Poland and Romania. Perhaps we can agree about the impact on religion and religious authority of the differentiation of distinct and autonomous social spheres, and of individual

---

2   Green, *The Passing of Protestant England.*

autonomy. Yet individual autonomy is very far advanced in the USA and nevertheless finds acceptable expression within the churches, including homosexuality, divorce and family disintegration. The same is true of the shift from the moral economy of scarcity which at one time included the imperative of child-bearing where perhaps one in two died in childhood and the survivors were potential economic assets, to an economy of affluence where even serious self-indulgence is more stupid than morally wrong. Affluence, especially when combined with the fruits of modern technology, provides endless alternative forms of entertainment, rivalling or surpassing the provision found in the churches. Yet affluence in the USA turns out to be entirely compatible with active Christianity, so even the impact of a moral economy of affluence depends to some extent on historical and cultural context.

This then is my *thematic index* for thinking comparatively about secularisation and the relation of religion to politics in Western and Eastern Europe. One of the most important is the way a religious, ethnic or ethno-religious conflict between groups firms up solidarity, especially where one of the groups constitutes a compact and geographically rooted minority. Moreover, a minority of this kind, whether or not with a distinctive territorial heartland such as one finds in Brittany and Wales, will first resist impulses for a dominant centre and then assimilate. In Britain the religious minority in the voluntary sector lost impetus with the loss of grievances, and so did the Catholic minority in Holland, which was very compact as well as having territorial heartlands in the south of the country.

Of course, people migrate out of an ethnic or religious minority. People have been leaving the peripheries of Ireland, Wales and Scotland for England, the British Empire and the USA for a very long time. Catalonia has looked towards Paris as well as Madrid and has received a massive flow of migrants from the south of Spain. Millions of Ukrainians are now in Canada, the USA, Argentina and Brazil. And this is to say nothing of politically or economically forced migrations, most notoriously deportations to Siberia, and the appalling effects of enforced famine in Ukraine. The borderlands of Eastern Europe are also 'bloodlands' where countries and peoples have expanded to the east or to the west, where enclaves like the Swabian Germans of Romania or the Bulgarians of Ukraine have settled for centuries, or like the Lemkos in post-World War Two Poland have found themselves in the wrong place at the wrong time and been forcibly removed elsewhere. To be at a border may motivate you to hold fast to your traditions, especially when you fear the hostile power on the other side of the border. Greeks, Hungarians, Serbians and Bulgarians have pictures in their heads of historical and mythic borders extending far beyond their present ones, and harbour illusory visions of their own ethno-religious homogeneity that lead to expulsions or refusal to recognise subcommunities. People also migrate to ex-imperial countries for economic reasons, so that Britain, France and Spain have more religiously diverse populations, including Muslims and non-European Christians, whose practice is often relatively high.

Spain

If we now turn to Spain, it is a square country with a natural centre which became the capital, Madrid, natural borders and several peripheries. After 800 years of war the country was unified under a Catholic monarchy, just as England was unified under an anti-Roman Catholic monarchy. That meant that Catholicism and Protestantism came to define the two countries, in particular in their rivalry with each other. Arguably Spain and England were early examples of nationhood achieved by a strong monarchy enforcing religious unity rather than through the mass mobilisations led by the Romantic intelligentsia in the nineteenth century. Jews and Muslims were eventually expelled from a united Spain, just as Jews and Christians left under the harsh regime of the Muslim Almohads in the years after 1147.

Apart from the early unification under a monarchy and the subjugation of the Church to monarchical control, Spain and England followed radically different paths. The Enlightenment in Spain, though manifested in the common European neo-classical style, was dependent on a centralising and anti-clerical Bourbon royal power in pursuit of economic reform in the absence of a middle class. This is very different from England where it flourished in the life of the middle-class coffee house. The English (and Scottish) Enlightenment had an extended life for over a century, and included thinkers from all the main religious traditions, Anglican, Scottish Presbyterian and also dissenting, in particular Unitarians. Perhaps one easily forgets the association of Enlightenment with orthodox as well as dissident forms of Christianity, and the way an orthodox Christianity emphasising lay initiative and individual conscience can eventually undermine confessional states. There was no equivalent in England of the Carlist movement supporting a legitimist cause and having some relation to North-Eastern separatism, except maybe the rebellions sparked off in Ireland in 1689 and in Scotland in 1715 and 1745 in favour of the Catholic Stuarts.

Both Spain and Britain had peripheries based on geography, but whereas in Britain these peripheries were defined by semi-mythic histories of ethnic difference with a variable link to language and by the pre-eminent role of different Christian churches – Calvinist in Scotland, Ulster and Wales, Catholic in most of Ireland – in Spain they were defined by elements of a local Catholic nationalism: strong in the Basque country but rather exclusive, sometimes violent and linked to race; weaker in Catalonia and more closely linked to language and culture.[3] Both regions were economically advanced. The link between the politics of the peripheries and the political divides of the nation was very different in Britain and Spain. Each periphery in Britain in the nineteenth century generated a distinctive political culture, but – with the very partial exception of Ireland, North and South – these cultures were linked to the overall rivalry of Conservatives and Liberals. In Spain, however, a massive and often violent struggle built up between Republicans and Catholic monarchists cross-cutting the struggle between autonomy and centralisation. Affected by a socialist, anarchist and syndicalist left in twentieth-century, Catalonia was both autonomist and anti-clerical. Britain was not torn apart by conflicts over religion *as such* and liable to turn violent and anarchic. Religion was diffusely related to national identity, but Anglicans did not identify the very existence of the nation with the dominance of their Church. Religious trade unions and political parties have had no place in British politics.

The Civil War beginning in 1936 between Republicans and Catholic nationalists in Spain and the subsequent imposition of Catholicism under Franco, including the suppression of local autonomy, were inconceivable in Britain. Nor can one imagine an elite Anglican group operating like Opus Dei in Spain under Franco to initiate a technical and business revolution and influencing the transition after Franco's demise.[4] Of course, the struggle in Ireland between Britain and the Republicans between 1916 and 1922 involved a symbiosis of Catholics with Republicans, but the social dominance of the established Protestant Church of Ireland had long ceased to be an issue. English attitudes to Ireland included a dislike of the Irish as politically troublesome, and there was also ambivalence towards them, with some regarding Catholic Ireland as dominated by priests and backward, and others regarding it as enchanted and uninfected by Protestant materialism

---

    [3]   Daniele Conversi, *The Basques, Catalans and Spain: Alternative Routes to Nationalist Mobilisation* (London: Hurst, 1997).

    [4]   John Allen, *Opus Dei: an Objective Look at the Myths and Reality of the Most Controversial Force in the Catholic Church* (New York: Doubleday, 2005); Joan Estruch, *Saints and Schemers: Opus Dei and its Paradoxes* (Oxford: Oxford University Press, 1995).

One element in my thematic index was the spread of the lower religious vitality of the centre to the peripheries even as these peripheries have gained greater political and cultural autonomy. In Spain that relationship is made more complicated by long-term historical differences between the north and the south that have led to higher practice in parts of the north and north-east, and a more colourful folkloric religion in the south. All the same, the Basque country, for example, much of which was strongly Catholic, has moved closer to the national norm. That norm shows sharp declines in belief, practice and clerical recruitment since the 1980s, partly as a reaction to the control exercised by Franco, even though the Church eventually distanced itself from the more authoritarian aspects of the regime and challenged its control of appointments.[5] The other reasons for decline, tourism apart, are standard ones already noted in Britain, such as industrialisation, urbanisation and the shift from a moral economy of scarcity to one of affluence, except that in Britain these mostly operated over a much longer timescale.

Changes have been so rapid that the Church, initially neutral towards the rival Social Democratic and Popular parties, has tended to support the more conservative Popular Party. As elsewhere, any attempt to control the intimate life of citizens seems doomed to failure, as the birth rates throughout most of Catholic Europe dramatically indicate. If even Ireland and Spain, both at the level of government and in the practice of lay Catholics, reject a political or legal subordination to official Church teachings, a shift has occurred that is most unlikely to be reversed. In Britain a Christian couple were not allowed to adopt on account of their negative views about homosexuality, while Spain has legalised same-sex marriage. So there is *convergence* after a history of *divergence*. However, we shall see that Eastern Europe is different.

Before that we might ask how far the British and Spanish empires reproduced their cultural templates in their colonial territories, thereby creating a situation where English and Spanish are the two pre-eminent international tongues, between them including over a billion people for whom they are first languages. Spain helped Americans in their revolutionary war, while Britain helped the Spanish colonies in their revolutionary wars, as well as helping expel the French in Spain in alliance with the Spanish army and the guerrillas. The two imperial systems were very different, given that Britain had a primarily commercial empire that made no attempt to convert whole populations to Protestantism, and in many areas inhibited missionary activity even though there was a

---

[5]   Audrey Brassloff, *Religion and Politics in Spain: The Spanish Church in Transition, 1962–96* (New York: St. Martin's Press, 1998).

relationship between the expansion of empire and the work of missionaries. In the very broadest terms, Spain exported a template of Catholic hegemony often in conflict with liberal anti-clericals of the kind that led up to the Mexican Civil War, while Britain exported a Protestant pluralism that characterised North America, Australia and British Africa, with the two established churches, Presbyterian in Scotland and Anglican in England, sometimes achieving a local shadowy dominance. Moreover in Canada, as in Britain, 'enlightenment' could be disseminated through the churches.[6] In any case the contradictory messages found in the Bible could include a rhetoric of liberation diffusely available throughout the Anglo-Saxon world for 'ringing the liberty bell', for example among the blacks of Africa and North America. Indigenous and subject peoples in Latin America also used the rhetoric of Christianity, including its millenarian eschatology, against Spanish hegemony.

Migration from Protestant countries was encouraged by radicals in Latin America because they associated them with modernity and progress, even though Protestantism only affected small sectors of the population until the mid-twentieth century with the rapid expansion of Pentecostalism and Evangelical churches 'in renewal'. The opposition to this expansion paralleled a similar opposition in Eastern Europe. Even when some pluralism was accepted, the traditional mainstream churches and the cultural nationalists alike supported local tradition and laid the blame for religious and cultural intrusion on America, some of it associated with new styles of popular religious music and participation.

Eastern Europe: Poland, Lithuania and Ukraine

In Eastern Europe we look at the shared histories of Poland, Lithuania and Ukraine. We begin by surveying geopolitics on a large scale before focussing on the gateways from Asia into the European peninsula, one of which is the contested borderland of Galicia, while another borderland lies further west in Transylvania. These are both areas where nationalism became associated with the Uniate Church. The Uniate or Greek Catholic Church has a significant presence on the western borders of Ukraine and Romania respectively, and in these areas it coexists with other churches in a pluralist environment. These gateways in the

---

6   Nancy Christie and Michael Gauvreau, 'Secularisation or Resacralisation? The Canadian Case, 1760–2000', in Callum G. Brown and Michael Snape (eds), *Secularisation in the Christian World* (Farnham: Ashgate, 2010).

south-east of Europe, situated where its protective mountains begin, lie at the junctions where expanding Asian empires, whether Islamic or Orthodox (at least by tradition), and empires controlling the European heartland, whether Catholic or (later) Protestant (at least by tradition), come into contention. The long-term vista is provided first by waves of invasion from Asia, including the devastations wrought by the Golden Horde, and then by the struggles between Russia, Austria or Austria-Hungary – later Germany, and the Ottomans.

Religious, political and nationalist cultures are affected in a very complicated way both by imperial triumph and experience of defeat or alien domination. Russia switched to communism with defeat in 1917 and back to Orthodoxy with effective defeat in 1989. Turkey and Germany both repudiated part of their historic faiths with defeat in 1917. Britain and America were most religious at the height of their power in 1870 and 1950 respectively; and from 1947 to 1989 America contrasted its religious faith with the atheistic 'evil empire' of Russia. Poland and Ukraine have been from time to time incorporated in Russia, and relate their religion to their victimhood. But Poland, though it has its own imperial history, including much of the territory of what is today Ukraine, has acquired an exclusive relationship between being Polish and being Catholic, whereas Ukraine is very broadly divided west and east. Even Lithuania, which shared its glorious past with Poland, has a less exclusive relationship with Catholicism.

Starting with Lithuania we find Catholicism powerful but not unchallenged, especially now that modernisation has introduced western-style consumerism, particularly among the younger age groups. There is a very close relation between being ethnically Lithuanian and being Catholic, just as there is between being part of a Russian community of some 5 per cent and being Russian Orthodox or an Old Believer. However, the initial assertions of Lithuanian cultural identity in the nineteenth century were associated with an emerging middle class which, though it included clerics alongside liberal intellectuals, also looked back to a pre-Christian paganism preceding the inclusion of Lithuania in Christendom by political fiat. The Catholic hierarchy regarded the Lithuanian cultural renaissance with some reserve, in particular because it might alienate and marginalise the Polish minority. All the same, the failed revolution of 1905 mobilised the whole country, including the peasantry alongside the intelligentsia, and the Catholic Church played a major role in the nationalist movement culminating in independence in 1918. It was during the political and economic trials of the later nineteenth century that perhaps one-quarter of the population emigrated, as also happened in Galicia.

The Church dominated the political arena through Christian Democratic and allied parties up to 1926, when Lithuania was taken over by a secular authoritarian regime with a populist and nationalist agenda but found it politic to compromise with the Church. During the Soviet occupation (1940–41, 1944–89) the Church was the only institutional vehicle of national resistance. It projected an image of suffering that united those who might otherwise have been lukewarm to religion, including some whose primary focus might have been language and the authentic culture of the folk or the Helsinki human rights agenda. However, after independence this alliance weakened, and members of the intelligentsia divided into a minority for whom the Church was still the primary focus of Lithuanian identity and others who to this or that extent invoked Lithuanian history in general and the pre-Christian past. There is also some tension between some younger priests and members of the older generation, for example over such powerful folk icons as Our Lady of the Gate of Dawn, Vilnius, a devotion that extends to neighbouring countries, especially Poland, as well as North America.

Today, while the Church remains a powerful force, and indeed helped swing the vote in favour of joining the European Union (EU), it faces a younger generation less conscious of external threats and with a fading memory of the intense emotions raised, for example, by Soviet attempts to replace the three crosses on the hill above Vilnius with communist symbols. There are even some young people who seek a more 'modern', participatory and personal faith in the autonomous Lithuanian variant of the charismatic mega-church (along lines similar to the Living Word in Uppsala, Sweden, and the Faith Church in Budapest) known as Word of Faith. Most of the people attracted to the so-called 'New Religions' in Lithuania, and likewise in Latvia, are in fact charismatic Christians. So far as nationalists are concerned, devoutly Catholic or otherwise, modernity, especially when it comes from America, takes second place to local tradition, as indeed it does throughout Eastern Europe. Rapid economic development, some affluence, along with tourism and consumerism have had an impact, and perhaps some 25 per cent now describe themselves as having no religion, a much higher figure than in Poland but about the same figure as one finds in Ukraine.

Polish Catholics in Lithuania are a rather compact ethno-religious group of nearly 7 per cent in and around Vilnius. Lithuanians and Poles not only share some common history but have more recently experienced nationalist rivalry, especially when Poland occupied part of the country after the Great War. Most Polish Lithuanians live and move within their own community and its educational, cultural and political institutions as well as having their own festivals and devotional sites. At the same time, parishes often have services in Polish as well as Lithuanian and priests are bilingual, and Poles do not question the authority of the Lithuanian Catholic Church.

Poland is the most believing and practising country in Europe, in part due to the role of the Catholic Church in standing in for the nation under foreign rule. It is also homogeneous, following the westward shifts in frontiers since 1945 and the elimination of the Jewish population by the Nazis. The historical sequence in Poland parallels the sequence in Lithuania, including a period of authoritarian rule between the wars. Romanticism uses religious imagery in a generic rather than a Christian way to express love and suffering, and Romantic poets and writers in Poland recast Christian messianic imagery to project the providential mission of the nation. Perhaps language under the influence of Romanticism was the core value for Poles, while under the communists the emphasis moved to religion.

There is no need here to rehearse the precise roles played by the Polish Catholic Church, the Polish Pope and the Solidarity trades union in the Soviet collapse. Domination by an atheistic regime resting on Soviet power rapidly created a duality between good Catholic patriots and bad atheistic communists, so that by the end of the 1980s the Catholic Church emerged as the most trusted institution in Poland and the key player in the politics of liberation and the establishment of democratic freedoms. This moment when the Church appeared to be the one rock of continuity and trust was experienced in several countries and, though weakened, has not entirely disappeared. Under dictatorial rule the broad symbolic resources of the Church did not need to be attached to concrete political policies beyond liberation, so that even in countries where the Church was relatively weak, as in the DDR and Bulgaria, opposition emerged behind its banners. People did not know what the Church stood for, but they intuited what it was against. The Church represented non-violent opposition with a human face.[7]

Unfortunately the Catholic hierarchy in Poland translated its accumulated moral capital into the right to speak for post-communist Poland, even though that capital rested on broad symbolism not adherence to Catholic teaching, particularly in intimate matters. Changes were made in the law respecting abortion and religious education in schools without a full debate of all concerned parties within civil society. As in Ireland after a similar experience of foreign rule, the Church felt it had the right to dominate politics and even suggest

---

[7]   Irena Borowik, *Church–State Relations in Central and Eastern Europe* (Warsaw: Zaklad Wydawyniczy, 1999).

how people should vote. Again, as in Ireland in 1937, a new constitution made explicit reference to God. However, there were now many people, including strongly practising Catholics, who felt able to choose over a much wider range than previously. The Church was now more differentiated and varied, and while one group might be represented by Radio Maria with its rather xenophobic and anti-Semitic tendencies and fear of Western Europe, others were ready to support left and liberal parties rather than the overtly Catholic party of Lech Walesa. As in Ireland, the Church remained secretive, not only about cooperation under communism, which happened in every country, but on issues relating to priestly abuse. When similar secrecy was exposed in Ireland, the Catholic hierarchy initially failed to realise that moral capital earned generations ago could be squandered, particularly when a newly independent intelligentsia was in charge of new media.[8]

In Ukraine no one version of Christianity has represented the nation against external domination. We could construct a typology running from situations where religions divided the nation and where it united the nation. In Albania three different confessions divided the nation north, centre and south; and its dictator, Enver Hoxha, actually forbade any exercise of religion. In Italy the nation was divided down the middle by the Papal States and by those who thought of Italy as a federation under the Pope and secular nationalists like Byron, Mazzini and Garibaldi, who focussed on the role of Piedmont and sought to create a mythology of the Risorgimento as a kind of analogy of the Resurrection. Greece, by contrast, could appeal directly to the Resurrection even though its nationalism combined a memory of suffering under Ottoman imperialism with a classical and a Byzantine heritage. In Ireland the unity of Irish identity and Catholicism was actually reinforced after independence in 1922 by partition from a North where the Protestants were in the majority and the Catholics regarded themselves as second-class citizens. In a situation where the Protestant majority in the North was only 60 per cent, religious solidarity was reinforced on both sides of the divide.

In Ukraine the proportions belonging to different religious confessions shifts from Uniates in the West, who are about 6 per cent overall, to the Kiev Patriarchate of the Orthodox Church and the autonomous Ukrainian Orthodox Church closer to the centre, until in the East the Moscow Patriarchate is dominant. The linguistic map also shifts from Ukrainian in the West to Russian in the East. These shifts find some echo in the division between those who look politically to Western Europe and those who look to Russia. These divisions

---

[8]   Borowik, *Church–State Relations in Central and Eastern Europe.*

were a major element in the Orange Revolution in 2004 sparked by suspected electoral fraud on the part of the pro-Russian political forces. Initially the revolution was a 'liminal' event as people came together and achieved a fervent sense of non-violent community. Yet, corruption and political dealing can all too rapidly resume their accustomed sway, as also happened in Romania after the liminal events at the end of 1989 and again in Moldova in 2007. There are always major groups who counter-mobilise to recover the ground lost in the brief moments of revolution The 2011 government declared the Orange Revolution of no great significance, just as some 2014 revolutionaries declared 'the Great Patriotic War' of no great significance.

One source of trouble lies in the history of borderlands that are also zones of transition. Like most nations in the transitional zones of Europe lying between rival empires, Ukraine has its own memory of a time when it extended over a large area and of other times when it was ruled over or wholly or partly incorporated in the Mongol Empire (as the existence of the Crimean Tatars bears witness), Poland-Lithuania, Austro-Hungary, the Ottoman Empire or Russia. The story of the rise of Ukrainian nationalism is too complex to rehearse here, though it seems clear that Russophilia was quite common among the Slavic population and that strong cultural links with Russia were formed. As always, culture heroes are invoked and poets write of devotion to the nation: in Ukraine poets like Taras Shevchenko; in Moldova Mihai Eminescu, at least for the Romanian section of the population. There has to be national poet or writer to express national aspirations and call up a history of heroism and suffering. The socialist writer Ivan Franko is particularly interesting for the idea of Galicia: he also compared the search for a Ukrainian homeland to the quest of the Jews and translated Byron, among other nineteenth-century Romantics. England lacks such figures, lacking a history of confusion and external oppression.[9]

The appalling anarchy and the infighting of rival groups, including the famous Ukrainian Riflemen, after the First World War was only brought to a tragic end by the incorporation of parts of western Ukraine into Poland, while most of Ukraine became a constituent Republic of the Soviet Union. To begin with this occurred under conditions favourable to cultural identity with the rapid progress of education and urbanisation, but then after 1928 there was a forced industrialisation and collectivisation which resulted in near-genocide, the suppression of Ukrainian culture and attacks on the cultural elite and all the churches. Throughout the Soviet period Ukraine remained the most religious

---

[9]   Larry Wolff, *The Idea of Galicia: History and Fantasy in Habsburg Political Culture* (Stanford: Stanford University Press, 2010).

part of the Union, and half the functioning churches were located there. Today regular practice may be as high as one in three, though it is at its highest in the far west of the country and lowest in the east. The attacks on religion included the suppression of the Ukrainian Autocephalous Church and the Uniate Church. In the Second World War, though some Ukrainians fought with or cooperated with the Nazis, millions of Ukrainians died fighting in the Red Army. The large Jewish population of L'viv was decimated. The Ukrainian population of L'viv today is often of relatively recent rural origin. After the confusion and devastation of the war, Ukraine became the spearhead of Soviet industrialisation until the breakup of the Union.

These are the barest outlines of an incredibly complex history providing a backdrop to the particular problems of religion and the politics of identity in a zone of transition. In Western Europe a comparable zone of transition between France and Germany became a focus for the bridging institutions of the EU as these built on a mythic structure of the Middle Kingdom of Charlemagne and a Catholic–Protestant rapprochement. That solution seems not possible in Ukraine. Instead we have multiple histories and something like the rival memories that haunt the northern borderlands like Latvia and Estonia, in spite of attempts to promote a straightforward narrative of national restoration. On commemorative and public occasions it is politically significant which church the officiating priests belong to, and the tensions between them in Ukraine are very like those in the divided Orthodox Church of contemporary Bulgaria.

In many countries placed precariously in vast and easily penetrated zones of transition both memory and history are haunted and contentious, and these are manifest in the fields of religion and politics. Not only will histories and memories vary in different regions in Ukraine but also in the diasporas of Europe and North America: Galicia is now a haunting memory in the USA. Many will favour one kind of history, especially in the schools, because it assists political mobilisation; others will adopt an East Slavic and more Russian-oriented perspective, or they may adopt various regional and ideological perspectives. At the same time, multi-ethnic and transnational histories may portray Ukraine as a zone pointing both to Asia and East Central Europe. Meanwhile, the politics of identity and of commemoration and their manifestations in religion fragment. The treatment of Mazepa as a past historical figure illustrates this fragmentation. Because Mazepa, fearing for his own autonomy, left Peter the Great to side with Charles of Sweden, he was anathematised in Russia and by the Russian Orthodox Church; and later in the Soviet period he was condemned as a figure of bourgeois nationalism. In independent Ukraine he appears on a stamp, but his memory and commemoration have been a source of tension within Ukraine and between Ukraine and Russia. Galicia in the west is a cockpit rather like Belgium, divided historically by ethnicity, language, class and appalling violence, as in 1846 and both world wars. It has played an important role in Ukrainian nationalism; and the Greek Catholic Church of the region, with its strong western orientation, has experienced a renaissance. The Roman Catholic Church mostly serves ethnic Poles and Hungarians. One further source of tension arises because in Soviet times official morality required the privileged and wealthy to hide the fact, whereas now differences are openly flaunted.

The tension between pluralism and centralisation is political and religious. Since Ukraine is a zone of transition it is the most plural of the large successor states to the Soviet Union, and there is rivalry between traditional churches for position and control of assets. In particular there is a rivalry between the western churches, with the Orthodox of the Moscow Patriarchate expressing the more favourable attitude to Russia in the east, especially among older people in the cities, and even cooperating with the communists. The official visit of the Patriarch to Ukraine was supported by the Russian government. Whereas in Russia and Belarus there is a clear hierarchy of political acceptability between traditional and non-traditional churches, this is much less pronounced in Ukraine. There has been a considerable expansion of Pentecostal, charismatic and Baptist churches, perhaps making up 2–3 per cent of the population. These churches represent transnational flows from and to Ukraine, although, of course, the traditional churches also have transnational connections.[10]

Commentary

I have selected my areas of comparison largely to bring out the themes of most interest to sociologists: centre and periphery; the role of 'the Other' in reinforcing solidarity, different degrees of homogeneity and pluralism, of the identification of nation and faith, and the role of memories of defeat and oppression, and of past cultural and political splendour. I have also emphasised the importance of geography for a compact seaboard nation like Spain; for nations like England and America, protected by sea and maybe able

---

[10]   Catherine Wanner, *Communities of the Converted: Ukrainians and Global Evangelism* (Ithaca: Cornell University Press, 2007). I should mention that in Soviet times many thousands of Jehovah's Witnesses were deported by what was known as 'Operation North' to Siberia, along with many clergy of the Greek Catholic Church, including its leader, who spent 18 years in the Gulag.

to pioneer different degrees of pluralism; and for countries like Ukraine and Poland exposed to movements of peoples and conflicts of empires. Whether the pattern of transnational religious pluralism represents the global future is one of the many questions sociology is not equipped to answer.

Chapter 11
No Logos without Mythos

By looking at Blake's 'Jerusalem' I want to show how it simultaneously plays a role as a hymn, a national song and a political anthem or manifesto. My object is to illustrate the close relation between religion, nationalism and politics, in particular their common participation in myth. I also want to indicate how all three modes of social being oscillate between mental fight and physical struggle. I take my text from the British playwright Jez Butterworth: 'There is no Logos without Mythos.'

Jez Butterworth is the author of a very successful play about Britain called *Jerusalem*, and for those who do not know, 'Jerusalem' is the British national song about the Second Coming which is sung by people of all political persuasions. It was written in 1808 at a time of continental war, revolutionary upheaval and political repression, by William Blake, a poet influenced by Emanuel Swedenborg and Jacob Boehme. It was set to music in 1917 at a time of mounting casualties, by a humanist composer, Hubert Parry, a great admirer of Germany torn apart by the war. Socialists sing 'Jerusalem' because Blake was a radical and his poem presents a prophetic and revolutionary vision of Albion, Albion being an archaic name for Britain. A New Jerusalem shall be built here, *one day*. Conservatives sing it because they think they *already* live in a Promised Land of liberty and justice, though maybe it needs sensible improvements from time to time.

Socialists and conservatives are in two minds about whether this shared vision is achieved by peace or a sword. We think peace and war are opposites, but in the visionary perspective of Apocalypse Now, or Apocalypse very soon, they go together. The Book of Revelation portrays war in heaven itself before the heavenly city of Jerusalem comes down on earth as it is in heaven. In Germany during the Radical Reformation there was violent mayhem in Münster before the Anabaptist movement was distilled into the peaceful Mennonites. In England during the Civil War beginning in 1642, the Fifth Monarchy Men tried to bring in the kingdom of Jesus by violence. The peaceful testimony of the Quakers only emerged in 1660 with the death of the revolutionary Republic. In both Germany and England radicals were simultaneously demanding perfection and sweeping away the demands of the moral law in declarations of antinomian liberty. Peace and war, perfection and moral anarchy go together in apocalyptic times. Religious ideas are ambiguous. They contain multitudes.

If prophets spoke like lawyers or scientists they would be of no account. Like most prophets, Blake is ambiguous. In his poetry Blake attacks legalism and the law embodied in commandments in favour of 'life, more life', but in his condemnation of the Pharisees, meaning perhaps the Church, he plainly believes that there is a higher law of perfect righteousness. In 'Jerusalem' his language is simultaneously cherishing and threatening, pacific and warlike. He writes: 'Bring me my spear: O clouds unfold!/Bring me my chariot of fire!/ I will not cease from mental fight,/ Nor shall my sword sleep in my hand/ Till we have built Jerusalem/ In England's green and pleasant land.'

Blake wrote during the Pandemonium of the Industrial Revolution. Socialists think he anticipated endless struggle, political revolution and apocalypse now. They overhear his reference to the unsleeping sword. Of course, if revolution can be achieved by what Blake called 'mental fight', so much the better. Indeed, Socialists see war as part of the corrupt world they are *fighting against*, so they may even describe themselves as pacifists. They are fighting for peace *and* struggling against war. They would prefer what Blake called 'mental fight', but maybe they need to come out on General Strike if pushed to the limit by the forces of evil.

When Conservatives sing 'Jerusalem' they overhear the reference to England's pleasant land, and they imagine a patchwork of green fields and cloudy hills with many a shared enclosure around an ancient church. These paradisal images were constantly reproduced in the Second World War alongside very different images of a dead sea of destruction and a barren landscape of crosses. As far back as the eighteenth century, and beyond, England has been pictured and sung about in benign images of a Promised Land of peace and plenty, like Israel in the reign of good King Solomon. This 'Fairest Isle' is defended like 'another Eden' against the corrupt continent by the Channel, specially created 10,000 years ago by a kindly providence. The defence of this precious earth requires ceaseless vigilance and an unsleeping sword.

This is a perfect text to illustrate how religious ideas work because the ideas appear to be religious in origin, but they are really not confined to religion and they are not really *ideas* at all. They are condensed *images*, pictograms to be read at different times by different people in very different lights. They emit an aura of the sacred and they can be backed up by Sacred Scripture. Blake's imagery is saturated in Scripture. But condensed images are easily translated into any number of political scripts. We may think there is a boundary between religion and politics, and Christianity itself sets an ambiguous boundary between God and Caesar, but the repertoire of religious images ignores our imagined boundaries. After all, it was created two and a half millennia ago by Israelites under threat, and they had no boundary between religion and politics.

Sacred Scripture is an explosive and dangerous mine where we dig up what we want. Sacred earth is not a New Testament notion, but there is enough material in the Hebrew Bible to give a religious sanction to the sanctity of place – whether that is a land or a temple or a city, or a holy temple in a holy city at the sacred heart of a holy land. Royalty is not a New Testament notion either, but the coronation psalms and the idealisation of Solomon have shored up sacred monarchy from the time of the Holy Roman Empire until yesterday. The coronation anthem written by a German Lutheran composer for a German Lutheran king, George II, when he was crowned in Westminster Abbey in 1727, begins 'Zadok the priest and Nathan the prophet anointed Solomon king'.

But even if we did not appeal to Sacred Scripture to shore up power we have the revered writings of the ancient classics to perform the same service. The ceiling of the Banqueting Hall in Whitehall, London, painted by Rubens in 1630, depicts the *apotheosis* of James I. Since Constantine the classical vocabulary of apotheosis has cooperated with the biblical vocabulary to shore up the sacred panoply of power. The vocabulary of power finds whatever dialect it needs to shore it up. We can take it for granted that power seeks to be taken for granted. All over Europe sacred kings traced their origins to Israel and to the ancient classical world. Christian shrines are sacred places, but 'sacer' comes from the pagan lexicon. So it is as difficult to draw a clear boundary around a *purely* Christian language as it is to confine religious language to religion.

I do not want to be misunderstood. I do *not* mean there is no properly Christian language. The New Testament contains a social logic of closely related signs. The break with territory, with genealogy and with the associated imperatives of collective violence and sexual reproduction translates into the Virgin birth, into bands of disciples and their female support networks, and into international brotherhoods and sisterhoods dedicated to celibacy (or purity), peace and the relief of the poor. The royal, priestly and covenantal traditions of Judaism mutate into the fusion of the suffering servant who is also the promised king, into our great high priest who takes our humanity into the holy of holies, and into the Good Shepherd of his People who is the sacrificial Lamb of God. In the New Testament, assuming post-AD 70 back projections, the local temple in Jerusalem is quite explicitly translated into the body of Christ as that is realised across every frontier wherever two or three are gathered together. The holy city is translated into a heavenly city for all nations, tribes and tongues, 'the mother of us all'.

Those translations represent a complete transformational grammar, but under the pressure of power they can be translated back into real sacred cities and holy lands. Paul's 'sword of the Spirit' becomes just a sword. The Norsemen in Norway were converted by force and they did not cease to be warlike just because they had been forced to be Christians. By the time the Normans had reached southern Italy and Sicily their geopolitical imagination saw the holy city of Jerusalem as yet another capital of Norman power. They saw themselves as successors to King Solomon and their ambitions are inscribed all over the great church of Monreale in Sicily.

So while we can locate a distinctively Christian language in the New Testament, in practice we are dealing with incredibly powerful religious and political creoles. If you prefer terms from linguistics we are dealing with floating signifiers. Just as a shared repertoire migrates freely across the boundaries between religion and politics, so it migrates across the boundaries between religion and nationalism. In Germany there was a time when Arminius was a national hero against the Roman Empire, just as Martin Luther was a national hero and *Ein feste Burg* against the Roman Church a millennium and a half later.

Winchester was the capital of the West Saxons in the ninth century, and in 1899 a statue was raised to King Alfred the Saxon warrior, with a distinctly Wagnerian look about it. However, the statue of Alfred in Winchester is a statement of *British* nationalism, when in actual fact the Britons were conquered by the Saxons and mostly driven into Wales, where they now have their own nationalism. This statue also commemorates a *Christian* king who defended Britain against the *pagan* Danes. It is a multipurpose artefact to help us tell what we call '*our* island story'. Yet even as I write I keep swinging backwards and forwards between referring to Britain and referring to England, because the language I am using is itself a creole. Indeed, it is a multiple creole because it is part Celto-British, part Danish and part English, but more importantly part English and part Norman French.

So we come to the crucial question: 'Who do you think you are?' We are all mixed up with mingled genealogies, and yet we have a shared story to tell: sometimes our story of Christianity, sometimes our national story, sometimes both together. The narrative is a kind of *Heilsgeschichte* which makes sense of who we are. It does not matter whether we are conservatives, liberals or socialists; whether we are Americans or Germans or Russians; whether we are Catholics, Protestants or secularists; whether we are followers of the light of Christ or of *the* Enlightenment, if there ever was such a thing. We all have our *Heilsgeschichte*. It is the story we tell to *others* in order to tell *ourselves* where we came from, who we are now and where we are going.

The story is not just any old narrative wandering into our distracted heads from nowhere, but part of the basic grammar of developed language out of which emerges religion. Language is made up of tenses, past, present and future, and it concerns what may be and what cannot be. It creates and reflects hope and frustration. So does religion. Religious language does what all language does. Just as we all tell stories about who we think we are, so we all use a language of hope and frustration. Moreover, we cannot say whether our images depend on and derive from the exercise of power, or whether the exercise of power depends on images. Religious language affects the world, reflects it, inflects it and deflects it. But there is no *It*.

Let me repeat my text: 'There is no Logos without Mythos.' We are inveterate storytelling animals, even though the story we tell is as much a redaction of varied elements as was the Bible when it was edited, maybe in exilic and post-exilic times. The library of books we call the Bible provides a wide repertoire for us to select from, and mixed messages for us to choose from, as circumstances dictate. Other times and other people will be drawn to different parts of the repertoire and they will each translate the message in their own tongue for their own purposes.

Today's Pentecostals read the descent of the Spirit as falling on untutored men and women and empowering them to prophesy and dream dreams as in the days of Joel. It is their global meta-language available across every barrier of dialect, class and nation. The Jesuits in Salamanca read the descent of the Spirit rather differently. In their University Church of the Holy Spirit they pictured the dove falling on the first chosen representatives of the universal Church and the Blessed Virgin, ordaining them to preach in Latin America, or China.

Now, this repertoire is kept available by the external storage provided by alphabetic writing and for the last 500 years since Gutenberg by printing. That brings me to my second text: 'Nothing is ever lost', which I take from Robert Bellah.[1] He discusses the evolution of religion all the way from certain biological givens to the associated emergence of developed language and religion, and then to what Karl Jaspers called the Axial Age two to three millennia ago. Bellah believes that there were various stages of development in human history, recapitulated in child development, which create enhanced capacities. He also believes that the achievement of narrative is not *superseded* by theoretical

---

[1]   Bellah, *Religion in Human Evolution*.

scientific knowledge such as was presaged in ancient Greece and achieved in the seventeenth century. So my first text, 'There is no Logos without Mythos', can be given a social scientific translation in my second text, 'Nothing is ever lost'.

The Axial Age took different forms: prophetic denunciation in Israel; ascetic renunciation in India; the wisdom of the philosophers in Greece and of the sages in China. Today we are still living with the tensions created then by the achievement of a critical distance from immemorial givens. Critical distance opened up new perspectives that enabled us to redraw the map of human possibility. Conditions of crisis and breakdown made people question the way things were ordered here on earth. They fostered religious transformation scenes that allowed us to see how far we had fallen short, through sin or weakness, or through imprisonment in the shadowy realm of Plato's cave, or immersion in Maya (or illusion) or defection from the Way of Heaven and Nature.

The dynamic unleashed by the visionary perspectives of the Axial Age expressed and fostered a critical doubt about the beneficence and power of the god-kings of Egypt or Persia in their role as good shepherds of their people. It raised the possibility of one true God over all and in all, and of a universal humanity under a universal law, and it asks who then might be the *true* king. The world religions as we know them are dramatic configurations and transfigurations dating from the Axial Age. They are the narratives generated by those transfigurations. They are the icons and rituals that carry them forward.

Here we come to the crux: a basic profit and loss account sometimes obscured by talking about functions and dysfunctions as though you could balance them up and come to a judgement. I want to say that everything has a large price tag and you *have* to pay it whether you like it or not. There is a social logic of strict entailment you cannot evade. In religion as in science you cannot have the perfume without the mustard gas. For example, the moment you embrace universality and the idea of truth you are entangled in a struggle with the partisans of particularity and of alternative versions of universal truth. The moment you embrace the need for good faith and sincerity all the way from Jeremiah to Luther you are engaged in a struggle against mere forms, bad faith and hypocrisy.

Having a Sacred Scripture entails gains and losses. The stable text eventually achieved by the Jews not only gave them hope in the promise of return but, through the social inventions of the synagogue and the Rabbinate, it enabled them to survive and live anywhere. But it also meant, on at least *one* interpretation, that they were stuck with 613 inconvenient commandments as a condition of the covenant between God and his people. Of course, you can also turn this cost into a profit. The Hebrew Scriptures are a kind of forensic rhetoric marvellously adapted for arguing the toss, even with God. But they also offer you an incentive to become even more argumentative to get round their inconvenient demands. That skill could be put to use all over again when the Jews were pushed out of the ghetto by Enlightenment and disagreed how much enlightenment they really wanted and whether it would give them a better chance of survival or lead to their disappearance because they have lost the social definition provided by the Law.

Perhaps the Egyptian pharaoh Akhenaten started it all, even though his top-down reforms ran into the sand. He closed temples, smashed icons and abolished priesthoods. Because he failed, the story as we tell it begins with Moses, though biblical scholars seem to think he is mostly a back projection anyway, like *the* Enlightenment. The Covenant between God and the people revealed to Moses on Sinai did not run into the sand, but it did lead to the same radical consequences as in Egypt. When Moses came down from Sinai and found the people worshipping the golden calf he had the same three options as revolutionaries ever since. There was the Leninist answer: savage punishment to save the revolution from dilution. There was the social democratic answer: you should lead by persuasion and example. There was the conservative answer: conserve the tradition and keep the commandments that you may live long in your promised land. Moses adopted all three.

The dynamic unleashed by truth, universality and sincerity, all those good and costly things, ensures that rituals will be challenged by anti-rituals. The mediation of icons and of priesthoods will be challenged by iconoclasm and a demand for lay access. The partial expropriation of hope and truth by power will be challenged by heresies and movements of purification, often among the excluded but also among counter-elites. That means that the controversies of religious history, for example, access to the chalice, are not about trivialities, but issues of central human concern. Access to the chalice, like the priesthood of all believers, is by implication about universal human access.

There is a particular cost exacted by permanent revolution. The evolution of revolutions and reformations is punctuated by permanent revolutions and permanent reformations: *semper reformanda*. These reformations and revolutions hide an enduring will-to-power behind a claim to nurturance, and behind the ritual recitation of an impeccable genealogy as *the* Party of Humanity. The Enlightenment did just this, keeping itself in power by hiding what was in practice its racism, its demand for assimilation, its exemplary violence, its imperialism and autocracy. Christianity did much the same 1,500 years earlier.

Let me illustrate the socio-logic of great possibilities and inevitable costs by sketching a modern version of Genesis. In the beginning certain generalised potentials were built into the psyche by biological evolution. These are: attention and intention; empathy and cooperation; fight and flight in the service of self preservation; competition, ranking, hierarchy and dominance, including dominance *through* nurturance; and violence both against individual rivals and collective enemies. Social solidarity with others engenders social solidarity against others 'from foragers to schoolchildren to nation states'. Unity and conflict go together. These generalised potentials roughly correspond to what sociologists consider the prerequisites of society as such. So if you do not care for the biological account you can always stay with the cultural account. Cain will always be prone to murder Abel. The charter of liberation chanted by one group to celebrate its exodus from slavery makes it so much easier to legitimate its oppression of some other group in land it believes the Lord its God, or manifest destiny, or history and geography, has given it.

Those who follow the Enlightenment narrative blame religion for whatever goes wrong. Root out religion, if necessary by violence, and all shall be well. But when you think of the course of the French Revolution and the great secular persecutions of the twentieth century it is very obvious the problem is more profound, more generic to our species. Unfortunately, by some triumph of unreason enlightened rational individuals cannot see it. It contradicts the story they tell. It disrupts their *Heilsgeschichte*. Our modern genesis story suggests that wars and rumours of wars are only to be expected. Unity implies conflict. There is always conflict over scarce resources, and scarcity comes in innumerable kinds. No need then to explain war *as such*, as distinct from particular wars. Moral hyperventilation about religion is waste of breath.

What really cries out for explanation is not war but the vision of non-violence in Buddhism, in Isaiah and the Sermon the Mount, and in the Abbé de Saint-Pierre's idea of Perpetual Peace. That vision is a projection of the Axial Age which provides the platform in consciousness on which we stand. That is the basis on which we recognise the disparity between Buddhism and the repression initiated by the Buddhist government and the monks in Sri Lanka. That is why we are shocked by the difference between loving your enemies and the Puritan cry in the middle of English Revolution 'Jesus and no quarter'. We rest with unquestioning faith on the religious advances we violently disavow.

PART III
Religion, Power and Emplacement

Chapter 12

The Historical Ecology of European and North American Religion

This chapter deals with some problems of representation. At one time I planned to inscribe the distribution of European religion (and by extension North American religion) in the past, and now, in terms of social and regional geography and geopolitical pressure points. That is part of the current interest in 'materialising' religion and it takes for granted that religion, like every other ideological form, is closely implicated in power and place, dominance and territory, and in the dynamic of their expansion and contraction over centuries. I eventually scaled this project down to the distribution of religion in terms of architectural symbolism, in cities of the national centre and cities of the periphery. The symbolism of buildings served as a synecdoche of wider patterns of power and place and of the relation of religion to political power and social hierarchy.

The chapters which follow are part of the torso of my attempt to sculpt basic patterns of religion in architectural symbolism. They are problematic because the focus on different patterns of religion and its ecology throws up problems about how far I include architectural forms that alter mentality, like the great railway stations built from the mid-nineteenth century on, that compressed, rationalised and universalised time, or forms that either take over from religion – like hospitals, art galleries and concert halls – or acquire an analogous centrality, like shopping centres, television headquarters and stadia.

Yet this supposed 'plan' was originally not a plan at all, only an implicit mental map derived from my own social experience of the conjunction of Protestant Nonconformity and Liberal politics, especially in parts of the west of England like North Devon, where my maternal grandfather came from. Methodism and political Liberalism together motivated my interest in peace movements and provided me with a mental map useful for envisaging the distribution of peace movements in my initial studies of pacifism. They also provided me with a closely related mental map of the distribution of religious bodies I labelled denominational, following a well-known usage in the sociology of religion. I simply envisioned that peace movements flourished on the north-east seaboard of

North America and the north-west seaboard of Europe, and that denominational religion – by which I meant the various movements emerging in the wake of Puritanism, Evangelicalism and Pietism – flourished in the same environment. In my sociological imagination the ecology of the one overlapped the ecology of the other: where you have Congregationalists, Unitarians, Quakers and Methodists you probably have peace societies. I had another closely related map based on the distribution of amateur choral societies singing oratorios, but to include that in what follows would introduce intolerable complications. I think it no accident that Boston was home to early peace societies and at the very same time home to the Handel and Haydn Society.

I begin with my implicit map of peace movements precisely because, in common with most of our personal equipment for moral guidance, it was naive and unsystematic. Such maps configure the contemporary cultural scene for us and organise the past; and, like the old Mercator projections of childhood, they retain something of their original power even as we revise them in the light of later knowledge and experience. For the purposes of this discussion they raise fundamental problems about how to represent changing patterns of religion, politics and culture over time as well as across cultural and geographical space. There is an inherent difficulty about representing changes over cultural space and changes over cultural time *simultaneously*, especially when the timescale extends back many centuries, as it has to when considering the origins of the peace sentiment or the emergence of denominations like the Congregationalists and the Methodists (or amateur choral societies). My interests might be focussed on peace movements and denominational religion in the nineteenth and twentieth centuries but the roots lay initially in the Reformation, and ultimately they lay in the eighth century BC. That may look like a rather startling extension of the time scale but it is entirely consonant with the argument that Marx was the last of the Hebrew prophets. Modern political eschatology, notably Marxism but also some forms of apocalyptic nationalism, has roots that reach as far back in time as pacifism – initially to people like Thomas Müntzer in the Reformation period, but ultimately to anticipations in the Hebrew Scriptures.

I hypothesised that pacifism and revolution were closely linked over nearly three millennia. Groups engaged in pacifist withdrawal anticipated a new and revolutionary order with a fluctuating mixture of chiliastic hope and despair, or else the seeds of defeated and disappointed revolution were retained in a sectarian capsule until they found opportunity to flower in more favourable social circumstances. The Quakers withdrew from 'the world' once the Puritan revolution had failed in 1660 and the monarchy had returned, but they emerged again in Philadelphia, one of the seats of the American Revolution. Over the centuries Quakers exercised a vastly disproportionate influence on movements for social amelioration in England and indeed all over the western world. Pacifism in the Hebrew Scriptures was originally associated with radical visions of a peaceable kingdom focussed on Jerusalem which emerged on the apparently insignificant margins of ancient empires in Israel and Judah in the first millennium BC. Then, and crucially, in the New Testament period, pacifism derived authoritative inspiration from the preaching of the non-violent kingdom of God by Jesus, beginning on the Galilean periphery of Palestine but coming to a climax in Jerusalem.

The 'primitive' Gospel created a template for a radical tradition which is conventionally labelled 'sectarian' by sociologists by way of contrast with the tradition of negotiated compromise with 'the world' located in the 'church'. That meant my geographical map of radical Christianity had to incorporate a timescale of two to three millennia, taking the temporal perspective back to the period of what Jaspers called The Axial Age, when profound reservations about the world, its corruption and its violence, appeared in several different cultural centres, both east and west, along the lines indicated by Weber as well as Jaspers.[1] Christian reservations about the world – understanding both nature and man as a good creation but ruined and in need of redemption, restoration and recreation – generated the dichotomy between 'churches' which negotiated with things as they were by inserting 'signs' of a better world and 'sects' which sought a new order representing the rule of God. Of course, at different times these Christian anticipations might combine with other visions of change: the hope of a New Jerusalem might combine with the heavenly city of the philosophers; and eschatology might combine with the classical idea of a *novus ordo seclorum*. All this is necessary background to mapping the ecology of radical 'sectarian' and 'churchly' traditions over the cultural area affected by Christianity.

These radical traditions were quite widespread up the time of the Reformation, and they included a radical dualism derived from Manichaeism at odds with the Christian belief in the goodness of creation, as well as a potentially heretical Neoplatonism. Tensions were built into the fabric of Christian cultures that emerged from time to time, given favourable conditions, which questioned the structures of hierarchy and priestly mediation, which rejected infant baptism and the real presence in the Eucharistic sacrament of the altar and condemned the idolatry of images of the divine, and all outward shows and external forms militating against the inward sacrifice of a pure and humble heart. Christianity

---

[1]   Bellah and Joas, *The Axial Age and Its Consequences*.

was infiltrated by a *double entendre* whereby the eternal and heavenly king was glimpsed in a vulnerable child and a hanged man, and the Queen of Heaven identified in a maid 'of low degree'. Its symbolism reversed the hierarchy of values in the world and placed the innocent child at the centre of its kingdom. Inward and outward peace might be established by the pure in heart through withdrawal from the temptations of the world, its erotic and aesthetic enchantments, its worldly wealth and pride of place and power, the better to seek salvation and obey the law of love for God and neighbour.

Alternatively, and much more rarely, peace might be established by revolutionary action to bring the longed-for kingdom violently to birth. Meanwhile the Church negotiated with mundane reality by infiltrating into its iconography images of radical change when 'all things should be made new' at the end of ordinary time, even as it also assumed the panoply of wealth and power and experienced the corruptions that always travel in the wake of wealth and power. Standard Christian iconography embodied a tension between the legitimation and the delegitimation of the powerful. The Church acquired wealth and built imposing basilicas, while recognising it was more difficult for a rich man to enter the kingdom of God than for a camel to pass through the 'eye of a needle'. This tension remained evident long after Christianity was established in the fourth century. The idea of the city of man and the city of God and the institutions of monasticism symbolised a perpetual tension between 'the world' as it is and the world as it might be, between a good but imperfect creation and a more perfect re-creation in the future. The heavenly city as contrasted with the earthly city is part of the *double entendre*, and the monasteries were often seen as intimations of the New Jerusalem even when they grew prosperous and powerful.

Sometimes the radical impulse was united with a reverence for the holy meal of the Eucharist understood as the equal participation of all Christians in a sacrifice of thanks and praise, as among the followers of Jan Hus in Prague. At other times all fixed worship was rejected as contaminated by the exercise of clerical power, as with many of the English Puritans, including John Milton. In any case the radical tradition had its own symbolic resources, refusing all forms of deference in the interests of the equality of all the redeemed before God. During the Reformation the reforming impulse bifurcated into two versions, magisterial and radical. The magisterial reformers devised their own varied understandings of the relationship between the city of man and the city of God, and between the kingdoms of 'this world' and the kingdom of Christ. They created yet more versions of the double structure built into Christian culture.

The radical reformers devised varied understandings of how to make God's kingdom come on earth as it is in heaven.

All this is a necessary historical prolegomenon to any exploration of the spatial distribution of Christianity in its numerous variants and the instantiation of their different symbolic repertoires. In charting this history some half a century ago I merely noted that the radical traditions found distinctive spatial locations, such as the Albigensians of southern France (to the extent that they really existed outside the minds of their persecutors), the Waldensians of Piedmont, the Quakers of Cumbria, the Bogomils of the interstitial area between western and eastern Christendom in Bosnia, and the Anabaptists of Münster. However, underground movements do not as a rule generate spatial monuments above ground. After all, they have been subject to persecution. In *The War on Heresy*, R.I. Moore has convincingly argued that accusations of religious deviance provided the common currency of social solidarity and of conflicts over place and power by rival potentates and patrons.[2] Later this common religious currency was converted by nationalism into treason and by secular ideology into political deviation. Radical sectarian movements flare up, sometimes in iconoclastic fire storms that leave no icons behind apart from hacked and eloquent remains or 'bare ruined choirs', even though Alexandra Walsham has identified the permanent marks left on the landscape of England by the Reformation.[3] The names of cities like Philadelphia, Providence and Bethlehem bear mute witness to an earlier radical presence. The severity of Dutch post-Reformation churches witnesses to a new aesthetic rejecting imagery, vivid colour and festival.

For various reasons, including the influence of the painter and publisher Lucas Cranach, the Lutheran Reformation retained a far greater continuity with the iconography, ceremony and music of the Catholic Church.[4] Beyond that, radical sects after the sixteenth century created religious and utopian communities partially or wholly segregated from the wider society on a model not unlike the monasteries before the Reformation, especially once they were able to expand in the relatively open spaces of North America. The monastic communities associated with the severities of Cîteaux can be seen as recreated in the Anabaptist communities of Canada. The same radical Christian impulse achieved spatial realisations in the monasteries and in utopian communities, and in both instances the poor in spirit were sometimes corrupted by 'the world'

---

[2]   Moore, *The War on Heresy*.

[3]   Alexandra Walsham, *The Reformation of the Landscape: Religion, Identity and Memory in Early Modern Britain and Ireland* (Oxford: Oxford University Press, 2011).

[4]   Steven Ozment, *The Serpent and the Lamb: Cranach, Luther and the Making of the Reformation* (London and New Haven: Yale University Press, 2011).

and even inherited the earth. It was said at the time of the Reformation that the Abbott of Glastonbury and the Abbess of Shaftesbury owned a sizeable slice of England: collective wealth and power is still wealth and power.

The radical sects and utopian communities, from Cistercian monasteries to attempts to build Jerusalem in 'England's green and pleasant land' in the nineteenth century, like the Quaker Ebenezer Howard's 'Garden Cities of tomorrow', are only one part of the story. Spatially they remain part of the townscape in places like Letchworth, Welwyn Garden City, Bournville and Port Sunlight. But there are also the fruits of Huguenot, Dutch and Quaker enterprise in the banks and enterprises of the City of London: the Bank of England, Lloyds, Barclays. A culture emerged in eighteenth-century London that shifted from the court to the 'chattering classes' in the coffee houses, and from Whitehall to the West End and Mayfair. That signalled a shift from radical sectarian protest to a commercial ethos that eventually rejected mercantilism in favour of free trade and believed that trade was the harbinger of peace and prosperity for all. Free Trade was the quasi-providential invisible hand bearing peace to the nations.

The peace movements founded in the aftermath of the Napoleonic wars combined Enlightenment hopes of Universal Peace with the hopes of a rational Christianity, some of it Unitarian in inspiration, and impulses from the older sectarian traditions of Mennonites and Quakers. As the nineteenth century progressed the representatives of the Nonconformist conscience found it easy to distinguish between a priestly religion linked to older social formations, including the military, and a religion of preachers linked to peaceful commerce; and by the end of the century this had morphed again into the politics of the secular conscience and an aestheticism profoundly hostile to war and to the moral severities of Puritanism. The spatial realisations of the commercial pacific spirit were concentrated in north-eastern North America and north-western Europe, especially in Protestant countries, but also in France. The idea of conscience gained maximum purchase in Northern Protestant Europe: conscientious objection to war found little purchase in Catholicism.

So far I have concentrated on providing a background for the spatial realisations and social geography of religion in relatively recent times, first with regard to the tension between sect and church and then with regard to the tension between Christian and Enlightenment hopes of progress in defeating war and establishing perpetual peace. At this point I need to expand the dichotomy of sect and church by introducing the sociological concept of 'the denomination' and the history of the 'Free Churches'. My characterisation of the

Denomination in relation to Church and Sect was a key step in my formulation of a sociology of sectarian pacifism and denominational (and commercial) 'pacificism'.[5] So far I have only provided generalised and implicit notions of the social geography of sectarian pacifism and commercial 'pacificism'. I have now to outline the social geography of the Denomination because the presence or absence of denominational religion separated from the state and prone to pluralism and schism seems to me to provide a diacritical marker of major cultural importance, and an obvious link with Halévy's theory of the role of Evangelical religion in preventing revolution in Britain.[6] On the map of Europe England and France were not only rival imperial powers but profoundly different, both in their susceptibility to revolution and in matters of religion: France had one dominant Church, whereas Britain had a relatively weak established Church and numerous 'denominations'.

That was the precisely the difference which my general theory of secularisation took as its point of departure. In the USA the denomination was the dominant form of religious organisation, and the USA arguably became the one country where the pluralistic implications of the Protestant principle of the perspicuity of the Gospel to individual scrutiny were fully realised. In England in the latter part of the nineteenth century Methodism and the other Free Churches were closely associated with the Liberal Party, and in the twentieth century helped provide leadership for the nascent Labour Party, along with Catholics, likewise excluded from the partial alliance between the established Anglican Church and the Conservative Party. Religion existed on both sides of the political divide and was also associated with geographical divides, not only the very different religious complexions of the four or five nations of the British Isles but also a north–south religious divide.

In my mind I entertained a model of difference between the two rival countries (and empires) of Britain and France, which turned on the presence of Methodism and denominationalism more generally in Britain and America, and its absence in France. More than that, the denomination as a form of Christianity was linked to relatively modest institutional claims, to pluralism and a certain pragmatism about institutional forms and ceremonies. The spatial distribution of the denomination demarcated America and Britain from all of continental Europe, while the existence of a state church in England linked England to the Protestant state churches of Northern Europe. Taken together, the total

---

[5]   David Martin, 'The Denomination', *British Journal of Sociology* (13, March 1962, pp. 1–14).
[6]   Halévy, *A History of the English People*.

pluralism of the USA, the partial pluralism of Britain and the state churches of Northern Protestant Europe provided my main categories for mapping the religion of the North Atlantic area and offered a major contrast both with Southern European Catholicism and with Eastern Orthodoxy. There was also a central zone where countries were divided between rival territorial churches, Protestant in the north of a country and Catholic in the south.

These half dozen or so categories, starting from the key difference between Catholic France and Protestant England, and the absence or presence of Methodism provided the diacritical markers for my general theory of secularisation. They were supplemented by one other category made up of countries where nation and religion were together united against foreign rule by a country of a different religion, like Poland and Ireland. There was a high degree of overlap between the map of the North Atlantic distribution of pacifism and 'pacificism' and the map of religion. I hope I have by now indicated just how my studies of pacifism led on quite naturally to the distribution of religion according to the categories just outlined in my general theory of secularisation. Each category generated a different trajectory of secularisation reflecting quite varied relationships between romantic nationalism and religion, between enlightenment and religion, and between revolutionary political theology and religion. For example, Northern Ireland combined Protestant nationhood and the Enlightenment, while Catholicism in the rest of Ireland ignored the Enlightenment in favour of romantic nationalism. France embraced Enlightenment and nationalism against religion, while the USA embraced Protestant nationhood and Enlightenment together.

There remained only the tension between centre and periphery. I first became aware of the difference between centre and periphery by looking at the contrast between Strasbourg and Alsace with Paris and the Paris basin, although I did not encounter the concept until I read Edward Shils.[7] Strasbourg exemplified a limited pluralism unaffected by the confrontation between religious and secular you find in Paris. But there are numerous other peripheries in Europe, some of them like Strasbourg at cultural junctions. It was above all the difference between Strasbourg and Paris, and the way the urban ecology in the two cities mirrored very different constellations of symbolic power, that led me to see cities of the centre like London and Paris as architectural documents expressing very different politico-religious constellations. The same difference helped me imagine a religious map of Europe and North America based on regional cultures like Catholic Bavaria centred on Munich and the Catholic Rhineland centred

---

[7]   Shils, *Center and Periphery*.

on Cologne, contrasted with the Protestant north centred on Hamburg and the Protestant east centred on Berlin. It was regional constellations of this kind with their distinctive histories that governed the flow and character of secularisation.

We are now better able to construct a modern map of religion and secularisation in Europe in historical depth. We do so keeping in mind the categories set out earlier and the different relationships between religion and nationalism, religion and Enlightenment, and alert to the presence or absence of revolutionary political ideology as well as the related presence or absence of denominational religion along the lines of the Halévy thesis. All that amounts to formidable complication. However, to achieve a comprehensive picture one has to build in even more historical background. Once again one has to step back a long way historically because today's map reflects many centuries of history, most obviously so in the local religious majorities reflecting the redistributions of population after the Treaty of Westphalia in 1648. For example, after 1648 Protestants belonging to minority confessions moved into areas where Protestants were in the majority, just as much later after the First World War Orthodox Greeks were expelled from Turkey and Muslim Turks from Greece; and after the Second World War minority ethnic groups and minority ethno-religious groups were redistributed across the map of Europe. That is why Königsberg with its old Lutheran cathedral is now Kaliningrad with its new Orthodox cathedral of Christ the Saviour completed in 2006 and overlooking Victory Square: an obvious gesture in stone back to the cathedral of Christ the Saviour in Moscow. When Königsberg became Kaliningrad it was only the most recent act in a very long historical play of the tensions between Germans and Slavs discussed in Chapter 15. Maps of religion reflect the migrations, voluntary or forced, of peoples and faiths and peoples with faiths, like the Huguenots who left France after 1685 for Germany, Britain and North America.

The broadest possible historical context for the geographical distribution of religion today is provided by the folk wanderings and the rise and fall of empires over the last two millennia. The contemporary map of religion in Europe and North America reminds us that religion reflects successive folk-wanderings and invasions into the heart of Europe, from the arrival of the Avars in what is now Hungary to the crossing of the Strait of Gibraltar by Muslim armies in the seventh century and the arrival of Muslim armies in front of Vienna in the late seventeenth century. As the Muslim kingdoms of Spain and the Ottoman Empire in South-Eastern Europe weakened, that movement was reversed, above all as the Russian Empire pushed southwards and eastwards. We need to see religion as travelling with peoples as they migrate as well as associated with the expansions of empires and with long-term resistance to empires in a constant movement back and forth. The map of the past is in front of our eyes now, and how people and peoples mentally construct that map creates yet more history here and now.

The Russians first resisted the Polish Empire and the Poles later resisted the Russian Empire. The Romanian and Bulgarian peoples resisted the Ottomans, and the Muslim peoples of southern Russia and the Caucasus resisted Russian expansion. And just as there were migrations into Europe, there were migrations out of Europe propelled by a mixture of economic, political and religious motives: for example, the Catholic Germans who left Germany on account of Bismarck's *Kulturkampf* against Catholicism; the Jews who left Russia for Germany, Britain and the USA to escape the pogroms. Today there are once more migrations into Europe following the drastic declines in European fertility, most frequently from Muslim majority countries once colonised by European empires but also from ex-colonies now mostly Christian, like Ghana and the West Indies. Europe once exported people: Scottish Presbyterians to Western Canada and to the South Island of New Zealand, Catholic Italians to North (and South) America. Now it is an importing continent. Flows of migrants run in every direction: Middle Eastern Christians to the USA, Christians from numerous places all over the globe to the Muslim states of the Gulf.

We can now examine the social geography of religion (and of secularity) in Europe and North America with a proper sense of long-term continuities and constant flows and counter-flows over centuries, and also with some awareness of the distribution of different types of religion. These types run all the way from the Byzantine traditions of a unity of peoples and a *symphonia* of Church and state to the individualised religion of Northern Europe and the denominational pluralism of the Anglo-Saxon world. We can most usefully begin with the 'collectivistic religions' of South-Eastern Europe. All over the Orthodox world, and in most of the Catholic world immediately adjacent, religion is embedded as culturally taken for granted and as part of the narrative of national survival and continuity. It is manifested in gestures, in folk practices like the veneration of icons in the icon corner, and in festivals like All Souls when people gather in graveyards to commemorate the dead.

Buildings are erected and tended because they provide markers both of national and religious histories. By implication sites of pilgrimage, like the church of Christ's Resurrection in Lithuania, may also celebrate the resurrection of the nation. The cathedral of Saint Sava in Belgrade, an immense monument started in 1935, recollects both the medieval Serbian kingdom and the traditions of Byzantium. At one time or other these various 'ethno-religious' monuments were forcibly secularised or profaned by Nazis or communists and then resacralised or rebuilt as symbols of national renaissance. By the same token, sentiments of national solidarity create absences as well as presences 'on the ground' because landscapes and townscapes simultaneously embody and exclude identities. The Swiss may well be tolerant and religiously lax, but they voted against minarets. Minarets are picturesque on holiday but at home they puncture a familiar sense of the relation between Swiss history and Swiss geography. Swiss mountains are guarantors of freedom and protect the integrity of Switzerland as another Eden. Similar sentiments were mobilised to prevent a Muslim structure being erected in New York close to the site of 9/11. The height and salience of buildings matters, which is why Orthodox structures in Bulgaria erected in the Ottoman period do not stand out too obviously. (In Melbourne the Catholic cathedral was erected 4 feet higher than the Anglican cathedral by an Irish-born ecclesiastic.)

The pressures of disputed borders and the consequent sense of threatened identities embodied in rival national narratives and myths, reinforced by memories of past greatness and historic expropriations, have over the past century ensured a far greater homogeneity than was once the case. There are parts of the Balkans where territory has to some extent been shared and sanctuaries and pilgrimage sites adapted for use by different ethnic and religious groups. There has been an appalling history of ethnic cleansing altering the ethno-religious map of multicultural emporia like Beirut, Istanbul, Sarajevo, Cracow, Vilnius, Salonika and L'viv. Salonika is now overwhelmingly Greek and L'viv overwhelmingly Ukrainian. Vilnius was at one time host to a large Jewish population; and Poland was far from being homogeneously Catholic. All this has changed over the last century and feeds into anxieties about the erection of mosques in Athens and fears of Pakistani migrants all over Greece. Greece and Cyprus both lie at major borders between civilisations where the sense of collective identity is heightened by the presence of 'the Other'.

A dangerous and contested border still runs through the Balkans between Rome, Byzantium and the Ottoman Empire. The recent hyper-nationalism of Serbia and its Church reflected more than the fact that Serbia lost a larger percentage of its population than any other country in the First World War; more than the sufferings of Serbs at the hands of Croat right-wing militias in the 1940s; and more than the transition in the 1990s from communism to nationalism as the main ideological pillar of the power of the sometime communist elite. Serbia has picked up geopolitical pressures over half a millennium and more, emanating from the Catholic centre of Europe to the north-west and the Ottoman Turks to the south-east. The dualistic Bogomil heresy took root along the fault line, as did subsequent conversions to Islam. There is a vortex surrounding the fault line through the Balkans that reinforces identities and memories of triumph and victimhood. Serbian religiosity is at one and the same time a marker of identity and an amalgam of folk practices.

In the case of Romania the relation between national identity and the Romanian Orthodox Church, manifest in relatively high levels of belief and practice, reflects a rather different concatenation of pressures: a long-term resistance to Ottoman domination, and tensions with Hungary to the west and Russia to the north-east. For a long time Hungarian-speakers in Romania, mostly Catholic and Calvinist, were suspected of forming a fifth column, while Germans, mostly Lutheran, were likewise suspect, and the majority of Germans found it politic to leave the country. As for Uniate Catholics, they were perceived as rival claimants for the role of Romanian national church, and subject to the same degree of persecution they suffered in Ukraine under the Soviets. Uniate Catholics were perceived in Romania and Ukraine alike as a fifth column of the Catholic West, and also subject to Polonisation in Poland.

If one wanted testimony to ethnic homogenisation all the way from Zagreb to Odessa one could find it in the changing distribution of confessional loyalties in the ancient city of Sibiu, (Hermannstadt in German and Nagyszeben in Hungarian). Since 1910 the Hungarians, Germans and Jews have mostly gone. In terms of religious statistics the Romanian Orthodox are now over 90 per cent where they were only 20 per cent; the Uniate Catholics and Calvinists 1 per cent where they were 8 per cent; the Roman Catholics 2 per cent where they were 20 per cent; and the Lutherans 2 per cent where they were 42 per cent. The Orthodox cathedral was finished in 1904, the Lutheran cathedral built in the fourteenth century, the Roman Catholic cathedral built around 1730 and the Reformed (Calvinist) church built in 1783–86 following the declaration of tolerance by Joseph the Second. Architecturally the city witnesses to an historic diversity, with the tiny German remnant worshipping in the oldest and most central building. Demographically the city witnesses to a contemporary monoculturalism. While the European West has shifted in a multicultural direction through migration, the East has become monocultural through extrusion and the redrawing of borders.

If we shift the focus to Central Europe the geopolitical base line extends back as far as the border between the Roman Empire and the 'barbarians' and raises such questions as to how far the northern border of the cult of the Dea Mater corresponds to the border of Catholicism after the Reformation. The Holy Roman Empire was centred in Germany at the heart of Europe, and under the Hohenstaufens extended to Italy. The geopolitical strategies of Charles the Fifth as Holy Roman Emperor were crucial to the substantial defeat of the Reformation in Central Europe, and so to its current borders. Later geopolitical theorists argued that whoever controlled the heartland secured overall hegemony, and in the long run the struggle for the heartland was fought out between Catholic Austria and Protestant Germany. The religious dispositions of all the peripheries of these two power centres reflected their partial assimilation and their resistance. For example, Czech secularity and Estonian secularity reflect resistance to one or other version of German-speaking cultural and political hegemony. Estonia and the Czech Republic are today among the most secular areas in Europe: in Estonia and the Czech Republic believers in God number some 15 per cent. Self-identified Catholics in the Czech Republic have now declined to about 10 per cent. East Germany, the former DDR, is also extremely secular on account of the fatal association of German nationalism with Nazism in the Second World War. That association inhibited the ability of Lutheranism to resist forcible secularisation by calling on the resources of a historic religious national identity, even though the eventual movement to bring down the communist government utilised the symbolic space of churches, like the Nikolaikirche in Leipzig and Stettin Cathedral.

The varied distribution of religious belief and practice in the Baltic Republics reflects the fact that they lie at a border constantly contested between rival hegemons, including Sweden and Poland as well as Russia and Germany. The vitality of religion, at least in this area, depends more on geopolitical history than on factors like degrees of 'existential security' sometimes cited as crucial. Tallinn as the capital of Estonia can be seen as part of a post-Protestant northern plain stretching from Birmingham to Amsterdam, Copenhagen, Hamburg and Berlin, and to Latvia and Estonia. Religion in this northern plain is individualised and secularised, especially in the major cities and capitals: a dramatic contrast with the collective and embedded religion of the southeast. The exception is Catholic Lithuania where the Catholic Church has long retained a positive identification with Lithuanian identity in spite of a history of forced Christianisation by Germans in the late fourteenth century and the promotion of paganism as the original faith of Lithuania by some contemporary intellectuals.

Russian attempts to replace Polish Catholic influence with Orthodoxy in the nineteenth century reinforced Lithuanian self-consciousness and Catholic identification; and discrimination against Lithuanian Catholics in secular employment stimulated the recruitment of talented priests who challenged the influence of secular nationalism in the intelligentsia and adopted programmes of social justice that pre-empted some of the appeal of socialism. After independence in 1918 the Catholic Democratic Party dominated politics up to 1926 and ethnic Germans were tolerated, along with Jews, who in Vilnius made up close to half of the population. After 1926 a new left-wing government tried to reduce Catholic influence. Once forcibly reincorporated in Russia in 1940 (and again reincorporated in 1944 after three years of German occupation) clergy were immediate targets of repression and the church developed a fortress mentality it still retains. Eventually believers agitated for human rights and created an underground church possessed of some genuine popular authority. Soon after independence was regained the reformed communists came to power and some of the moral prestige gained by the Church under occupation evaporated. When a socially conservative government was elected in 2008 people suspected the social ambitions of the Church, and a growing urban middle class open to media influence found the Church a rather ambiguous presence. Nevertheless some 80 per cent of the population identify with Catholicism, some 30 per cent claim to attend church on holy days and another 30 per cent claim to attend at least once a month. Lithuania and Poland were once united and have a common history of resistance to Russia, which in the second half of the twentieth century became resistance to enforced secularisation.[8] Today the two countries are among the most practising in Europe: in Poland 80–90 per cent of the population believes in God, and 50–70 per cent regularly attends church.

Amsterdam represents the secularity of northwest Europe and can be regarded as the capital of religious indifference. It provides a major hub linking the secular Northern European plain and the secular world of Britain and Scandinavia. Though the religious indifference of Amsterdam on the contemporary scale dates from the 1960s and the collapses of the separately integrated social and religious 'pillars' of Dutch society, the story properly begins with the Eighty Years' War of independence against Catholic Spain and the iconoclastic fury that accompanied it. Out of the carnage there arose a burger society interested in trade and commerce and inclined to a degree of tolerance, rather than a society of kings and priests. This was the great period of Dutch sea power and of creative achievement in the arts; and the modern representation of identity might well be the Rijksmuseum, both in its original and highly controversial form as the Gothic creation of a Catholic architect in a society cherishing a Protestant founding narrative and in its renovated form as a statement of an identity now based on certain values, in particular artistic creativity. Whereas in Sicily they might haul an icon of the Virgin through the streets in procession, in

---

⁸   Ališauskienė and Schröder, *Religious Diversity in Post-Soviet Society*.

Holland in 2013 they hauled Rembrandt's *The Night Watch* to the Rijksmuseum as a representation of the public face of Dutch society. Holland is an example, with Germany and Switzerland, of a bi-confessional society, and all three show a decline in religion, most obviously in the Protestant sector. In what was, during the mid-twentieth century a strongly practising society, the Dutch have become highly individualised religious consumers: about one in four speaks of belief in God and one in three of belief in 'a higher power'. The proportion of the spiritually unaffiliated increases, in particular among young educated urban dwellers: these people conceive of a transcendent dimension quite apart from institutional attachment and seek a harmonious relation to the environment. Among those aged under 30 in 2010 religious affiliation was as low as 30 per cent; and the Catholic proportion of the population has dropped from 40 per cent to 25 per cent, with only about 1 per cent present at mass on any given Sunday.

The United Kingdom and the northern countries of Scandinavia are as secular and individualised as the European northern plain, though they differ in not having historic territorial emplacements of Catholicism. Scandinavia has long been characterised by formal identification with the majority churches, so that even now most young people are confirmed, but levels of active participation on Sundays are less than 5 per cent. The United Kingdom has seen declines in belief and practice since the 1960s following a brief post-war stabilisation, and also a secular transition in the peripheries: Scotland and Wales have both drawn closer to the dominant pattern of religiosity in England.

France and Belgium are very different and quite exceptional in their degree of explicit secularism rather than mere secularity. Both countries have experienced outright conflict between Catholicism and secular liberalism and socialism, and splits over religion running through the whole society, as well as serious religious revivals in the late nineteenth and early twentieth centuries. Ideals of *laïcité* focussed on curbing the influence of the Catholic Church go back to the time of the French Revolution when peasants were finally converted into Frenchmen. In both France and Belgium identification with Catholicism has dropped to around half the population and practice to around 5 per cent on any given Sunday.[9] Spain and Italy have also experienced major splits between Catholicism and secular liberalism and socialism, but have considerably higher reserves of Catholic identification and belief and higher levels of mass attendance. In Italy regular mass attendance may be as high as 20+ per cent, perhaps reflecting the fact that the political memory of collusion with Fascism is more distant than

---

[9]   Institut Français d'Opinion Publique (IFOP), *Analyse: Le Catholicisme en France en 2009* (www.ifop.com).

in Spain as well as reflecting the post-war influence of Christian Democracy. There is also a lurking memory of an earlier tension between the Church and Italian liberalism and nationalism: the statues to Arnold of Brescia in Brescia and of Giordano Bruno in Rome that were put up in the late nineteenth century memorialised heretics in order to further the cause of the Risorgimento. The younger generations in both Spain and Italy are little influenced by Catholic moral teaching and there are major problems of recruitment to the priesthood. Birth rates indicate that Catholic moral teaching on contraception is utterly null and void for most Catholics. Italy legalised divorce in the 1970s and Spain legalised same-sex marriage in 2005. Even Malta, a country where there is still majority practice, legalised divorce in 2012. The most obvious popular expressions of religion are in pilgrimages and festivals, including pilgrimage centres rooted in a strong local identity, such as Montserrat in Catalonia, El Pilar in Aragon and Santiago in Galicia.

If one were to try to summarise the situation in Western Europe one might say that with economic security and urbanisation there has been a demobilisation of identities, whether these are religious, national or political. The national centres become precarious and local identities assert themselves, as in Scotland and Catalonia. Ireland has long been dominated by nationalism, by Catholicism and by a nationalistic Catholicism nurtured in the Protestant Ascendancy and maintained against the nationalistic Protestantism of Ulster. With prosperity and the easing of the situation in the north of the island, including the amelioration of practices of exclusion and discrimination, as well as the increasing influence of liberal professionals and a liberal media, there has been a degree of demobilisation and what Roy Foster has called the 'Protestantisation' of Ireland. Foster notes a shift to individual moral choice and a rejection of laws imposed by ecclesiastical fiat that now extends throughout Western Europe.[10] In Spain same-sex marriage and abortion might be opposed by the Church but they attract the support of the majority.

The decline of Social Democracy in Northern Europe and of Christian Democracy in Southern Europe provides another indicator of demobilisation. The decline of Social Democracy is related to the achievement of most social democratic goals and the rising costs of welfare, and the decline of Christian Democracy to a diminishing Catholic base and the demise of communism in the East and the West alike. Practising Catholics, for example in all the countries of 'Latin' Europe, tend to the centre right but they are a diminishing and

---

[10]   Roy Foster, *Luck and the Irish: A Brief History of Change since 1970* (Oxford: Oxford University Press, 2008).

ageing constituency; and at the same time the fortress mentality of communist electorates in France and Italy with their associated union power has dissipated. The politics of commitment based on mass institutions has given way to a search for the centre ground based on pragmatic calculations of electoral advantage in an atmosphere of scepticism about politics and politicians. In successive years of recession electorates simply opt for whichever party is not responsible for current austerity. Populist parties of the right express frustration with austerity, and in Britain and France as well as Austria and Greece they pick up lower-class anxieties about migration.

The rise of 'spirituality' expresses an individualistic resistance to institutions and finds expression in technologies of the self and concern for the environment, even though spirituality still retains major links with organised religion. The areas that were once religiously distinct, especially in the peripheries, have assimilated more to the centre, and there are now substantial religious and ethnic minorities where once there was a religious monopoly. Migration has resulted in Muslim minorities of over a million in Spain and Italy, and in the rest of Western Europe the proportion of Muslims edges towards 5 per cent or even 6 per cent, mostly concentrated in the major cities: Vienna may cease to be a Catholic city within a generation or so even though its architectural profile is dominated by churches. Prejudice against minorities, in particular Muslims, is declining, as is prejudice against sexual deviation, though more so in Western than in Eastern Europe. The major secular icons in public space are clusters of banks as in London and Frankfurt, sports stadia, media headquarters, art galleries, universities and hospitals. That is why revolutionaries first seek to take control of media headquarters and terrorists attack the architectural symbols of contemporary financial and military power. Perhaps the centre of industrial Milan, built on the car industry and the fashion industry, symbolises the rivalrous and complementary sources of contemporary social power: the cathedral, the Brera Art Gallery and the Galleria Vittorio Emanuele II, built between 1865 and 1877, looking back to London's Burlington Arcade, and linking the cathedral with La Scala Opera House.

The four maritime nations of Western Europe laid down the social geography of religion in North America, and topographical names are the most eloquent testimony to the past (including a Native American presence even in places where Native Americans are scarce on the ground, like Manhattan and Massachusetts). New York was New Amsterdam up to 1664, with a Jewish as well as a Dutch presence, and in the immediate vicinity of New York you can follow a trail of place names with a Dutch provenance like Flushing, Harlem and the Bronx.

Here one needs first to keep in mind the conflicts between the English and the Dutch for maritime supremacy, initially settled in favour of the Dutch, and then to remember the religious and political affinity between the two Protestant nations. When William of Orange became king of England in 1688, his advent was immediately followed in 1689 by a Bill of Rights that provided something like a first version of the American Bill of Rights roughly a century later. The Civil War in England that ended in the restoration of the monarchy in 1660 ended in America with the deposition of the monarchy in 1776.

The hinterlands of Boston, Plymouth and Jamestown in Virginia are scrambled maps of England and the influence of these maps fans out southward to Charleston, westward to Philadelphia and northward to Portland and Bangor. All these areas reproduce something of the varied ecclesiastical ecology of England, Scotland, Wales and Ulster: classical looking churches and meeting houses on an English eighteenth-century model, often rebuilt, that may be Episcopal, Congregational, Unitarian, Baptist, Methodist or some Protestant Church founded much later. As far south as Savannah in Georgia you find the characteristic emplacements of towns founded on an eighteenth-century model but with a wider representation of denominations than you might expect in England, and Episcopal churches no more central than the others.

Classical architecture, domestic and ecclesiastical, extends all over the South, as well as throughout the middle states and New England: much of it in an early nineteenth-century Greek style that reflected Jefferson's idea of America as the new Athens, as exemplified in the building of the University of Virginia.[11] Later one finds the emplacements of a nineteenth-century Gothic continuous with English neo-Gothic and neo-Romanesque, such as Andrew Jackson Downing's St. Patrick's Cathedral in New York and Henry Hobson Richardson's Episcopal Trinity Church in Boston. American universities and their chapels reflect the expansion of different denominations: Baptist foundations at Brown and Chicago; Congregational foundations at Harvard and Yale; Scottish Presbyterian foundations at Princeton; Methodist foundations at Boston, Duke and Emory. Sometimes these universities are associated with some form of industrial enterprise, for example, tobacco at Duke, Coca-Cola at Emory; and they alternate between the eighteenth-century classical model and the nineteenth-century Gothic model, in particular Gothic university chapels on the scale of an English cathedral like those in Duke and Princeton.

---

[11]   Margaret Malamud, *Ancient Rome and Modern America* (Oxford: Wiley-Blackwell, 2009).

Place names are just as eloquent of an expansive and ambitious French presence only really brought to a halt at the conclusion of the first world war of 1756–63. From Maine and Vermont in the north to New Orleans and Louisiana in the south, the French presence sought to contain the westward expansion of the English, Scottish and Scots Irish in an arc that includes the massive Catholic emplacements on the heights of Québec and Montreal, as well as Detroit and Des Moines. The Catholic Cathedral-Basilica of Saint Louis, King of France, overlooking Jackson Square in New Orleans, retains the same centrality it would have in Europe. Place names also provide potent reminders of the Spanish presence. Today the most striking traces of the Spanish *imperium* are found in missions set up by Spaniards from the late seventeenth century onward up to the 1820s, such as San Juan Capistrano in California and San Antonio de Valero (the Alamo) in Texas. Spanish influence can be picked up all over what is now the southern border of the USA: from St. Augustine in Florida, to the western coast of California, and northwards beyond the San Francisco Bay area. Proceeding further north you encounter a Scottish influence with massive emplacements all over western Canada as well as in the western Maritimes.

These foundations represent a redistribution of the patterns and architectural styles of Europe ultimately meeting, mingling and competing on a basis of near equality. There is hardly anywhere in Europe where Methodists and Catholics compete on equal terms, but they do in Kansas. The cities of Eastern and Central North America, above all Chicago – as well as cities like Toronto in Canada – are multicultural emporia that in their churches simultaneously witness to a pullulating Protestant pluralism and to wave after wave of migrants. The migrants come from Ireland, Italy, Greece, Poland, Russia and Ukraine; and they include blacks from the American South, the West Indies and West Africa, as well as Hispanics from Mexico, Central and South America, Puerto Rico, the Dominican Republic and Haiti. All the cities of the American South, traditionally dominated by Baptists and other Protestant denominations, now have vast sectors, including the suburbs, occupied by blacks and by Hispanic migrants. The cities of the West Coast from San Diego to Vancouver have Chinese, Korean, Japanese and Philippine populations, and these have fanned out all over the land mass of North America. Every city has major mega-churches, like the Crystal Cathedral or Saddleback Valley Church, Lake Forest, California, or Lakewood and Second Baptist in Houston: like shopping malls, churches have grown vastly in size and in the range of their facilities.[12] One finds

---

[12]   Scott Thumma and Dave Travis, *Beyond the Myth: What We Can Learn from America's Largest Churches* (San Francisco: Wiley/Jossey-Bass, 2007).

a Chinese Presbyterian church in Toronto and a Korean Presbyterian church in Boston, and they may easily share a block with a Brazilian or Nigerian Evangelical or Pentecostal church. This social geography of religion intersects with the political map of North America: 'white conservative Protestants' in the South voting Republican; Hispanics, blacks, Liberal Protestants, Jews and 'seculars' voting Democrat; Catholics shifting from their old Democrat allegiances to a more evenly split allegiance.[13]

The ecology of American religion splits fairly easily into the North-East, which is relatively secular (for example Vermont), with a very strong Catholic presence in the major cities; the West, also relatively secular (for example Oregon); the South which is still white conservative and Protestant, with expanding sectors of Hispanic migrants; and the Midwest, which remains disproportionately German and Scandinavian Lutheran, often of a conservative complexion. The proportion of Americans identifying themselves as Christian may be much the same as in Europe, at about 80 per cent; but the proportion regularly attending church is more than twice as high, and belief in God very much higher. Even those who in increasing numbers (among young men up to 20 per cent) identify themselves as having 'no religion' often believe in God, pray and accept the label 'spiritual'. Given the Hispanic and Irish backgrounds of many in the 'no religion' category the figures may pick up disillusion with the Catholic Church after recent scandals.

In this chapter I have tried to provide the broadest possible context for the attempt in the next two chapters to inscribe my general theory of secularisation in terms of the dispositions of religious power in cities of the centre and cities of the periphery. In the initial sections I have sketched the fundamental dynamic of cultures influenced by Christianity and the types of organisation to which that dynamic gives rise. I have then broadened out from implicit mental maps of the distribution of different kinds of Christianity to trace in outline the categories set out in the general theory, such as the Protestant state churches of Northern Europe, the areas of mixed confession in north-central Europe and the areas of major political conflict over religion in southern Catholic Europe, as well as the embedded collective religion of Eastern Europe, the partial pluralism of the UK and the total pluralism of North America. I have not attempted to build in the process of functional differentiation, mainly because that is dealt with in the chapter following.

---

[13]   Corwin E. Smidt, *American Evangelicals Today* (London and New York: Rowman and Littlefield, 2013).

Chapter 13

Inscribing the General Theory of Secularisation and Its Basic Patterns in the Space/Time of the City

Translating the General Theory

From time to time I have tried to translate a revised version of my *A General Theory of Secularization* in spatial terms, using a framework loosely based on Edward Shils' contrast between centre and periphery, and focussing on the architectural dispositions of capital (or central) cities like Paris or Berlin, often as these are contrasted with the architectural dispositions in 'peripheral cities' like Strasbourg or Munich.[1] Architectural dispositions represent physically the distributions of secular and sacred power as they change over time. They visibly demonstrate whose flag or emblem flies in the high and holy place, and they manifest the forms in which such symbolic statements are confronted and contested. In this chapter I offer such a translation for Europe and North America, before focussing in the next chapter on England, with particular reference to London.

Preliminaries: The General Theory

First I need to indicate yet again the nature of my 'General Theory', recollecting that since 1965 I have always argued that secularisation was both a descriptive and a prescriptive concept and that it is best understood as a linked set of general tendencies heavily inflected by particular histories. The world is not destined to follow in the steps of either France or Sweden, and the Western European pattern is not universally normative. Modernity is not all of a piece.

In the context of modernisation, which began very early in Britain and late (say) in Albania, the general theory assumed there were some general empirical

---

[1]   David Martin, *A General Theory of Secularization* (Oxford: Blackwell, 1978).

tendencies towards secularisation. These empirical tendencies were channelled by processes of functional differentiation, which in turn were inflected by the relation of the myth of the nation to religion, whether positive or negative, and by the thrust of the national version of the Enlightenment. France was a nation where the myth of the nation and its version of the Enlightenment were both negative towards religion, and the USA a nation where they were both positive. Relations of hostility or friendliness with respect either to religion and the nation or to religion and Enlightenment, or both together, were often dramatised in crucial dramatic events. Major examples are the Anglo-American revolutions of 1642–60, 1688–89 and 1776–86, the French Revolution of 1789 and the Russian revolutions of 1917 and 1989. One also needs to take into account the failure of revolution, for example in Germany in 1848 and 1919, bearing in mind that the myth of the German nation and the thrust of the German Enlightenment were relatively favourable to religion.[2] One also needs to take into account the enlightened autocracies in Germany, Austria and even in Turkey and Russia that achieved an interim and partial top-down 'modernisation' until they collapsed under the pressures of the 1914–18 war. Below I briefly indicate the kind of architectural emplacements created by these imperial systems, and their later reincarnations in 'enlightened' dictatorships.

Other important influences on the course of secularisation are whether the religion is Protestant, Catholic or Orthodox; whether it is a monopoly, as in Latin Europe or Scandinavia, a duopoly, as in Germany and the Netherlands, or a competitive free market, as in the USA; and whether a nation has been oppressed, as in the cases of Ireland or Poland, or has been the centre of an empire, as in Britain and Russia. At this juncture I suggest something of the variable impact of types of religion on my basic patterns, without going into the immensely complicated issue of the extent to which early Christianity made available a repertoire presupposing a space between the 'world' (or the *saeculum*) and faith, in particular between the political world and the community of faith. This can take very varied and paradoxical forms, all the way from the Investiture Controversy between papal and imperial power and the American 'wall of separation' between Church and state, a spatial image translated in spatial terms in nearly every American city outside the South-West.

---

[2]   The range of Enlightenments is brought out in David Sorkin, *The Religious Enlightenment: Protestants, Jews, and Catholics from London to Vienna* (Princeton: Princeton University Press, 2008).

The Variable Impact of Different Types of Religion

Where the religion is Protestant/Evangelical, there are various potential developments. One of these is a radical development of the individualistic deposit in Protestantism. Under specifically European conditions individualism easily undermines the sense of active corporate belonging in the body of the Church, which is increasingly regarded as a 'service station'. Maybe individualism, when disseminated in a society where the Church can be viewed as a service station, also assists the rise of modern 'spirituality'. In the USA, however, churches are not service stations but active voluntary associations filling the space between the citizen and the state. The size of such a space is always an important variable, and in the USA, where the space is maximal, the effect of individualism has been to accentuate the rise of pluralism and a competitive free market, though 'spirituality' also emerges, particularly on the west coast. At the same time, Protestantism can be partly taken over by the idea of the nation understood as a new Israel, a tendency that has been particularly strong in Anglo-American societies. England donated the idea of the nation as a new Israel to the nascent USA via the Puritan Revolution in 1642. In the same way, Sweden donated the idea to Finland.

Where the religion in question is Catholic, monopolistic and established there is a strong tendency to forge an alliance with the *ancien régime* and to retain a religious monopoly, which in turn stimulates anti-clerical and even anti-religious movements, as in France, Italy and Spain. If Catholicism is part of a duopolistic religious system – as in Germany, Holland and Switzerland – it tends to build up its own institutional world, including political parties, parallel to the Protestant institutional world. If Catholics are a minority then they may shift politically into the progressive column, as in Australia and the USA but also in late nineteenth-century Germany. Where Catholicism is the majority faith of a nation oppressed by another nation, religion and nation tend to fuse together, as in Ireland, Lithuania and Poland.

The link between Orthodoxy and nationalism is strong, and it reaches back to the Byzantine legacy of caesaro-papism, and to the concepts of autocephaly (or autonomous governance) and of a *symphonia* between Church and state. The link with nationalism persists whether or not the nation is oppressed or a great empire, though it is also true that the link between religion and nation is often strengthened by oppression or by political circumstances, real or semi-mythical, which lead a nation to regard itself as a collective martyr or messiah. The consequences for religious vitality of the mythical invocation of national defeat, for example the defeat of the Serbs at Kosovo in 1389, or of victory, for example the Russian victory over Napoleon in 1812, or of sacrificial expenditures of blood and treasure are too complex and variable to be canvassed here, though their monuments and sites of recollection are scattered all over Europe.

Some Spatial Translations at Centre and Periphery

These complex and variable relationships constituted a limited set of basic patterns of secularisation and of relations between the sacred and secular power which I began to translate in a spatial form some years ago. I did so by identifying the architectural dispositions at the heart of capital (or central) cities like Washington, London, Paris, Amsterdam, Budapest, Vienna and Berlin and juxtaposing them with the architectural dispositions in contrasting peripheries. Selecting the contrasting peripheries is a delicate matter because there are usually several candidates. In Britain it could be Glasgow, the traditional 'second city', or Manchester or Liverpool. Glasgow was certainly a serious candidate.[3] For various reasons I selected cities like Dallas, Edinburgh (or Dublin), Strasbourg, Debrecen and Munich as my 'peripheral' cities. I also related my heartland cities to Rome, Athens and Jerusalem because for Christian countries these are the three 'cities of perpetual recollection', though Paris might be seen as city of perpetual recollection on its own account.

For the purposes of this discussion I look at Washington (including some of the alternatives to it on the North American continent) and at London, Amsterdam and Paris. Washington, London and Amsterdam have had relatively positive relationships between their national myths and religion, and between their versions of the Enlightenment and religion. Paris, however, exemplifies mostly negative or at any rate strongly contested relationships. Amsterdam has a special importance because it arguably inaugurated a secular mutation within Protestantism parallel to, and following on from, the secular mutation of Catholicism in Venice and Florence: the cumulative ascendancy of the commercial over the religious.

Taking Washington first, its sacred field is the creation of a specifically American Enlightenment. It embodies classical (and Masonic) ideals of the *res publica*, and sets the two national cathedrals, Episcopalian and Catholic (and any

---

[3]   Cf. David W. Smith, *Seeking a City with Foundations: Theology for an Urban World* (Nottingham: Inter-Varsity Press, 2011). David Smith traces a changing skyline from the medieval cathedral to the emergence of the commercial 'lower town' and of the idea of the Holy Commonwealth, and then onto the nineteenth century and iconic buildings like the City Chambers, and finally to the tower blocks and shopping malls of today.

number of other denominational buildings), at a distance, symbolising the wall of separation between Church and state. Washington was conceived by a French architect, and is an unusually pure case of a unified political vision. At the same time, America is a continent and can also be represented by other cities along a spectrum from quasi-establishments to total fragmentation. This spectrum picks up just at the point where Europe (notably England and Holland) leave off, and exemplifies the long-term logic of pluralism. New York, which was New Amsterdam until 1664, picks up the theme of the cumulative ascendancy of the commercial ethos, with the edifices of the ethnic migrant communities tucked in the interstices, for example St. Patrick's Cathedral. Other North American cities indicate other major possibilities, some of them referring back to continental Europe, notably Spain and France. Santa Fé is dominated by a cathedral square which affiliates it with Guadalajara in Mexico, and New Orleans has a cathedral square which affiliates it with Montréal, a city where the commanding heights are quite self-consciously dominated by Catholicism. Boston, Savannah and Philadelphia represent mutations of the British combination of establishment and increasing pluralism. Philadelphia, one of the two epicentres of the Revolution, for a long time allowed no building to exceed in height the statue of one of the founding deists, Benjamin Franklin; and it is perhaps no accident that the nearest 'religious' edifice to the government centre is the Scottish rite Masonic temple. Boston, the other epicentre of the Revolution, has several churches that stand for rival quasi-establishments, like the historic Congregational Church on the Common, the (now Unitarian) King's Chapel, the Old North (Episcopal) Church and the Episcopal Church of the Advent on Beacon Hill. Arguably, the real sacred site is the city centre itself, 'set on a hill' and presided over by a Senate House resembling the Dome of the Rock. If you want explicit European and British genealogies in Boston you mostly have to locate them within religious buildings, not in public space, for example the genealogy of British Methodism celebrated in the iconography inside Boston University Chapel. At the same time the boulevards of Boston refer back architecturally to Paris as a (secondary) 'city of perpetual recollection'. After all, France has adopted the role of godmother to the American Revolution, a claim it symbolised in its gift of the Statue of Liberty for the centenary celebrations of 1876.

Stepping westward in the USA the centres increasingly fragment. Though Dallas, Texas, has massive Methodist and Baptist emplacements close to the centre, and an increasing and mainly Catholic Hispanic architectural presence, there is at its heart the secular Thanks-Giving Square occupied by an edifice resembling the Great Mosque of Samarra and dense with inter-faith symbolism.

At the end of the westward trail Los Angeles is completely decentred, and so, perhaps, may have been the appropriate city to host the origins of the decentred faith of Pentecostalism. San Francisco is dominated by a secular pyramid structure while retaining architectural echoes of a more traditional Hispanic format. In San Francisco, and in most Californian cities, you encounter the architectural presence of the Far East, for example the Japanese, the Chinese and the (mostly Protestant) Koreans, and the eastern influences that have fed into Californian spirituality.

The centre of London exemplifies a pattern of secularisation and of the relation between secular and sacred power very different from the centre of Washington. There is no revolutionary wall of separation between Church and state because England has experienced the evolution of an increasing pluralism alongside a continuing but decreasingly dominant establishment. In London the upper end of Victoria Street represented the relation of Church to state in the juxtaposition of Westminster Abbey (with St. Margaret's) and the Houses of Parliament, while the Methodist Central Hall opposite the Abbey represented the challenge of Protestant voluntarism, and the Catholic Westminster Cathedral at the other end of Victoria Street represented the challenge of the largest ethnic Church. Unlike revolutionary Washington and revolutionary Paris (or enlightened and autocratic Berlin and St. Petersburg), London has no unifying or governing axis, and attempts at creating one have always been successfully resisted or simply failed to materialise, like the plan set out by John Nash of which Regent Street is a fragmentary and modified version.

Paris is as different from London as London is from Washington, and the three great cities represent a triangle of fundamental possibilities, all of them exported with variations to the rest of the world: Paris to Santiago, Bucharest and Buenos Aires; Washington to Canberra; and London to Budapest. In Paris rival monuments symbolised a prolonged struggle culminating in the separation of Church and state in 1905. On the one hand there were embodiments of the sacred as understood by radical republicanism and by the myth of the 'universal' revolutionary nation, and on the other hand the sacred as understood by the international Catholic Church. This latter is still a live option, indicated by the notion mooted by ex-President Sarkozy, of positive *laïcité*. The national Panthéon and the revolutionary Place de la Bastille faced off Notre-Dame (originally at the centre of a complex spatial symbolism including La Sainte-Chapelle), La Madeleine and Sacré Coeur.

An important bifurcated extension of the French model was initiated in Turkey, where a new explicitly secular capital was set up in Ankara by way of contrast to the old Ottoman capital in Istanbul. However, the return of the repressed in the new migrant suburbs of Ankara is an indication of de-secularisation rather than anything 'post-secular'. An analogous bifurcation, this time of the Anglo-American model, can be found in Tel Aviv, which stands in relation to Jerusalem as Ankara stands in relation to Istanbul. Tel Aviv is a self-consciously modern city, referring back to modern planning by the British architect Patrick Geddes and distinguished by fine modern architecture in the Bauhaus style. It is secular and Zionist in its inspiration, and memorialises people who fostered the modern use of the Hebrew language and of an associated national culture, as well as the pioneers, for example those who broke the British blockade or died in the attempt. There is no religious revival evident in Tel Aviv. In Israel religious revival is most obviously located in the massive emplacements being erected by the largely Sephardic and North African religious movement known as Shas in the environs of Jerusalem.

Amsterdam is a city where the dispositions of symbolic power seem less obvious than in (say) London, its historic Protestant rival. If one assumes that the Dam is the symbolic centre of Amsterdam, it can be read as sending out a message about the dominance of money and commerce, just as the architecture of the houses on surrounding canals sends out a message about the dominance of the merchant and banking classes. Amsterdam does not have triumphal avenues or vistas such as one finds in Paris. The 'New Church' opposite the Dam, now secularised, is not at all dominating, even though it reminds us of the role of Calvinism in the rise of Amsterdam. Amsterdam is, perhaps, the first example of a city where the symbolism of its architectural disposition speaks loudly of commerce rather than Church, and its numerous successor cities include not only New York but St. Petersburg. One might trace a sequence from the Venetian ghetto to the Jewish communities in Amsterdam, London and New York, and one which included the migration of the commercially active French Huguenots. The symbiosis of Protestantism and Jewry, and the social role sometimes played by sects like the Dutch Mennonites and the Old Believers in Moscow, is closely bound up with the long-term secularising power of money. The longer roots go back to the abandonment of the prohibition of usury, a readiness to trade with infidels and the embrace of naked power in both Venice and in Florence, explicitly articulated for the first time by Machiavelli. An implicit secular practice finally became explicit in Machiavelli and the architecture of the Medicis.

The Cities of Enlightened Autocracy

One has to recollect, however briefly, another pattern of 'internal' secularisation inscribed in the cities created by enlightened autocracy. The Enlightenment is far too easily associated with liberty and fraternity when it has just as often been associated with autocracy and/or imperialism and racism, as in France. Vienna and St. Petersburg are two great creations of eighteenth-century enlightened autocracy where an interim modernisation or internal secularisation was achieved by a governmental subordination of the Church. Joseph the Second of Austria may have been a partial failure, but he is the model par excellence of the enlightened imperial autocrat. A parallel internal secularisation is also present, if more modestly, in London in its enlightened architecture from 1680 to 1830.

Both Vienna and St. Petersburg are conceived in terms of major axes, spaces and vistas conveying a sense of concentrated power, passed through the lens of classicism in the later manifestations of St. Petersburg under Catherine and Alexander. These cities look back to a prototype in the architectural projects of Louis XIV, which in turn look back to Rome. In Vienna (with its reminiscences of the Parisian boulevards) there are distinct centres associated with the royal palace and St. Stephen's Cathedral, providing an echo, however faint, of the Church–state distinction and the sense of an independent power base found in Catholicism. In St. Petersburg the Orthodox tradition of a union of Church and state is inscribed in the Peter and Paul Fortress, but in the rest of the city the churches are interspersed among other monuments without dominating them, exactly as they are in imperial Berlin, and indeed in Edinburgh's eighteenth-century New Town. In Berlin (and in Potsdam, its variant of Versailles) the churches are part of an ensemble, and some of the key ones, like Berlin's Protestant cathedral, are royal mausolea or otherwise connected to the monarchy. In all three imperial cities the museums and the emplacements of high art and music, in particular the opera houses, are as important as the churches, Moreover, at the point of political breakdown in the wake of the (first) Great War they were in the course of emerging as foci of political radicalism and distinct versions of artistic and philosophical modernity, rivalling those emerging from Paris. As already suggested, Ankara should also be regarded as the creation of an enlightened autocracy, following the 'shy Enlightenment' attempted by the late Ottomans, who pursued a modernisation largely on the basis of the French model.

One finds a somewhat different disposition of power if we look at Munich as a periphery of Berlin, or alternatively as a centre of what was once another possible Germany, affiliated to Catholic Austria. Here we have a more emphatic division into two centres, one of them Catholic and focussed on Church and market, and the other classical, overlooked by what is now the Amerikahaus. A space was created here marked by monumental Egyptian columns within which the power of the Nazis could be displayed, just as it was in 1938 in the central spaces of Vienna.

Some Spatial Translations in Cities on the Peripheries

Munich is an ambiguous example of what is meant by a periphery. Another example might have been Frankfurt, where German democracy almost achieved success through the assembly that met in 1848 in the Paulskirche. I now offer two rather different examples of the relation between centre and periphery: first *within* a country, Holland, taking Amsterdam as the centre and Groningen as the north-east periphery; and then *between* countries, where a sometime satellite city like Helsinki becomes the new centre of an independent nation.

Earlier I characterised Amsterdam as a city representing the power of commerce, and in that respect it is the north-west European Protestant realisation of a process begun in Catholic – but anti-papal – Venice, notably the role of credit in the hands of the Jewish ghetto, as well as the role of banking as developed in Florence. In one way Venice is saturated in Catholic religious symbolism, but the Lion of St. Mark and its many ancillary symbols represent the triumph of the city, first over neighbouring cities and then over ecclesiastical power, so that the Cathedral of St. Mark is the Doge's own peculiar as much as Westminster Abbey is the peculiar of the British monarch. Commercial Amsterdam, which also had its important Jewish community, is the Venice of the North, and not only because of its canals. But where can one locate a peripheral city?

One candidate is Groningen, the largest city in the Protestant north-east, except that in a small country this periphery is more a mirror of the centre than a contrast. Like Amsterdam, it was forcibly converted to Protestantism, and the Catholic population mostly expelled, in the war of liberation from the Spanish, alias the Civil War – though Amsterdam looked southward, whereas Groningen was a city of the empire. Today it is predominantly a university city which resembles Amsterdam in being a place where those of no declared religion are in the majority, though surrounded by a countryside of Protestant villages and small townships which are both Calvinist and Re-Reformed. Its main churches are empty and in civic ownership, like the New Church in Amsterdam. It has a history as a 'red' city like Bologna, to which it has related itself quite consciously, and it is the site of the foundation of the Dutch workers' movement. As Amsterdam is to Venice so Groningen is to Bologna. Up to the 1940s it had a Jewish quarter, housing up to 10 per cent of the population in an area now mainly occupied by Muslims.

Helsinki, Edinburgh and Dublin were once cities on the periphery, closely replicating the style of the centre, but they now symbolise the resurgence of an independent nation. In its original form Senate Square in Helsinki combined Church, state, law enforcement and university in a single architectural ensemble expressly echoing the classical style of imperial St. Petersburg. It is literally overlooked by the Orthodox cathedral on a nearby eminence, whereas the emplacements of the Finnish national vernacular, of the (highly secular) Jugendstyl, and Finnish modernism are concentrated elsewhere in the city. Today the square hosts vast gatherings expressing the intensity of Finnish nationalism, which is, incidentally, a cause enthusiastically espoused by the Finnish clergy. In the same way the centre of Dublin, with its two Anglican cathedrals, is a largely eighteenth-century creation expressing the Anglo-Irish Protestant ascendancy, while in Edinburgh – the self-styled Athens of the North – the eighteenth-century New Town expresses the union of 1707. Helsinki, Edinburgh and Dublin have been cities of the periphery, embodying symbols of the power of the centre for a period, prior to nationalist resurgence.

Peripheries are important and have to be read architecturally as counterpoints to the centre. We need to envisage them as existing in different degrees of dependence and difference from the centre, both between countries, as in the case of Helsinki in Finland and St. Petersburg in Russia, and within them, as in the case of Paris and Strasbourg. Moscow can be seen as the centre of Slavic spirituality and St. Petersburg as a rival centre embodying an Enlightened opening to the West. The cathedral of Strasbourg was recovered for Catholicism with the forcible incorporation of Alsace in France in 1681, while a German church was built in Strasbourg after 1870 to symbolise the forcible incorporation of Alsace in the German Empire.

Transitional Areas

Of course, Strasbourg is also placed at a point of ethnic, linguistic and religious transition, which means it is not simply a city of the French periphery in the way Barcelona, Santiago and Saragossa are cities of the peripheries of Spain – though Barcelona can also be seen, so far as culture and communications are concerned, as a junction or point of transition, since it is as much a periphery of Paris as of Madrid. Strasbourg has to be read alongside other cities that are placed at major junctions between civilisations, such as Timisoara, Sarajevo, Salonika and L'viv. Not only are they countercultural in relation to a national capital but multicultural in relation to the pull of rival centres of power. The different churches and synagogue sites of L'viv are eloquent of its role as a contested meeting point and of its incorporation in different polities and spheres of religious influence at different times. Only recently the Church of the Transfiguration changed hands after an unhappy struggle and passed back to the Uniates, Orthodox in liturgy but united since 1596 with Rome, and therefore much persecuted and suppressed in Soviet times. As a transitional area Western Ukraine has been much more resistant to Soviet atheism than elsewhere in the former Soviet Union, and is now a religiously plural society with a large Evangelical minority.

The three cities of Strasbourg, Brussels and Geneva lie at, or close to, transitional areas of religio-political and linguistic dispute in Western Europe, and were natural places to select to house the key institutions of the EU. What had been sites of conflict became the sites of reconciliation. Those Christian Democrats who imagined a reconciled Europe in the late 1940s were very conscious of the meanings attached to the transitional areas, in particular the mythic status attributed to the coronation of Charlemagne at Aachen in AD 800 and the role of the Middle Kingdom of Lotharingia. It is one of the oddities of the sociological 'optic' that this massive role of religion in post-war European reconstruction, including the creation of the Strasbourg Parliament, was ignored. The importance of religion has only belatedly been realised on account of Islam, even though its influence on European voting behaviour has been in continuous decline.

Religion and Region, Spatial Niches and Geopolitical Boundaries

I hope it is by now possible to envisage how one might map sites of symbolic power on a continental scale as well as articulate the varying relations of centre and periphery within nations and between them. However, the relations of centre to periphery just canvassed are not the only ones. There is, for example, a massive difference between the religion of the Mediterranean littoral, the Central Alpine hub extending into Bavaria, and the Anglo-Dutch-Germanic north. Arguably there is a Mediterranean kind of religiosity not at all confined to the Northern Mediterranean, and it is interesting that the monastery of Montserrat in Catalonia is not only the symbolic mountain focus of Catalonian nationalism, but conceives itself in religious geopolitical terms which include the south as well as the north of the Mediterranean. The Anglo-Germanic north includes a northern plain dominated by the major capitals of secularity: Birmingham, Amsterdam, Hamburg, Copenhagen, Berlin and Tallinn. Then there are the distinct spiritualities surrounding the (mainly) Lutheran Baltic and the (Celtic) Irish Sea, as well as the spiritualities of the Celtic fringe extending from the Celtic west of the British Isles, including Cornwall, to Brittany and to Spanish Galicia. Starting with Hungary, Croatia and Slovakia and moving east the dominant form of faith has a very strong ethno-religious character. This extends from the troubled Balkans to the equally troubled Caucasus, and both are regions where empires have contended over centuries and religious borders have been coterminous with intense local ethnic identities. The fractures run along the lines between geopolitical tectonic plates.

There are some other ways in which geography, and in particular geographical niches, affects the distribution of religion, including pilgrimage sites, and by extension affects patterns of secularisation. In Switzerland, for example, Catholicism is more associated with the mountain cantons and has a major pilgrimage site in the mountains at Einsiedeln, whereas Protestantism is more associated with the low-lying cities as well as being more extensively secularised. One might expect Geneva to be a Protestant pilgrimage site, but there seems to be little devotion attached to its major monuments, no doubt in part because Protestantism is an inward faith lacking tangible foci or the sense of sacred place that sustains both Catholicism and Orthodoxy.

One has to take into account the shape and geographical configuration of a country. Whereas the geography of Switzerland actively shapes its internal religious and linguistic fragmentation, the geography of Denmark shapes its religious and linguistic homogeneity, although history has also played its part, in particular a traumatic defeat inflicted by Prussia, which removed the German-speaking southernmost provinces. Denmark is a peninsula with associated islands and is almost uniformly flat. The Lutheran folk-Church includes the vast majority, but the absence of competition or the presence of a religious or ethnic 'Other' (until the recent arrival of 150,000 Muslims) results in a low-key religious identification which takes the country of Denmark for its focus as much as Christianity. Denmark, by almost submerging faith in state and nation, represents one Protestant mode of secularisation, while Holland represents another mode through the merging of faith with commerce. The USA combines both modes, but with very different consequences for religious vitality.

Resistant Niches, Small and Large

Copenhagen, a city strategically placed to command the entrance to the Baltic, ranks with Amsterdam and Berlin as one of the capitals of secularity. Historically the northern tip of Jutland has nurtured a Pietist spirituality, and one can locate similar niches in other parts of Scandinavia and in Northern Europe generally: such as south-west Norway, central and northern Finland; and in Holland the northern Protestant area of Friesland and southern Catholic areas like Limburg. Indeed the northernmost areas of Britain have provided niches able to sustain a distinctive piety, for example the Protestant fishing villages of north-east Scotland and the Protestant and Catholic islands off the Scottish west coast. However, in a world of global communications none of these peripheries is large enough to sustain itself against encroachment from the secular centre or to compensate for losses due to migration from periphery to centre. There is no equivalent in Europe to the kind of massive Pietist periphery you find in the American South. Most peripheries in Europe or North America, or indeed anywhere, are defended by some degree of linguistic difference: a different language, as in North Wales, Brittany or the Basque Country; or a variant of what claims to be the standard language, as in south-west Norway.

Some of the largest peripheries in Europe are found in rather 'square' countries like Spain and France, though perhaps one might also include Germany here. Germany has a massive 'periphery' in Bavaria, with a distinctive religious and political character and major pilgrimage sites, such as the Vierzehnheiligen. Spain has four peripheries – Aragon, Catalonia, Galicia and the Basque Country – each with major pilgrimage sites, while France has a western periphery with a pilgrimage site at Mont Saint-Michel, an eastern periphery with a pilgrimage site in the Vosges, and southern peripheries with a major pilgrimage site at Lourdes. Taizé is distinctive because a Protestant pilgrim site in a Catholic country, though very different from the other Protestant pilgrimage sites commemorating persecution and martyrdom in the Cévennes. Taizé brings together large numbers of young people, many of them spiritual seekers such as one finds all over Europe. These seekers mingle with more traditional kinds of pilgrim, for example at Santiago. It might well make sense to see remote pilgrimage sites like

Lourdes in France and Fatima in southern Portugal as outposts of resistance to the pressure exerted from the centres of those countries by radical secularism.

Elongated countries tend to nurture very different kinds of religiosity and may even face serious separatist tendencies. Czechoslovakia was an elongated country created, like Yugoslavia, after the Great War; but after the end of communism it divided into the highly secular Czech Republic (especially secular in Bohemia, the scene of major post-war upheavals and massive expulsions) and a consciously Catholic Slovakia. Italy is also a religiously divided country: the religious and political landscape of the south, beyond Ancona, is quite distinct from the rest of the country, and was traditionally the stronghold of Democracia Cristiana. Milan, the 'middle city' arguably looks north to Central Europe. The Veneto has been a religious region, whereas the region of Bologna, situated in what used to be 'red' Emilio-Romagna (and originally part of the Papal States), has historically been a stronghold of anticlericalism. The British Isles are also elongated and fragmented in a way that encourages the formation of religious and political niches, particularly in areas like the Scottish Highlands. The mountains of North Wales have been a stronghold of religious and linguistic difference as well as nationalist politics, and nowadays they shelter an alternative hippy culture. Ulster east of the River Bann is mainly Protestant and Scots-Irish, whereas west of the Bann is mainly Catholic. It is a general rule that a faith under political and military pressure holds out in mountain areas, as Protestants did in the Cévennes and the mountain areas on the Italian–French border. Religions also shelter in islands protected by the sea. Irish nationalists have regarded the island character of the country as mandating both national and religious unity, and the islands of Malta and Cyprus are among the most religious countries in Europe.

The Inner Ring and the Processional Ways of the Centre

These outposts on the periphery can be contrasted with pilgrimage sites or sacred cities much older and closer to what might be called the political heartlands: Chartres in France, Porvoo in Finland, Uppsala in Sweden, Canterbury in England or Nizhny Novgorod, Vladimir and Zagorsk in Russia. This Russian centre is, of course, contested over the centuries by an alternative centre and an alternative nationalism in Kiev as well as St. Petersburg. Not only is there a symbolic resonance attached to the inner protective ring (the Île-de-France, the Home Counties) but also to the processional ways within the capital city, either because they express established power, as in the Champs-Elysées, or because they provide venues for revolution and protest, most iconically the storming of the Winter Palace in 1917, at least as represented on film. Here one recollects the removal of the signs of communist triumph from the city centres of Europe, particularly in Hungary where they have been collected in an amusement park outside Budapest. However, memorials to Russian soldiers have only occasionally been treated in this way, and an attempt to displace such a monument in Estonia was officially described in Russia as a 'desecration' and as 'blasphemous'. East Germany is notable for its retention of mementos from the communist period in the naming of its streets and squares, and this includes not only early pioneers of socialism like Rosa Luxemburg or heroes like Yuri Gagarin, but communist dictators like Walter Ulbricht.

Ethnic Nationalism and Homogenisation

The multicultural character of much of Western Europe is far from universal in today's world. On the contrary, where nationalism is based on common ethnicity and language, ethno-religious minorities may be threatened with ethnic cleansing, which means that countries become increasingly homogeneous. The exchange of populations between Greece and Turkey in 1922 provides a particularly dramatic example, but the process is ubiquitous and continuous, and includes the evacuation or virtual expulsion of Christians from the Middle East, including historic Armenia; the expulsion of Muslims from Bulgaria, Crete and parts of Russia; and the ethno-religious consolidations following the wars that attended the break-up of Yugoslavia. Russian anti-Semitism, both under the Tsars and the Soviets, as well as the horrors of the Holocaust and Nazi plans for the elimination of the Slavs, can all be understood as part of this nationalist frenzy.

Empirical Correlations and Functional Differentiation

Perhaps I have sketched in sufficient detail the spatial embodiments of the religious and the secular to suggest what is to be attempted in the next chapter by way of an analysis of London in the context of England. However, I still need to suggest how one might translate and map in spatial terms certain key components of a general theory of secularisation, such as the empirical trends associated with modernisation and the process of functional differentiation.

There are various empirical correlations between social-geographical milieux and varying kinds of religious belonging or believing, such as the difference between a working-class or migrant *banlieue* and a middle-class suburb, or between a rural periphery and the industrial or financial city, or between a mountain hub and the cities of the plain. For example, one could contrast the religiosity of the mountain hub of the Massif Central (or the Protestant Cévennes) with that of the surrounding lowlands, and above all with the secularity of the Paris Basin. Or, one could contrast the religiosity of the Alpine hub of Europe with the cities of the plain: Vienna to the east; Geneva, Zurich and Bern to the north; and Milan to the south.

Functional differentiation is a concept equally central to urban geography and sociology. At its simplest it refers to the process whereby sectors of social life are separated from ecclesiastical control, beginning with law, commerce and administration and eventually extending to education and welfare. The autonomy of education has included the autonomy of the arts and the sciences. The autonomy of art was initiated in the Renaissance with the invention of the art gallery in Florence and the creation of an apostolic succession of artistic genius initiated by Vasari. All the great art galleries which today are custodians of an aesthetic spirituality and provide venues for the celebration of the artist as spiritual hero go back to Florence. At the same time welfare, primary socialisation and the family mostly retain some relationship to religion, depending on the type of secularisation pattern and the type of religion, given that differentiation is also a theological principle, based on the distinction between God and Caesar, the city of God and the city of Man, and variably interpreted by different traditions. If the art gallery represents one translation of the role of the medieval cathedral, the hospital represents another; and how far the historic relation to Christianity (commemorated in London by St. Thomas' Hospital or Barts) is retained depends on particular histories and national traditions. In Germany and in the USA – or, for that matter, in sub-Saharan Africa – the link between the churches and welfare of all kinds is particularly close.

In Protestantism there is either a process of assimilation to the state or else an initiation of various forms of voluntary pluralism, while in Catholicism there is an emphasis on the doctrine of the two swords which often issues in Church–state conflict. In Orthodoxy there is a *symphonia* of Church and state which is often associated with ethno-nationalism. Here I simply offer a contrast between the two ends of the spectrum, Protestant and Orthodox, which is also in some degree a contrast between West and East.

Some West–East and Protestant–Orthodox Contrasts

In Orthodoxy there is minimal space between Church and state, or between religion and politics. The Church of the Divine Wisdom in Constantinople was integrally linked to the imperial palace, and the principle of *symphonia* is as much a political reality in Russia today as it was an architectural reality in Byzantium. The Kremlins in Nizhny Novgorod and Moscow combine religious and political power, as does the Peter and Paul Fortress in St. Petersburg. In varying degrees the autocephalous successor churches of Byzantium have declared their independence, as part of the project of national independence, but they have usually reproduced the Byzantine spatial and political proximity of Church and state and of Church and nation in their architectural dispositions, in particular the new cathedral of Saint Sophia in Belgrade and the rebuilt cathedral of Christ the Saviour immediately opposite the Kremlin in Moscow. The Orthodox cathedral in Bucharest is in the immediate vicinity of the Parliament building, while the Alexander Nevsky Cathedral in Sofia is a reminder of the protective role exercised by Russia towards its Bulgarian 'younger brother'.

So to some extent the functional differentiation of some ecclesiastical and governmental buildings in Catholic Europe has a theological root in the doctrine of the two swords and the two cities, as well as in sociological process. It can also be seen as having a contingent or accidental character given that the collapse of the Roman Empire meant the Church had (eventually) to take over such administrative, educational and welfare institutions as were viable in the difficult and destructive times of the 'folk-wanderings'. Whatever weight one assigns to theological or 'accidental' factors, the pull of collaboration between the elites of Church and state is often as much in evidence as their functional differentiation, for example the magnificent clump of religio-political power on the Castle Hill in Prague or the architectural manifestations of Erastian Protestant folk-churches you find in the central islands of the Old City of Stockholm.

What are the architectural differences introduced by Protestantism? One obvious difference is the relative absence in Protestantism of a tangible sense of presence, including divine presence in sacred space. Protestant churches often have a severe aesthetic, represented in art by paintings of Dutch church interiors and focussed on the preaching office rather than the altar, and on the aural rather than the visual. Protestant churches do not dominate their surroundings, and have fewer side chapels for specific devotions. Nor do Protestant symbols dominate the city skyline. Instead Protestant cities are more likely to be overlooked by civic or national heroes, for example the statue of Benjamin

Franklin in Philadelphia or, at a less commanding level, the historical figures that mark the length of Commonwealth Avenue in Boston, Massachusetts, and the Victoria Embankment in London. Two interesting cases of what might seem to be Protestant memorials at the heart of cities, the monuments to Kossuth in Budapest and to Hus in Prague, are actually more nationalist than religious, and symbolise the role of Protestantism in the emergent myth of the nation.

Exemplary Destructions and Reconstructions

Destructions and reconstructions characterise all three traditional forms of Christianity. The Reformation was iconoclastic in two ways: in its destruction of statuary and in its destruction of the monasteries as the abode of religious virtuosi. A parallel destruction followed the political revolutions of 1789 and 1917 and occurred as part of the anti-religious and anti-clerical movements that have characterised Catholic and Orthodox cultures. The fate of the great abbey of Cluny is one of the most dramatic instances of revolutionary destruction, and one only has to look to (rebuilt) Speyer, likewise seriously threatened with destruction by the revolutionary French, to gauge that architectural loss. There were equally violent attacks on churches in Russia under Stalin, and in Spain, especially by anarchists, during the Civil War (1937–40). Whereas Protestant churches more usually succumb to a slow inner secularisation, Catholic churches are liable to be attacked or even destroyed in times of revolutionary fervour. After the post-war communist take-over in Poland the government punished the resistant city of Cracow by building a vast industrial suburb outside it, without a church. However, the new population drafted into the suburb eventually built there one of the largest churches in Poland. The church in Nowa Huta, like the memorial to members of Solidarity shot down in protests in the Gdansk shipyard, is a major symbol of the fusion of nation and Church in resistance to alien rule.

The history of the Cathedral of Christ the Saviour in Moscow provides an exemplary instance of a severe seesaw between a religious nationalism and revolutionary atheist nationalism. Built in a rather old-fashioned style to celebrate the defeat of Napoleon in 1812, it was demolished by Stalin in 1931 to make way for what was to be the tallest building in the world, initially to celebrate Lenin but eventually to celebrate Stalin himself as part of the ubiquitous cult of personality. However, this building was never put up and instead a people's swimming pool was erected over the site, until in the 1990s the cathedral was rebuilt and in due course received the body of Yeltsin for the first religious state funeral since 1894. At that point the intelligentsia, who had previously lamented the destruction of the cathedral, began to lament the disappearance of the swimming pool and the popular camaraderie associated with it.

Monuments of Nationalism and Revolution

The ideals of revolution and of revolutionary nationalism, sometimes seen as manifested in economic power and progress, have their own architectural embodiments: for example the Eiffel Tower erected in Paris in the 1880s; its miniature version in Guatemala City; and a potential rival installation in St. Petersburg which was never built, designed to flash the message of communism to the city and the world. Albert Speer had equivalent plans for triumphal architecture celebrating the Nazi revolution. Art galleries and museums are also repositories of national pride, either because they tell the story of a repressed national spirit that eventually triumphs over imperial oppression or supposed cultural inferiority, for example the National Museum of Norway, or because they are emporia of loot garnered in times of imperial power and cultural expansion, like the British Museum and the museums of Berlin. National museums are often based on the collections of monarchs and aristocracies that pass later by gift or expropriation to the nation. The Louvre is a special case because remodelled by Napoleon to be a gallery for the people, though it is no less an emporium of loot on that account.

Today there are museums that express 'the politics of regret', like the International Slavery Museum in Liverpool, a city which was, with Bristol, among the great centres of the slave trade. The politics of regret and 'recognition' have been embraced in much of Western Europe over the last few decades since the demise of political colonialism – but not in Eastern Europe, let alone Turkey. Oppressed nations in Eastern Europe have their museums memorialising oppression, like the museums in Vilnius and Budapest, but they are very unwilling to recognise the extent to which they have also been oppressors; and in Russia there is a memory of resistance to Nazism followed by triumph, with little recognition of wounds inflicted as well as heroically borne.[4] Berlin, Vienna and Paris are the sites of notable Holocaust memorials as well as museums.[5]

---

[4]   Aleida Assmann, *Cultural Memory and Western Civilization: Functions, Media, Archives* (Cambridge: Cambridge University Press, 2012). Cf. Pierre Nora, *Les Lieux de Mémoire* (Paris: Gallimard, 1984, p. 92).

[5]   Jan Assmann, *Religion and Cultural Memory*, pp. 21–2.

Then there are the churches explicitly built to rebuke revolutionary triumphalism, such as the Sacré Coeur in Paris erected about the same time as the Tour Eiffel, and Gaudí's Church of the Holy Family in Barcelona, with its symbolic references to the sanctity of work and the family. An architectural complex which might equally illustrate functional differentiation, both theological and sociological, as well as the clash of the Church with a revolutionary nationalism is the Via della Conciliazione linking the Vatican with Rome as the national capital. It symbolises the conclusion of several decades of hostility between Church and state, Church and nation. The low points of the papacy were reached in its relationships with Napoleon and the loss of Rome to a newly unified Italy of 1870. However, in the course of the late twentieth century it gained more in spiritual prestige and salience than it lost earlier in temporal power.

Mapping Migratory Trails

Another theme needs only cursory mention here prior to a proper treatment in the analysis of London. This theme concerns the migrant trails across the continent and across particular countries, as well as localised urban concentrations of migrants. Clearly the most important of these migrations are of Muslims from Africa to Southern Europe; of Turks, above all to Germany and Austria; of Indonesians, Turks and Moroccans to Holland; and of people from the Indian subcontinent to Britain. Muslim migrations have greatly raised the political and cultural profile of religion in Western Europe. The other major migrations have been of mainly Christian populations from the so-called Global South, for example of Caribbeans to England and of Ghanaians to Holland.

Religious Niches: An Anglo-American Comparison

England (more broadly, the British Isles) is made up of geographical niches likely to foster different versions of the Christian religion. I have already referred to the remote peripheries found in the north-east and north-west of Scotland as well as the north of Wales and the west of Ireland. These are either more Catholic than the centre or more Protestant. North Wales, as already mentioned, has been different from South Wales both religiously and linguistically, and South Wales today has been extensively secularised and anglicised. The myriad local chapels of a major town like Swansea have given way to a few larger and comparatively successful Evangelical churches.

One can plausibly divide Britain and the USA into religious regions. In the USA there is the Pietist Evangelical and predominantly Baptist South (including Texas); the semi-Hispanic South-West; the semi-Lutheran Midwest; the relatively secular mountain states; the mainly Catholic northern cities like Chicago; the spiritually experimental Pacific Coast; and the mainstream Protestant/Catholic and semi-secular north-east coast. The British regional equivalents fan out from London to the north and to the west, and some of them have historical connections with the regions in America – most notably the connection between Ulster and the Scots-Irish of the American South, and between East Anglia and New England. There are distinctive forms of religion in the West Country and Cornwall, beginning at Bristol, and also in the north of England, in the lowlands and the northern Highlands and Islands of Scotland. At the Reformation, Catholicism retired to the margins, for example north Lancashire, though it remained dominant in Ireland. The growth of Puritan Protestantism, both within the established Church and in an emerging voluntary sector, was relatively strong in the East Midlands, East Anglia and London, and its intellectual capital was Cambridge. It was also strong in lowland Scotland. It is entirely appropriate therefore that the most prestigious universities in America should be Puritan foundations on the north-east coast: at Cambridge, Massachusetts; at New Haven (Congregational); at Providence (Baptist); and at Princeton (Scottish Presbyterian). The second wave of evangelical Protestantism in Britain, both within the established Church and in a rapidly expanding voluntary sector, took root in the industrial West Midlands and the industrial North. This wave was paralleled on the rapidly moving American frontier and produced a second tier of American universities, beginning with the founding of Boston University (Methodist) in 1838 and followed by institutions like Emory and Duke. The Holy Spirit Empowerment movement, beginning in the northern town of Keswick in 1875, with strong Protestant Irish and Cambridge connections, fed into American holiness movements and eventually – with reinforcements from the Welsh revival of 1904 – into the emergence of Pentecostalism in 1906 at the end of the frontier trail in Los Angeles.

Chapter 14
England and London

English Religious Geography and Migratory Trails

From the 1840s on in Britain the changing religious geography mainly depended on the migration of ethnic groups bringing their faiths with them, and the pattern of settlement ran on all fours with that in America, though on a much smaller scale. The Irish arrived at the east-coast port of Liverpool, creating a semi-Catholic culture in west Lancashire, and moved across the country to the urban north-east coast and the Scottish urban south-west, and also downwards via Birmingham to particular parts of London. The Jewish migrants were mostly from Eastern Europe and were particularly numerous in the last two decades of the nineteenth century. They moved in the reverse direction, travelling north from East London to Leeds, Liverpool, Manchester and Glasgow. The Muslim, Sikh and Hindu migrations arrived after the Second World War, and they followed a similar trajectory, concentrating in East London and in certain Midland and northern cities like Leicester and Bradford. The parallel Caribbean and (later) West African migrations, largely Protestant and sometimes Pentecostal, also settled in the inner London suburbs, and indeed in inner suburban areas all over the country, like St. Paul's in Bristol. As for the Anglican Church, it remained relatively strong in the outer London suburbs, in the rural shires and particularly in a band running from south-west through Oxford (the conservative and political university) to Lincolnshire and cross-ways to the main migrations.

This religious geography has been mirrored in political geography, with Catholics, Jews and Muslims in the big cities voting for Labour (as they vote for the Democrats in the US), making inner London a Labour stronghold, with further strongholds in Liverpool, Manchester, Newcastle, Glasgow and the mining areas of Yorkshire and South Wales. Historically, Nonconformists, especially in Wales, the West Country and northern Scotland, have voted for the Liberal Party, which at one stage was inclined to promote religious disestablishment and could be seen as a civil rights movement for groups newly emerging and mobilising in the industrial cities, and as a party well disposed (except for the Liberal Imperialists) to Irish self-rule. Naturally the Scots-Irish in Ulster voted Conservative and Unionist, and also had links with conservatives in the American South. Seventeen of America's presidents have been of Scots-Irish background, compared to one (Irish) Catholic. We can now consider how far this national religious and political geography is mirrored in London.

How Is This Religious Geography Mirrored in London?

London is two cities. One, known as 'the Square Mile', is set on a hill. It is the centre of financial power, and jealous of its historic self-governance. The other is the City of Westminster, historically the centre of royal power and now the centre of parliamentary power. Both cities are almost completely occupied by the historic emplacements of religion, government and finance, and both were seen from the mid-eighteenth century to the mid-twentieth century as at the heart of empire: two architectural realisations of the imperial theme are Soane's original (c.1800) Bank of England and Constitution Arch (1846), both appropriately classical. There are two other powerful sites downriver. To the north of the Thames there is Canary Wharf, a new financial centre without any distinctive religious marker, whose name is a reminder of the historic role of London as a great port. To the south is Greenwich, a magnificent group of buildings, including important churches, set by or beneath a hill, with royal, naval and – at the Observatory – scientific associations.

Traditional Emplacements and Incipient Functional Differentiation: Law and University

The traditional emplacements of established religion in Westminster and the 'City' – such as the 'royal peculiar' of Westminster Abbey, St. Paul's Cathedral, St. Bartholomew's Priory and St. Bride's Church – are probably set on pagan holy sites, and St. Paul's Cathedral was for 1,000 years the centre of a cult of St. Erkenwald. St. Bride's recapitulates the history of London, being the site of a Roman temple, a Saxon church and a medieval church, and now of a (rebuilt) Renaissance church. Its current association is with the press, and it contains a memorial to John Winthrop, the first governor of Massachusetts.

St. Bride's is not alone in that. Several of the churches in Westminster and the City have North American associations, and are minor pilgrimage sites recalling the so-called 'first British Empire' (1655–1776) and marking a continuing transatlantic association, as for example the insignia of all the American states in the stained glass set behind the altar of St. Paul's in gratitude for American succour in the Second World War. These churches are also reminders of a radical London which was aligned with eastern England in siding with Parliament and the Puritans in the Civil War. For centuries London, like the established Church, has looked towards North America and a global empire, whereas in medieval times it faced towards the continent, as the name Lombard Street indicates.

Today there is little to remind anyone of medieval mystery, sanctity and sacrament – apart from names like Paternoster Row and Amen Court, or churches of the nineteenth-century Anglo-Catholic revival like St. Magnus Martyr or the Ely Place church of St. Etheldreda reacquired by the Roman Catholic Church in the 1870s. The Temple Church may be a medieval Crusader church, and built in the round because that is how medieval people imagined the temple in Jerusalem, perhaps unintentionally on the model of the Dome of the Rock, but its contemporary role is to act as the church of one the legal profession's Inns of Court. It is characteristic of England that the sacred places symbolising the ancient links between religion and law remain in place and in use, unlike in the USA or indeed *laïque* France, even though the two spheres are functionally quite distinct. The same links are observable in the older universities, but in London the functional differentiation was made very explicit with the founding of University College in 1826 and of Bedford College for women in 1849. Neither college had a chapel. King's College in the Strand, founded by royal charter in 1829, represented an attempt by the Established Church to restore the link between Church and university, but the Senate House is a massive essay in neo-Egyptian, not unlike some of the imposing buildings of continental Fascism, and it suggests a distinctly secular ethos.

If London University mostly represents a functionally differentiated sector animated by a secular ethos, in spite of the Anglican foundation of King's College, the military retains a surprisingly close link to the Church, in part because of the social and religious origins of the officer corps, particularly among Scottish and Ulster Protestants as well as Anglican independent schools. The elite Guards units are stationed in quarters adjoining Buckingham Palace, where they have a major chapel. Most military units have a chapel, an association which is enhanced wherever there is a close monarchical connection, as at Windsor. However, there is an interesting contrast between the modest establishments of London and the grandiloquence of analogous establishments in Paris: the Chelsea Hospital is not remotely on the scale of the military monastery of Les Invalides, conceived under Louis XIV as part of a vast programme of monumental buildings. Nor are the streets of London named after generals – or intellectuals for that matter – as in Paris.

Internal Secularisations? The Impact of Enlightenment and Nationalism

It is also possible to discern an internal secularisation even in Westminster Abbey and St. Paul's. Both churches are mausolea of great men in war, politics, science and the arts. Wellington and Nelson are buried in the crypt of St. Paul's. Both have been iconic national heroes but are certainly not candidates for beatification. The churches of central London – dating from about 1680 to 1830 and running geographically from Christchurch, Spitalfields, in the east to St. George's, Hanover Square, in the West End – are the light-filled temples and the Protestant auditoria of a rational civic cult. St. Martin-in-the-Fields, Trafalgar Square, the royal parish church, is closely affiliated to the dominant classical style of New England and much of North America; and even St. Paul's, though it looks to the Baroque, rejects the Counter-Reformation opulence of the European continent. Looking at the heartlands of established religion in London one might think that secularity had secured its first triumph at just the point in the late seventeenth century when some scholars have identified the secular crisis in European consciousness.

All the same, a different picture emerges if one looks before and after the 'long eighteenth century' because the City churches in particular were built over medieval sites within a medieval street plan, and reproduce an ancient guild structure modified by relatively modern forms of activity, for example the Royal Air Force church of St. Clement Dane's. The churches of the City proper cater mainly for a weekday working population, and have each developed a different character at different times, depending somewhat on the incumbent, for example the tradition of political debates at St. Mary-le-Bow.

Counter-Movements: Evangelicalism and Anglo-Catholicism

The Evangelical movement beginning in the eighteenth century and the Anglo-Catholic movement emerging nearly a century later have claimed sites in or near the central area, with outposts in the fashionable West End and what has been historically a poor East End, crowded by successive waves of migrants:

Huguenot, Jewish, Pakistani and Bangladeshi. St. Mary's Bourne Street and All Saints Margaret Street are major Anglo-Catholic churches in the West End, and major architects like Pugin and Butterfield embraced versions of Gothic as a warm and compassionate Christian style contrasted with a cold, pitiless and secular classicism. The East End is also famous for Anglo-Catholic churches, now often decayed, which were built there in the nineteenth century to serve the poor. The same purpose inspired the Anglican settlements and the Free Church Missions, such as the West Ham Mission. If the Anglo-Catholic spirit is at a low ebb the reverse has been true of the Evangelicals. All Souls, Langham Place, located in what nearly two centuries ago were the new wealthy extensions of London northward, housed the first wave of an Evangelical revival, while Holy Trinity, Brompton, situated in another wealthy extension of London further west towards the 'village' of Chelsea, housed a major (and now widespread) charismatic revival, attracting many young business executives. The atmosphere here is in marked contrast with what one would at one time have encountered at the 'progressive' church of St. James, Piccadilly, with its market and distinct air of the New Age and the arts. To the north of Piccadilly, in opulent Mayfair, there is the Third Church of Christ, Scientist, a first outpost of American therapeutic faith to serve those, particularly women, whose needs were more intimate and personal than material. Pevsner comments that it looks surprisingly secular, and it could easily be mistaken for a city insurance office. The Christian Science movement, with its massive cathedral-like headquarters in Boston, Massachusetts, is in recession, but it belongs to the genealogies of the centrality of the self and plays a role in the triumph of the therapeutic. Like so many therapeutic movements it has a problem in maintaining generational continuity.

The Fundamental Configuration: Establishment, Voluntary Sector and Ethnic Church

So far I have sketched the religious dispositions and emplacements of the London heartlands and their historic extensions in the eighteenth and nineteenth centuries to west, north and east (and holding the South Bank in reserve for later). I need to focus on the religiously three-way thoroughfare of Victoria Street. There is Westminster Abbey with St. Margaret's church at one end, linked directly to the power-centre in the neo-Gothic (and in terms of a deliberate choice of architectural style, Christian) Houses of Parliament. Then, at the other end, and set slightly back, is the Roman Catholic Westminster

Cathedral, begun about the beginning of the twentieth century, in a deliberately non-English style (and one matching its musical repertory) based on Siena and St. Irene, Constantinople. Finally, there is the Methodist Central Hall, directly opposite and challenging Westminster Abbey, in Edwardian baroque.

Here we have in symbolic conjunction the key elements of the historic religious semi-pluralism of England: the established territorial church, the largest ethnic minority church and the largest form of religious voluntary association. The third of these is a preaching auditorium, nowadays far too large for its small congregation but ideal for secular civic and political occasions and protests, beginning with the first assembly of the United Nations after the war. The other great preaching auditoria of Free Church Nonconformity, nowadays often serviced by American preachers, are Westminster (independent congregational) Chapel, the City Temple, Whitefield Memorial Church and Spurgeon's (Metropolitan) Tabernacle, rebuilt on a smaller scale after destruction in the war. The City Temple belongs to the conservative Evangelical Alliance and might well be seen as very close to the ethos of St. Helen's, Bishopsgate, indicating that the Free Churches are now present in semi-detached sectors of the established Church. Conservative Evangelicalism, with its ambiguously fundamentalist fringe, finds the Anglican parish system ideal for forming 'gathered congregations'. Institutional separation hardly matters, and what the French call the disaggregation of religion is realised in flows of religiosity which pay scant heed to denominational boundaries.

The Spatial Evanescence of the Protestant Voluntary Sector

The fate of the Nonconformist King's Weigh House Church and of the Methodist Kingsway Hall indicates what has befallen historic Protestant Nonconformity. The former, set in Mayfair, first developed in a high church liturgical direction and is now occupied by an ethnic congregation belonging to the Ukrainian Catholic Church. The latter has become a hotel. Religion in the form of voluntary association – sometimes with radical political associations, as with Kingsway Hall – does not cherish architectural expressions on sacred sites; and its memorials, apart from Wesley's Chapel to the north in the City Road, tend to be graveyards, such as the Moravian graveyard and Bunhill Fields, also by the City Road.

The Protestant national narrative, historically dear to Nonconformists, is now largely forgotten: for example the unnoticed statues on the Victoria

Embankment to William Tyndale, translator of the English Bible, and to Robert Raikes, founder of the now virtually defunct Sunday School movement. The Smithfield Protestant martyrs are also unremarked. The exception is the highly controversial statue to Oliver Cromwell, complete with Bible and sword, set up in 1889 in front of Parliament; but the motives behind its erection may have been as much political as religious. Again, the association of Free Churches with particular strands of political movement, sometimes radical and revolutionary and sometimes pacifist, means that Church and movement flourish and decline together. The Methodist Central Hall was built when Methodists and other Nonconformists had their maximum representation at Westminster during the time of the radical Liberal government of 1906. The Unitarians, who were quite disproportionately represented in the radical nineteenth-century elites and were also prominent in the radical agitations of the French revolutionary period, are now represented by a bookshop on an historic site in Essex Street and through their cultural activities as wealthy industrialists, for example the Courtauld Institute and the Tate. Perhaps one might include the Freemasons under Unitarianism: they have complex roots in both Judaism and Egyptian mythology and links to Anglo-American deism. Winston Churchill and Edward VII were both Masons. The 'Brotherhood' was founded in 1717 and has its headquarters in an inter-war Grand Temple (Art Deco with hints of Egyptian splendour) in Great Queen Street.

Ethnic Migratory Trails in London

The name Courtauld in the context of Unitarianism aptly introduces the theme of successive migrant groups, beginning with the Huguenots and other Protestant groups, with churches, some of which are close to the heartlands of the establishment – for example the Lutherans at St. Anne's and the Dutch church at Austin Friars. The French Protestant church in Soho Square, dismissed by Pevsner as just another office building, reminds us that Soho was once identified with French migrants. Today Soho is a louche district, densely populated by migrants of all kinds, and its principal churches are Notre Dame de France and the Catholic church of St. Anne's in Soho Square. This is a rather different milieu from that of the high-powered Jesuit church of the Immaculate Conception in wealthy Mayfair or the Brompton Oratory in fashionable Knightsbridge, built in the style of Il Gesù in Rome, and with a mainly traditionalist Catholic congregation.

The ethnic faiths, concentrated in different parts of the UK and the Republic of Ireland, are likewise concentrated in different parts of London. They can be taken in turn: the Irish, the Welsh and Scots Presbyterians; the Jews, the Greeks and other Eastern Orthodox; the Italians, the Poles and other Catholic migrants; the Caribbean and African Christians, mainly Protestant; and successive waves of Indians, Sikhs and Muslims. The Irish initially settled in quite poor inner areas, and stayed there for a long time with little social mobility before the mid-twentieth century and relatively little erosion of religious practice prior to the 1960s, though priests did complain in the mid-nineteenth century of poor mass attendance among the early migrants. Some Irish settled in the north-west inner suburbs like Kilburn, in inner areas just north of the river like St. Giles or immediately south of the river, in the Borough. There seems to have been relatively little of the tension between Catholics and Ulster Protestants that was exported to Liverpool and Glasgow. There was, however, some tension between Irish Catholics and the remnants of English Catholicism, with its aristocratic sprinkling and distinctive ethos, especially as the Irish became numerically dominant and stayed dominant – even after the arrival of Poles in the further western suburbs during the war and (later) other Catholic refugees from communist Europe.

There are, of course, two kinds of refugee: the poor or oppressed looking for a better life; and the rich, who may be in diaspora after persecution, like the Armenians, or a displaced elite as in the case of the Russians and (to some extent) the Poles. The suburbs of west London stretching along the M4 corridor, house major concentrations of Poles, consisting mainly of refugees who stayed in England after the Second World War. The Russians and Armenians both have their cathedrals in wealthy Kensington, whereas the Greeks have their cathedral in Bayswater, an uproarious migrant area, though the clientele of the cathedral includes wealthy conservative Greeks and groups surrounding the Greek ex-royal family. The main Serbian Orthodox church is also in Bayswater. Many Greeks, Cypriots and Italians live in the immediate northern suburbs, the Italians in Clerkenwell, where they have a magnificent church, and the Greeks a little further out in Camden.

The Scots and Welsh Presbyterians established churches in London, the Welsh in a church in Charing Cross Road, now used to sell Australian food, and the Scots in the upmarket area of Pond Street. However, both communities tended to assimilate to English Nonconformity and failed to establish a religious presence commensurate with their numbers or their social and professional influence, which was disproportionate, since both groups were 'bible black' cultures, valuing literacy and education.

Jews and Muslims

The Jews are, of course, another 'bible black' culture, and their combination of hard work, intelligence, supportive networks and aspiration has created a pattern of social and geographical mobility that has made them rivals to the Scots in the professions, the media and in politics. As in the cases of the Scots and the Welsh, mobility has meant some secularisation and loosening of ties to the religious community, so that Jewry has become an ethnic as much as a religious category, and one suffering considerable leakage due to intermarriage and emigration. The Jewish community has been simultaneously secularised itself and a force for secularisation in the wider society, due to its position in many of the command posts of the media and the university. Half of Britain's Jews live in London, and are concentrated in the better-off suburbs of North London. After an enforced absence of nearly four centuries the Jews were invited back into England in the mid-seventeenth century. They were mainly Sephardic, and their first synagogue, Bevis Marks, was built, with Quaker assistance, in the City in 1700–01. In the mid-nineteenth century they still numbered only some 40,000 until the worsening situation in the Pale of Settlement, including Russian-occupied Poland, resulted in a massive migration of people who initially settled in London's impoverished East End, for example the area of Spitalfields which had once been settled by Huguenot refugees. Once the Jews had become economically and geographically mobile, and had moved to the more salubrious slopes of North London, the same area was occupied by Muslim migrants, many of them from Bangladesh. Jewish sacred buildings – whether we are talking about the large Orthodox synagogue in the West End or the Liberal synagogue near Lord's – do not draw attention to themselves as do, for example, the ornate and deliberately oriental-looking synagogues of Berlin and Budapest. They blend into their environment as easily as the people who attend them, and have the appearance, indeed the reality, of functioning as community centres. Perhaps that is some indication of the way Jewish devotion is centred on the family rather than on a distinctive ecclesial institution.

The reverse can be true of mosques, though minarets are usually not high and dominating. It is an established principle of sacred buildings that height establishes dominance, and a tall minaret in a sensitive area, or the proximity of a proposed mosque to the new Olympic stadium, automatically arouses resentment. Even the large Saudi Arabian mosque in the wealthy inner area of Regent's Park is set back and half hidden by trees, while the Ismaili centre in equally wealthy Knightsbridge does not advertise itself as a place of worship at all. These are the religious foci of rich migrant communities, very different from the communities from the Indian subcontinent. The famous Finsbury Park mosque was for a while a focus of Islamic radicalism, but it is not on the kind of prime site occupied by the Ismaili Centre.

Perhaps it is significant that it is not at all easy to identify a Buddhist presence architecturally, apart from a statue of the Buddha in a park facing the River Thames, though there are certainly many British adepts, particularly in the upper middle class of Hampstead and adjacent northern suburbs inhabited by the intelligentsia. One Buddhist centre lies out in deepest leafy Surrey in Haslemere, while the UK's very first mosque is also in suburban Surrey at Woking. Buddhist organisation seems associational rather than based on temples, at least for British Buddhists, whose philosophical understanding of Buddhism is (as in the USA) very different from the everyday Buddhism of South East Asia and of migrants from that area.

However, the architectural presence of Hinduism is less elusive, for example the magnificent new temple in the outer suburb of Neasden, celebrated in the media as proof positive of the diversity of multicultural Britain. Indian Hindus concentrate in particular suburbs, notably in the far western suburb of Southall, an area where there are also many Sikhs. The Chinese presence is also indicated by ritual markers and festive decorations, for example for the Chinese New Year, in Soho and in the traditionally Chinese parts of what used to be the port area of East London.

Minority Faiths, Including Christian Migrants

The Buddhist presence in the leafy interstices of suburban Surrey provides a reminder of how minority faiths may prefer locations well away from the vast conurbation, perhaps as part of their protest against the modern urban lifestyle. East Grinstead, for example, is home to the Anthroposophists as well as the Scientologists, and a major Mormon temple is not far away. However, the most visible, and strikingly modern, Mormon place of worship is the Church of Jesus Christ of Latter-Day Saints in Kensington in the centre of the museum sector.

Apart from Muslim migrants, the largest migrant minorities are Christian, many of them from the Caribbean and sub-Saharan Africa, though there are also Christians from Asia, particularly Korea. In parts of South-East London black migrants provide the main Christian presence. It is not possible to specify in detail the vast number of churches, from the Nigerian Cherubim and Seraphim to the Brazilian Universal Church of the Kingdom of God, except to notice that many of the worship venues are not immediately identifiable as churches. Perhaps one famous building, and one certainly looking like a church, can stand in for the rest. The Elim Pentecostal Kensington Temple is as much an advertisement for multiculturalism in its way as the Neasden Hindu Temple. It claims to include among its large throng of worshippers some 169 ethnic groups. Its position in the heavily migrant Notting Hill area, just north of Kensington, is arguably iconic. Notting Hill was the site of the first inter-ethnic riots in Britain, in the fifties, and it has since become internationally famous for its annual street festival.

London's Processional Ways

One does not think of a Protestant country like England as traversed by pilgrim ways and processional routes, and it is certainly true that London is conspicuously lacking in the broad avenues that provide processional ways in Paris, Vienna and Berlin. Proposals to build these – for example from St. Paul's to Westminster and a Via Triumphalis from Regent Street to Buckingham Palace – have always failed to materialise, as though the democratic spirit (or the British talent for 'muddling through') rejected urban grandiosity as both continental and oppressive. At the same time, St. Paul's is certainly a focus of perspectives, protected by law; and it is also the place where great national occasions of mourning or celebration take place, for example the huge congregations, including much of the American community, that gathered there for a service after the events of September 11th.

Processions and pilgrimage routes are eloquent of what, quite literally, moves people: there are the processional routes of state; the accepted trails for different kinds of protest; and the pilgrim ways that typically lie outside the city and run from ancient site to ancient site, whether Christian or pagan, or both at once. Perhaps the most astonishing procession of state, and one which was also an occasion of popular mourning, followed the death of Princess Diana. It ran from Kensington Palace to Westminster Abbey, and then along Whitehall on a long journey north to Diana's last resting place, which itself became a place of pilgrimage. The expressions of grief that accompanied her death gave the impression that England was no longer a northern Protestant country but syncretistic and almost Latin in its ethos. Such improvised rituals of contemporary 'spirituality' are eclectic expressions of public and personal grief with candles and flowers and invocations of RIP that indicate the continuity of the religious impulse detached from confessional specificity. Yet the sense of grief over Diana was as short-lived as it was heartfelt.

By contrast, the gatherings in Whitehall on Remembrance Day to recollect the grievous losses in the wars of the twentieth century have infinitely greater staying power. They are carefully choreographed occasions of Church and state which have even gained in public participation of recent years. It also tells a lot about a country where the grave of its 'Unknown Warrior' is situated, and in England it can only be in Westminster Abbey.. The Cenotaph in Whitehall was conceived by Lutyens as an empty tomb in apposition to the occupied tomb in Westminster Abbey.

Processional Ways of Protest and the Counter-Cultural South Bank

Trafalgar Square and the routes leading into it provide spaces for protest marches, and these have a very varied character. Trafalgar Square contains South Africa House, so this is where many protests against apartheid were held. The famous annual Aldermaston March against nuclear weapons ended in Trafalgar Square, and it combined representatives of the Christian pacifist and anti-war traditions and the idealistic morality of the left-leaning educated middle class. The Aldermaston March dates from the fifties and belongs to an older era, but the same elements have been present in contemporary protests against the Iraq war, with the addition of Muslim marchers. The Festival of Light was a different kind of moral protest, defending traditional virtues against the erosions perceived in the sixties. One of the most interesting processions was of the bishops to the Lambeth Conference protesting against the plight of the developing world, and addressed by the prime minister outside Lambeth Palace. Something of contemporary currents and counter-currents was revealed in the controversy over what sculpture should occupy the fourth and empty plinth in Trafalgar Square: candidates already installed in rotation have included sculptures of a woman disabled by thalidomide and of Jesus Christ, and Charles Darwin has also been proposed. Clearly it is a site of contemporary contestation, in part by way of explicit contrast to the imperial heroes elsewhere commemorated in the Square. There is a study to be done of the varied sites of protest, comparing the 'Occupy' movement in London (including the occupation of the forecourt of St. Paul's Cathedral) and New York with major eruptions in Taksim Square and Jerzy Park, Tahrir Square, Rio de Janeiro and other Brazilian cities, and the 'Pussy Riot' protest in the Cathedral of Christ the Saviour, Moscow.

The South Bank of the Thames has been for centuries the site of a counter-culture, beginning with the Globe Theatre and the criminal population that lived in Southwark. Near Southwark Bridge there used to be a plaque commemorating those, like John Penry, who were executed in the 1590s for opposing the union of Church and state in favour of voluntarism. This site can, with historical imagination, be seen as a symbolic marker presaging the First Amendment of the US Constitution, setting a wall of separation between Church and state nearly two centuries later. The major Edwardian baroque building directly facing the Houses of Parliament that used to house the civic government of London, the Greater London Council, was perceived in the Thatcher era to be a symbolic stronghold of the left, and turned into a commercial hotel rather than the Hotel de Ville. City government was later re-sited on the South Bank downriver by Tower Bridge. The Royal Festival Hall, National Theatre and other buildings, like the Hayward Gallery, inherit the same left-wing civic spirit, going back to the Festival of Britain in 1950; and there are monuments celebrating Nelson Mandela, as well as the Republican side in the Spanish Civil War. This complex of buildings marks one of the early victories of architectural modernism. The spaces further along the South Bank downriver are now post-modern venues for alternative musical events, while a converted power station now houses the decidedly post-modern Tate Modern art gallery, beyond which lies the Globe Theatre, recreating the Shakespearean glories of the Elizabethan era. Even religion shares in the distinctive flavour of the area. Southwark Cathedral was the centre of the radical and demythologising movement in the Anglican Church initiated in the 1950s by John Robinson, the bishop of Woolwich, a district much further downriver. His approach was admired or dismissed as 'South Bank religion'. Also on the South Bank, but upriver, and symbolically and dangerously aligned with the historic centre of royal power across the water, is Lambeth Palace. This was the heart of establishment, but its occupants over the last few decades have often been at odds with the political establishment, indicating an increasing distance between ancient foci of power. The Church–state link is now loose enough to dampen any enthusiasm for disestablishment such as was promoted by the Free Churches in the nineteenth century, especially as the state Church now acts as an umbrella for religious concerns in general. What became separation in the USA became in England a loose symbolic recognition whereby the Anglican

Church acts as master of ceremonies for national occasions, such as Remembrance Day in Whitehall and the funeral of Margaret Thatcher.

Pilgrimages of the Outer Ring

Other pilgrimages take place away from the centres of urban power, whether they are organised by Christians or pagans. All over Europe, not excluding England, the decline in church attendance has been accompanied by an increasing interest in pilgrimage, expressing several motives and motifs: an unfocussed spirituality mingled with nostalgia for community; a recollection of a Catholic past, as in the pilgrimage to Walsingham; and a sense of alienation from the rational bureaucracy of the city. An enthusiasm for pilgrimage, and for visiting cathedrals, mingles a tourist interest and a vague spirituality with a sense of the numinous and of places and ancient sites where 'prayer has been valid'. The pilgrimage to the rebuilt abbey on the island of Iona is part of the religious myth of Scotland, and the pilgrimage to Holy Island part of the myth of the Christian North-East.

Other ancient sites, like Stonehenge, attract people with an interest in pagan rituals embedded in the rhythms of the natural world as well as in sustainability, in ecology, in living naturally and in ideas of the goddess. The mysterious mount at Glastonbury, with its nearby abbey, is the site of the UK's largest pop festival, even though its 'alternative' spirit has been diluted by commercialism as well as contradicted by an annual Christian pilgrimage.

The Religions of Shopping and Mass Entertainment

Almost at the opposite end of the spectrum are the vast cathedrals of what has been called the religion of shopping: aspirations and dreams of fulfilment through goods as well as the good. The older form of the religion is found in the great stores of Oxford Street and nearby, such as Selfridges and Liberty, while the newer form lies much further out in the vast emporia of Brent Cross in North London, Westfield in West London and IKEA in Croydon in South London. Perhaps the nearest venue in London to resemble the classic nineteenth-century gallerias of Milan and Naples is the Burlington Arcade, just off Piccadilly. The arcade is close to the meeting point for every visitor, the statue of the Angel of Christian Charity (popularly misidentified as Eros) in honour of the great

Evangelical reformer and promoter of the Factory Acts, the Earl of Shaftesbury, who gives his name to nearby Shaftesbury Avenue.

Closely allied to the monuments of the world of shopping are the monuments of modern communication: the BBC's Broadcasting House in Portland Place, just north of Oxford Street, and Bush House, built by Americans in imposing business classical style. Both Bush House and Broadcasting House have scriptural inscriptions, indicating what was originally serious moral intention and commitment to an educational ethos. The BBC, under its first Scottish Presbyterian director, originally stood for a union of faith, culture and the national myth, but this union has been dissolved since the sixties. The other institutions of mass entertainment are the finely appointed football stadia, which arguably revive classical traditions such as were celebrated at Delphi and Olympia. These are now far more salient than the traditional sacred turf at Lord's Cricket Ground. Perhaps it is worth noticing that the modern versions of contemporary global sports were formalised in nineteenth-century industrial England.

Educated Seriousness: The Case of Music

However there remain pockets of educated seriousness, some still with a religious connection, most strongly in the sphere of music, traditionally the most religious of the arts. This can be traced in the evolution of musical taste and its architectural embodiments, beginning with the great monuments to Victorian seriousness connected with the Great Exhibition of 1851 in Kensington, in particular the Albert Hall, built on the model of the Coliseum, as well as the Natural History Museum and the Victoria and Albert Museum. This complex of buildings parallels those of the museum area in Berlin, and it owes much to the inspiration of the Prince Consort, Albert of Saxe-Coburg. It represents a union of the sciences, commerce and the arts for progress, education and the inculcation of betterment and moral seriousness that lasted up to 1914. In the high Victorian period in the late nineteenth century the main musically serious expression of this was a popular choral tradition centred on the works of Handel, Mendelssohn and Haydn – above all Handel's *Messiah*, which had its most extensive influence in the northern industrial districts of Yorkshire and Lancashire, and in Wales. There was also, of course a popular brass band movement and a flourishing interest in male voice choirs, as well as a conscious recovery of folksong and the carol. All of this belonged to an atmosphere of self-help and educational aspiration which strongly overlapped the world of the churches, even in London. Then a series of shifts took place in the elites, beginning with the aestheticism of the nineties and focussed later between the wars in the Bloomsbury Group, named after a wealthy district around the University of London, which tended to replace moral with aesthetic seriousness. Popular Protestantism faltered, though a deposit of seriousness remained, for example in the Workers' Educational Association (WEA). In the course of the Second World War it was still assumed that the object of education, when not simply utilitarian processing to improve the working skills of the masses, was to induct ever wider ranges of people into high culture. That included greater access to serious music, which increasingly meant the western orchestral and primarily continental canon. A literature was produced, in particular by Penguin Books, designed to introduce the arts, music included, to wider audiences.

About 1960 several semi-related changes occurred: a loss of confidence in educational mission, including the mission of the BBC; a vast expansion of a popular and commercial youth culture; a sense that Protestant massed choirs were provincial compared with small professional choirs and the continental operatic and orchestral tradition; and the collapse of access to a continuing contemporary high musical culture outside a tiny musical elite. That collapse coincided with the demise of the specifically English musical renaissance, dating from the 1880s, and its related religious aspects. A huge sector of musical activity continued to be associated with churches; but it was devalued, and was replaced by a vague sense of the 'spiritual' value of music, given that explicit faith was deemed no longer tenable. The Promenade concerts promoted by the BBC were and are a major expression of this unanchored spirituality. Mostly, however, spirituality is so personal and inward that it lacks concrete expression or public institutional form, apart from the eclectic expressions of public grief (and occasionally of celebration) mentioned earlier. Examples would be responses in Liverpool to the death of John Lennon, and to spates of teenage killings in London. Often there are both spontaneous expressions and a recourse to traditional sacred venues, Anglican or Catholic, and sometimes, in the case of black communities, Pentecostal.

The Plastic Arts

Art, especially painting, now rivals music as the focus of educated seriousness, though the emergence of Brit-Art and the kinds installation art favoured by the Turner Prize would suggest that seriousness has been partly displaced by commercial sensation and counter-cultural gesture. At the same time, so-called blockbuster exhibitions have attracted huge numbers to the National Gallery, the Royal Academy, Tate Britain and Tate Modern. Many of the UK's most famous artists, like Auerbach and Freud, are of foreign extraction, and the same has been partly true of sculpture. One undoubted international figure in painting has been Francis Bacon, and that raises the wider question as to why the art of earlier periods when life was hard for most people was mostly affirmative, whereas today when life is relatively easy art has been despairing.

The issues raised by contemporary art are too complex to be discussed here. However, it is perhaps worth referring to the contrast between the millennium exhibition put on at the National Gallery and focussed on the image of Christ, including its theological as well as aesthetic dimensions, and the eclectic mixture that made up the 'faith' sector in the Millennium Dome. The National Gallery exhibition attracted huge crowds and an extensive correspondence, particularly from those who were surprised at the depth of iconographical meaning in the pictures displayed, as well as from those who were otherwise disappointed at official attempts to play down the religious significance of the millennium. Of course, if one compares this lost iconographical language with the total saturation exemplified in Renaissance Venice, and its integration with the power and glory of the Venetian Empire, one has an index both of what secularisation meant then and what it means now. Religious language then was integrated with power structures, whereas now it is one sector of a fragmented iconic field.

Holy (Pentecostal) Spirituality in the Developing World: Another Movement in Contrary Motion

My final contrast is between architectural dispositions of religious and political power in Europe, and for that matter the USA, and the architectural dispositions of many of the cities of the developing world. The idea for a spatial realisation of religious dispositions came to me personally in Jamaica, where the European idea of Establishment mingles with the pluralism of North America and the developing world. At the centre of a small Jamaican town the Anglican church stood next to the police station; the traditional voluntary churches occupied the main street, while Pentecostal churches thronged the periphery.

Whereas in Europe impoverished areas might be sparsely supplied with churches, in the developing world – from Manila to Seoul, and Santiago, Chile, to Accra – they will be honeycombed with small Pentecostal churches or else with mega-churches. Mostly the European relation between established political and religious power will remain in place, though in Seoul the conspicuous architectural link is today between the mega-church of Paul Yonggi Cho and what has been the Protestant-dominated legislature of Korea. The impoverished and almost entirely black suburbs at the centre of Johannesburg are honeycombed with small Pentecostal churches, while the immense black suburb of Soweto is dominated by two buildings, the hospital and the Rhema mega-church. As already indicated, these churches of the developing world are now flourishing in the migrant suburbs of Northern Europe, and are often the liveliest centres of religion in what are the secular capitals of the world. They are also to be found all over the migrant suburbs of North America.

Postscript: Some Implicit Genealogies

My aim has not been primarily to restate the general theory of secularisation, but rather to suggest how it may be inscribed in the space/time of the city, and beyond that to bring out some less obvious genealogies of the secular and of what one has to call the dialectic of sacred and secular. One such dialectic might be successive waves of evangelisation and secularisation: beginning with the monks in the Roman imperial and medieval periods; continuing with the friars in the cities of the later medieval period; and then bifurcating into a Protestant genealogy running from the Puritan to the Evangelical Revival and the Charismatic or Pentecostal movement, and a Catholic genealogy running from the Counter-Reformation to the revivals of the nineteenth and twentieth centuries. The Catholic genealogy is usually neglected in sociological historiography.

Another less obvious genealogy is only implied by inscription in the space-time of the city because it would involve a prolonged excursion into the history of commerce and of the military. It is the explicit embrace of power politics and the power of money in Renaissance Florence and Venice manifest in the Bank and the Arsenal. The Twin Towers in New York (along with other massive emplacements from London and Frankfurt to Doha) were the pre-eminent realisations of these closely intertwined powers in the twentieth century. Linked with that epoch-making development in Renaissance Italy was the emergence of the artist as spiritual hero and of a canonical succession of artist-heroes illustrated in museum and art gallery. Thereafter art and business have been both in conflict and complementary in a long succession that came to a climax in twentieth-century Paris and (later) in New York. This long succession includes bohemianism as reinforced by Romanticism, and has today mutated into the post-modern and the art of ephemeral statement or defiant gesture. The prime embodiment of what has to be called the turn to the aesthetic is the modern museum, which from the Guggenheim to the Museum of Modern Art (MOMA) is central to the contemporary city. As the emergence of bohemianism indicates, the aesthetic not only includes an invocation of the sublime but a celebration of the amoral and hedonistic. An alternative focus to the museum would be the modern hospital, with its roots in Christian philanthropy and its translation of holiness into holism and health.

Another implicit genealogy is realised in the architecture of the long eighteenth century from about 1680 to 1830, and in the secularisation of Nature associated with Newton, later completed for biological nature by Darwin. The long-term realisation of that sequence of dramatic change is located in the autonomy of the secular university understood as a translation of the universal Church, above all in the massive emplacements of science. Yet another genealogy can be located in the tradition of Enlightened Autocracy, not just in its imperial manifestations but in modern 'Enlightened' Dictatorships. Enlightenment has been far more ambiguous in its historical realisations than it has been given discredit for. Another momentous bifurcation manifests itself here between the more modest Palladian and Grecian strand mostly adopted in Anglo-American culture and the monumental classicism of autocracy practised in Central and Eastern Europe, for example in Berlin and St. Petersburg.

If modern spirituality floating free from institutional and creedal location cannot achieve lasting architectural inscriptions over time it must achieve expression in the uses of space, above all in venues for mass festivity or collective mourning. Every city from Paris and London to New York and San Francisco has such spaces, which (like the art scene) combine high secular finance with simply hanging out. The problem is that privatised spirituality as realised in the relationship of client and therapist needs no external markers. By contrast, the simultaneously moral and communal spirituality of the developing world signified by Pentecostalism is massively inscribed in the contemporary city from Manila to Kiev.

Chapter 15

Moscow and Eurasia: Centre and Periphery, Ethno-religion and Voluntarism, Secularisation and De-Secularisation

This final chapter brings together themes treated earlier in the context of the distinction between centre and periphery. I attempt to treat the distinction between centre and periphery alongside the distinctions between ethno-religion (or religious nationalism) and voluntarism, between faith (or ideology) and power, between secularisation and de-secularisation – and to do so in the largest possible global context of Moscow and western Eurasia. Dealing with Moscow and Eurasia has the advantage of allowing me to discuss scientific atheism when it had its 'Constantinian moment' between 1917 and 1989 and had to face the problem of realising its proclaimed principles in the concrete circumstances of the here and now. Once principles became mired in the dynamics of power they underwent deformations precisely analogous to those it excoriated in the practice of religion.

To weave together the themes outlined in the previous paragraph requires a map of the terrain in historic time and geographical space, and some indication of how very different centres such as Moscow and London relate to very different peripheries such as St. Petersburg and Bombay. It is an old dictum of geopolitics that whoever controls the centre (or 'the heartland') controls the world. Such a dictum foregrounds power and control, and that is important because the dynamics of power and control are constants: the language of conflict may resonate with the rhetoric of 'holy war', as when the Muslim Turks were defeated at the gates of Vienna in 1683 by a Christian coalition; but the reality as seen by historians turns on the power plays of rival political centres like the Hapsburg, Ottoman and Romanov empires. Yet for sociological analysis faith and functionally equivalent ideologies like nationalism and communism are also important. Soviet power may operate like Romanov power, and the power exercised by scientific atheism may operate like the power exercised by

Russian Orthodoxy; but there remain analytically relevant differences between faiths and secular ideologies like nationalism and communism.

We need therefore to integrate physical and political geography with the changeful history of ideas and of religion. Ideologies and faiths are not static, and for the particular purposes of this analysis that means taking into account the emergence of national churches and voluntary denominations during the last three centuries of the history of the Reformation. That history includes the momentous shift from gesture and liturgical enactment to personal faith and considered assent to beliefs. Word displaces gesture and this displacement was broadly accomplished in the North and West of Europe, and even to some extent in Counter-Reformation Catholicism. But it was successfully resisted in the South and East of Europe. To this day religion in Russia remains embedded in gesture, obeisance and image rather than in discourse, personal faith and intellectual assent, and that helps account for its survival under prolonged attack and persecution on the part of scientific atheists who believed it was only necessary to dismiss faith as false cognition and mere superstition.

Once Christianity takes the form of voluntary denominations and territorial churches the dialectic of heartland and margin alters. In the early modern period North America received migrants who were attached both to territorial churches and to voluntary denominations, and as soon as denominations provided the main form of religious expression the dialectic of heartland and margin shifted accordingly. During the eighteenth century what became the USA was increasingly defined by a generalised Protestantism rather than a territorial church; and in the nineteenth century the dialectic of centre and periphery found expression in the tension between the intellectual Protestantism of the North-East and the populist Protestantism of the South.

The appearance of territorial churches and voluntary denominations also affected the way empires expanded in the early modern period. We have to link the *specific* geopolitical location of a nascent empire, like the British or the Russian, with the *changing* character of its religion. Consider first the nature of the geographical centre: for example whether it expands outwards from a large land mass through military power, as it did in the three centuries of Russian imperial expansion; or projects power from an island round the globe through naval power, as it did in the three centuries of British imperial expansion. Once that difference is grasped then we need to take into account the way the territorial church expands *alongside* the expansion of the empire, as it did in the Russian case, and the way rival denominations both took advantage of the opportunities offered by empire and distanced themselves from the imperial project, as in the British case.

This British mode of imperial expansion explains just why a voluntary denomination like Methodism was never likely to become the territorial faith of Britain's Indian Empire. It also explains why a relatively weak territorial church like the Church of England with numerous rivals was never likely to take the form elsewhere that it took in England, though in parts of Africa or in Australasia it might retain a special status. This is where analysis becomes complicated because it has to take account of the geographical size and demographic weight of the centre relative to the periphery in the two contrasted cases. Russia is large relative to its periphery, though of course there was a point in its early history when it had not achieved the dominance it eventually came to possess. The island of Britain was always small relative to what became its vast and populous periphery, and was in any case divided into several nations with two or three territorial churches. Some degree of pluralism was built in from the start on account of the rivalry between territorial churches and voluntary denominations.

All this is simply to indicate that the expansion of a territorial church across a contiguous land mass, as in Russia, was bound to be very different from the spread of rival churches and voluntary denominations in colonies scattered all over the globe, as in the case of Britain. Of course, there are other models of imperial expansion besides Russia and Britain. The spread of Iberian Catholicism in Latin America occurred through a combination of naval and military power projected far across the Atlantic in another continent. It reflected a prior history of eight centuries of struggle between Islam and Christianity that had ended with the suppression or expulsion of Jews, Muslims and Protestants alike to create a homogeneous state. The Spanish and Portuguese empires expanded from several weak centres within Latin America, like Mexico and Brazil that were later to evolve into the weak centres of a very partially realised nationalism. Latin America never constituted a single empire focussed on a major centre comparable to the island of Britain or the heartland of Russia. The French Empire provides yet another model of imperial expansion. Apart from Canada, which became a relic on another continent of a Catholic France that no longer existed, the expansion of France occurred after the territorial faith of Catholicism had been challenged and partly displaced by the equally territorial ideology of a nationalistic French Enlightenment. The expansion of France southward from outposts on the southern littoral of the Mediterranean occurred against the background of the anti-clericalism animating the later years of the Third Republic. French imperialism used Catholicism instrumentally, and the criteria of inclusion in 'French civilisation' became cultural and linguistic rather than religious.

My prime focus is on the dramatic difference between Britain and Russia. In Russia three centuries of subordination by, and resistance to, the pagan Golden Horde and its Muslim successors resulted in an attempt to impose a religious monopoly that in alliance with an autocratic Enlightenment set out to incorporate many foreign peoples and alien faiths. In due course an Orthodoxy that looked back to Byzantium fused with Great Russian nationalism. In Britain an initial expansion that united the two islands (Britain and Ireland) inaugurated another imperial expansion across the contiguous territories of North America that from 1776 onward proceeded under the auspices of the colonists. After 1776 the Second British Empire expanded in far-flung colonies in India, sub-Saharan Africa and Australasia. An empire based on sea power exercised from the Atlantic littoral projected power around the globe. Whereas the second city of Russia was St. Petersburg, the second city of the British Empire was 'neo-gothic' Bombay where subcontinental power was established through the University of Bombay and Bombay's railway terminus, and Indians were remoulded as Britons.[1]

When you contemplate the heartlands of Eurasia you notice the vast northern plain that stretches from East Anglia in the British Isles to the Urals. That plain constitutes a 2,000-mile zone of contention, and contrasts with the numerous ecological pockets in Southern Europe created by mountain and valley all the way from the Carpathians in the south-east to the Alps in the centre and the mountains of Spain and Portugal in the west. In Northern Europe that great plain provides the backdrop first for a history of confrontation between the various centres of religious and political power around the Baltic – whether Danish or Swedish, German or Russian – and then for another superimposed history of confrontation between Berlin and Moscow. In Southern Europe a very different ecology provides a backdrop first for a confrontation between the centres of religious and political power around the Black Sea, above all the Russian and Ottoman empires, and then for another superimposed history of confrontation between the powers of the Western Mediterranean and the Ottoman Empire in the Eastern Mediterranean with its European epicentre in the Balkans.

That brief sketch shows what is involved in integrating religious history with political geography and geopolitics. When we move the focus of attention to Moscow in the geopolitical heartland of western Eurasia, we encounter a vast zone of conflicting pressures: north and south, west and east. There is a pressure from the north, beginning in the tenth century with the southward movement of the Varangian tribes and concluding with the Russian defeat of the Swedes and

---

[1]   Daniel Brook, *A History of Future Cities* (New York: Norton, 2013).

the Russian advance along both the southern and northern littorals of the Baltic in the eighteenth and nineteenth centuries. Nor was that nineteenth-century Russian advance entirely conclusive: the Baltic States gained, lost and regained their independence; and the fortunes of the cause of Finnish independence and of Greater Finland ebbed back and forth between 1918 and 1945.[2]

There is a pressure from the West that includes the expansion of Poland-Lithuania into Ukraine and the littoral of the Black Sea from the sixteenth century to the eighteenth,[3] and concludes in struggles between Germany and Russia that ended in favour of Germany in 1917 and in favour of Russia in 1945. There is a pressure from the Islamic south that encounters the advance from the eighteenth century onward of the Russian Empire into the Balkans and the Caucasus that also incorporates Christian Armenia and Georgia. Finally, in the nineteenth century there is the eastward expansion of the Russian Empire into Muslim Central Asia that in its furthest reach includes Kamchatka and Alaska. There is even a sizeable Orthodox Church in Japan founded in the 1860s. The Russian Empire successfully incorporates the Tatars into its core, but it encounters continuous resistance at the periphery – for example Muslim peoples in the Crimea, Central Asia and the Caucasus – as well as a desire for national independence on the part of Armenia and Georgia.

The expansion of imperial Orthodox Russia, of its imperial atheist successor and of the reviving Orthodox *imperium* of the early twenty-first century has resulted in a series of cross-border relationships, some of them on a global scale. These include ethnic and ethno-religious groups *within* Russia: such as the Lutheran Germans, the Catholic Poles, the Orthodox Bulgarians; and the various deported peoples such as the Estonians, the Pontic Greeks, the Crimean Tatars and the Jews. The Jews were long confined within the Russian Pale, where they endured numerous pogroms, and in the twentieth century were for the most part driven out of their urban strongholds like Odessa, Vilnius and L'viv either by Russians, or by Germans or by local ethnic majorities. In the latter half of the twentieth century they mainly migrated to form a powerful minority in Israel. These groups can for the moment be set on one side since their sad and terrible histories are well known.

---

[2]   The Finns derived their sense of being a new Israel from the Swedes, as the Americans derived their sense of being a new Israel from England. Karelia in particular focussed dreams of the providential destiny of Greater Finland that were powerfully evoked in the wars of 1940–45.

[3]   Norman Davies, *Vanished Kingdoms: The History of Half-Forgotten Europe* (London: Penguin, 2011).

These cross-border relationships also include the Russian Orthodox churches and the Russian ethnic *diaspora* in the West: above all in France; the Russian minorities in the Baltic and the newly independent states of Muslim Central Asia; the Orthodox peoples and churches of the Balkans, notably Serbia, as well as Orthodox Christians in the Middle East, notably Syria; the 'bloodlands' where the European West meets the East, notably along the disputed and shifting borders of Belarus and Ukraine, especially Galicia, Volhynia and the Western Ukraine; and finally the vast rival centre of China, above all Beijing and Shanghai, at the eastern end of the Asian landmass. The most geopolitically important cross-border relationship was to have been realised by the road from Moscow to Beijing planned by Stalin to connect Russian power to what was then its Chinese satellite. Now that the relationship has been largely reversed the economic and demographic encroachments of China across Russia's far eastern frontier are watched with increasing anxiety.

Some of these cross-border relationships are historically of very long-standing. Russian monasticism has a historic connection with Mount Athos, and has from time to time been far from at ease with the central control of the Moscow hierarchy. There are also links between Moscow and the autocephalous churches of the Balkans and the Baltic that vary between fraternal sponsorship in difficult situations and resented attempts at control and manipulation. All these relationships involve negotiations and tensions with the political centre in Moscow and with the Moscow Patriarchate as a religious centre that since 1991 has been increasingly linked with the political powers that be. Here we simply need to indicate them on a map of tensions between centre and peripheries. Russian art provides another version of the map. For example, in the Tretyakov Gallery in Moscow, founded in the nineteenth century by an Old Believer businessman, one can observe first the transition from the medieval tradition of icons to western-style painting, the fascination with France and Italy, the loving celebration of Nature in the heartland, for example in the paintings of Levitan, and then the slow incorporation of the Russian Orient and an interest in the Middle East that parallels a similar movement in France, Britain and Germany. Russia has its own version of Orientalism.

There was nothing foreordained about the eventual supremacy of Moscow at the centre of the geopolitical heartland. The story of the struggle between St. Petersburg, created by Peter the Great (and later Catherine the Great) as a 'New Amsterdam' looking onto the West, and the modernity it represented, and Moscow as the focus of Orthodoxy in the Slavophil heartland, is very familiar. St. Petersburg stood for the classical and baroque style of Enlightenment autocracy up to the building of the cathedral of Our Saviour of the Spilled Blood in a resolutely 'Russian' style reminiscent of St. Basil's in Moscow. But there is also a somewhat less familiar story of an earlier struggle for pre-eminence in the heartland that had echoes in the struggle over the precise dates of Russian/ Ukrainian Christianisation. The other contenders for pre-eminence were Kiev, in particular the cathedral of Saint Sophia, and the ancient cities of the golden ring east of Moscow – Vladimir, Suzdal and Novgorod. These older cities are now treasure houses of early Russian art and architecture, and useful resources for the tourist industry. Each of these candidates for pre-eminence drew on the inheritance of Byzantium to legitimate their claims, long before Moscow asserted its right to be the principal inheritor of the Byzantine legacy with the fall of Constantinople in 1453. The migration of icons from Kiev to Vladimir and Suzdal, and the eventual migration of the artistic charisma of Rublev to Moscow, retell the story of the migration of power. Centuries later in the age of nationalism, the migration of art following conquest, and the transfer of artefacts like the Elgin Marbles to metropolitan museums, tell a parallel story. The history of art and archaeology provides rich illustrated books of the changing dispositions of political power.

In the Russian Empire archaeology and Byzantinology in particular are implicated in politics. For example, those archaeologists who uncovered the trails of many peoples across territories putatively occupied for ever by Slavs paid for their discoveries with their careers, and even their lives. Neal Ascherson tells the story of successive migrations during centuries of confrontation between city states on the Black Sea set up by Greeks, Venetians and others, and the various nomadic peoples that perennially crossed the steppes, beginning with the Scythians and Sarmatians in the first millennium BC. The former congratulated themselves as representatives of civilisation, whereas the latter were cast as mere barbarians.[4] Much later, as the Russian Empire moved south towards the Black Sea, 'the people of the land' either submitted or fled. From the point of view of Russian imperial ideology attempts to tell the story of the migrations of earlier peoples impugned the right of Russians to occupy their territory. Neal Ascherson also draws attention to groups he identifies as 'outpost' peoples. The Cossacks played the role of an outpost people representing the spirit of the imagined centre, as the Krajina Serbs did in the Balkans and the Protestant Irish in Northern Ireland.

---

[4] Neal Ascherson, *The Black Sea: The Birthplace of Civilisation and Barbarism* (London: Jonathan Cape, 1995).

The dispositions of religious and political power in the architecture of Moscow tell the story of the millennial *symphonia* between Church and state derived from Byzantium. As in so many other Russian cities representing the earliest manifestations of Russian power, for example Vladimir and Novgorod, the Kremlin represents the close proximity of Church and state. The Moscow Kremlin acts as a synecdoche for centralised autocracy and is both theatre and text.[5] Red Square combines political, religious and economic power, with St. Basil's cathedral at one end and at the other the recently rebuilt Kazan cathedral, close to the rebuilt Resurrection Gate, and the sometime Upper Trading Rows, now the GUM megastore, in between. The symbolic destructions and rebuildings are eloquent testimony to the violent lurches of Russian state ideology from Orthodoxy to communism and back again to Orthodoxy. The destruction and rebuilding of the cathedral of Christ the Saviour opposite the Kremlin reinforces that testimony. In 2007 it provided the venue for Yeltsin's funeral, the first state funeral in an Orthodox church since 1894, but also in 2011 for the 'iconic' protest of the Pussy Riot punk group over the collusion of Church with state, and in particular the relationship of the Patriarch to Putin.

Much of nineteenth-century Moscow has been destroyed, though a handsome commercial district remains on the other side of the river from the Kremlin. The Novodevichy Convent represents another monument to the *symphonia* of Church and state and, through its aristocratic connections, it testifies to the relation of Orthodoxy to monarchy. It was built to commemorate the victory of Basil III over the Poles at Smolensk in 1514, and for a period provided the fortress-like walls of the city. Its cemetery rivals Père Lachaise in Paris in housing the dust of some of the most famous Russians, including Solovyov, Shostakovich, Prokofiev and Chekhov. The Danilov Monastery is now the headquarters of the Russian Orthodox Patriarchate after decades of secularisation as a juvenile prison.

The Lenin Mausoleum remains the focal sacred site of the communist period, but there are many other architectural testimonies to the years 1917–89. Perhaps the most characteristic monuments of communist times are the apartment blocks put up in the style of Stalinist neo-baroque; but there are many other examples of the style, such the skyscrapers known as the Seven Sisters, including the Foreign Ministry and Moscow State University. Perhaps the most notorious monument of the regime is the (reconstructed) Lubianka, originally the headquarters of the All-Russia Insurance Company. The much

---

5   Catherine Merridale, *Red Fortress – The Secret Heart of Russia's History*. London: Allen Lane 2013.

advertised commitment of the regime to science is represented by the Academy of Sciences, known as the 'Brains' building from the sculpture on its roof, and the achievements of Soviet science are dramatically represented by the Gagarin monument. The Metro is, of course, the most famous of all the achievements of Soviet engineering and architecture. What the casual observer easily misses is the kind of ambivalence about religion and its relation to Russian memory and history signified by the Glazunov art gallery. Ilya Glazunov, born in 1930, painted Soviet politicians like Brezhnev and was also a right-wing nationalist who celebrated Christianity and 'Eternal Russia'. He was honoured by Putin.

Ethno-Religion at the Centre, Ethno-Religions at the Periphery and Voluntarism

There are two kinds of pluralism: there are rival ethno-religions occupying adjacent or overlapping territories, as in Ukraine, especially Western Ukraine; and there is a rivalry between ethno-religions and voluntary denominations. It is always possible for migrant ethno-religions to maintain a more or less tolerated presence in the heartlands of another religion based on a distinctive contribution to the economy, for example the migrants who were invited to assist in the creation of St. Petersburg. That is why the Nevsky Prospect is dotted with their different churches. Where an ethnic group is threatened with absorption by a more powerful ethnic group the bonds of territory and kinship are vigorously reinforced to secure survival, as they were in Poland and Lithuania when those countries were threatened with absorption by Russia. In such circumstances conversion to any other religion, whether the religion of the dominating nation or the faith of a voluntary denomination, is rendered very unlikely and attracts severe sanctions amounting to expulsion. The Chechens in the Caucasus have been very resistant to any form of conversion, though they accept in some degree the presence of a Russian minority. In recent years so much Russian blood and treasure have been spent in the virtual recreation of Chechnya, including the rebuilding of the capital, Grozny, that some Russians would be only too glad to concede independence. Once the Islamic nations of Central Asia gained their independence the Russian Orthodox minorities came under very considerable pressure, and many Russians either decided to leave or were attacked and virtually extruded. At the same time large numbers of Uzbeks, Kazakhs and Chechens continued to migrate to the Russian heartlands, so that Moscow – like London, Vienna and other European capital cities – hosts a very large Muslim population of over 2 million, mostly keeping their heads down and worshipping in 'house mosques'. The newly independent Islamic nations have as a rule been governed by autocrats in the Soviet mould and have suffered 'cults of personality' and associated policies of repression reminiscent of Nicolae Ceausescu in Romania.

Armenia and Georgia are resistant to conversion in the same way as the Islamic Republics, though there have been some modest movements of conversion to Evangelical Christianity. The pagan population of the Mari El Republic in eastern Russia was subject to considerable pressure to conform to Orthodoxy but succeeded in maintaining enough resistance for intellectuals to stimulate a contemporary pagan revival.[6] Of recent years, pagan revivals all over Europe and Eurasia seek to revive earlier religious patterns by building them into partially 'invented traditions' as the original faith of the 'folk'[7]. Of course, sometimes Christianity itself plays the role of the religion of the folk, for example among the Turkic people of the Gagauz in southern Moldova.

Nationalism on either side of the frontier between Christianity and Islam seeks religious, linguistic and ethnic unity, and in this Russia and Turkey are alike. Turkey is of course the residual nation state that rose in the wake of the Ottoman Empire. That empire had extended deep into Europe and into what is now Russia, and had passed through a phase when religion was 'nationalised' under Suleiman the Magnificent (or the Law-Giver) as it was later under Peter the Great, and another phase when a 'shy Enlightenment' was instigated in the late nineteenth century under Sultan and Caliph Abdul Hamid the Second.[8] With the Ottoman collapse, a multicultural empire within which religions and ethnic groups more (or less) coexisted rapidly morphed into a secular modern nation state that either extruded peoples of a different faith or, in the case of the Armenians, committed a still unacknowledged genocide.

---

[6]   Sonia Luehrmann, 'A Dual Quarrel of Images on the Middle Volga: Icon Veneration in the Face of Protestant and Pagan Critique', in Chris Hann and Hermann Goltz (eds), *Eastern Christians in Anthropological Perspective* (Berkeley: University of California Press, 2010, pp. 56–78).

[7]   Mariya Lesiv, *The Return of the Ancestral gods: Modern Ukrainian Paganism as an Alternative Vision for a Nation.* Montreal: McGill-Queens University Press 2013.

[8]   In the sixteenth century, following her excommunication by the Pope, Queen Elizabeth, as head of a 'nationalised' Protestant Church, made overtures to Suleiman concerning an anti-Catholic alliance. Geopolitical interests also coincided in the nineteenth century on account of British fears about Russian advance to the Mediterranean until disrupted by popular revulsion over 'the Bulgarian atrocities'.

The extrusion of deviant ethno-religions in secular Turkey paralleled similar extrusions in Russia and was fuelled by memories of Muslims arriving in Turkey after expulsion from Russia, south-eastern Europe and Greece.[9] In contemporary Russia ethnicity, culture and religion form a united front against ethnic or religious intrusion; and a brief period of openness after the fall of communism was quickly followed by legal and other sanctions against alien religious and cultural influences. An Orthodox atheist is more acceptable than a believing but alien Christian. Jehovah's Witnesses are subject to severe social sanctions as heretical, alien and American. In the Soviet period Witnesses in the Western Ukraine were deported en masse to Siberia in company with Uniates (Greek Catholics) who were totally repressed on account of their western affiliations and forcibly united with the Russian Orthodox Church.

Although voluntary denominations or rival ethno-religions have difficulty making converts in the heartlands, they find conversion easier at break points and cultural junctions. In the fifteenth and sixteenth centuries Islam gained its hold in Bosnia in the borderland between the Western and Eastern traditions of Christianity where – the issue is a matter of dispute among historians and has obvious political overtones – the Bogomil heresy had already provided a substantial slipway. In the twentieth century Evangelical religion made headway in multicultural Transylvania where Catholic and Calvinist Hungarians mingle with Orthodox Romanians, in the interstices of Serbia and Croatia, in the Western Ukraine and in Belarus. Belarus is interesting because it remains a tyranny in the old Stalinist mould under the heel of an autocrat describing himself as an 'Orthodox' atheist. It lies at a religious border which includes Catholic Poles and a lively evangelical community that may have as many active believers as the Orthodox.

Secularisation, De-Secularisation and 'Post-Secularity'

Casual observers may suppose that the Church acting virtually as a department of state under the Tsars from the time of Peter the Great on was merely supine. However, Diarmaid MacCulloch shows that there were numerous signs of dissent and spiritual vitality prior to the revolution of 1905 led by the Orthodox priest Gapon and the revolution of 1917.[10] The story of the spoliation and

---

[9]   Cf. Ildiko Beller-Hann and Chris Hann, *Turkish Region: Culture and Civilization on the East Black Sea Coast* (Oxford: James Currey, 2001).

[10]   Diarmaid MacCulloch, *A History of Christianity: The First Three Thousand Years* (London: Allen Lane, 2009).

persecution of the Church hardly needs further rehearsal here beyond the partial relaxation that occurred in 'the Great Patriotic War' and the return to repression under Khrushchev. Repression had destroyed the infrastructure of the Church, and developments in industrialisation, urbanisation, media and education had reduced the active members of the Church to a smallish minority dominated by *babushki* who often saw the Church as a private club for the practice of 'folk Orthodoxy' and had scant regard for priestly authority. Oddly enough some of these elderly women had in their youth been involved in young communist associations and had imbibed something of their ethos.

However, a change was signalled by a decision in 1984 to turn the 1,000th anniversary of the Christianisation of Russia into a national celebration. Partly this was because the central government preferred the historic Russian Church as a religious partner rather than Catholics, Baptists, Evangelicals, Adventists and Pentecostals who were rapidly expanding and whose administration might lie outside its control. From the point of view of a government concerned to maintain state oversight of religion it made sense to license new Orthodox parishes in border areas with substantial Russian populations along the Chinese borders in the far east and Kaliningrad in the far west. Evangelical and Pentecostal populations were emerging in places as remote as Uzbekistan and Kyrgyzstan.

Thereafter in the years of *perestroika* and *glasnost* under Gorbachev the Church emerged from the shadows. Nikolai Mitrokhin summarises the situation in 1990 as one that set the agenda for a decade and a half. The Church finally had a measure of independence and could elect its own leader. However, the murder of the archpriest Aleksandr Men – a brilliant Jew who appealed to the intelligentsia as well as more widely – maybe by extreme nationalist agents, split the intelligentsia into two camps: one with a wider outlook which included developments in the Orthodox diaspora; and another which consciously assimilated itself to the spirit of 'the folk' as embodying a higher wisdom.

1990 was also the year when the schism in Ukraine led to major changes in the policy of the Moscow Patriarchate towards the Church in what soon was to be an independent country. Though the historic heartlands of the Church might be seen as centred on Moscow, the liveliest sectors during and after the Soviet period lay in 'peripheral' regions that escaped two waves of murder and anti-religious militancy. These included Moldova, Western Belarus and Western Ukraine, areas that contained a large proportion of functioning churches and provided both revenue and clergy. Moreover, from the 1990s on in the Baltic States, in Transcaucasia, Moldova and Western Ukraine, national democrats saw ethnic and religious factors as closely related and instituted the full-scale restitution of Church property.

Mitrokhin writes: 'A considerable proportion of the priests ordained in the 1960s–1980s had grown up in the villages of Transcarpathia, Volhynia, Galicia and Polesye.'[11] These priests were influential all over Russia. From a low base line the number of monasteries and registered parishes in the Russian Church as a whole rose rapidly from 1987 to 1989. They existed alongside unofficial groups and secret monasteries that had long maintained themselves outside the controlled sphere of the Patriarchate as well as secretly ordained nuns, communities of monks and hermits in the remote mountains of Abkhazia and 'elders' dispensing solace and spiritual direction. A rapid increase in the number of parishes and a surge in support for religion, especially perhaps among intellectuals, over the years from 1988 to 1994 revealed a drastic shortage of clergy and inaugurated a period in which the Church opened new schools and theological colleges. Tractor drivers of modest education became priests without giving up their day-jobs, and some bishops became weary of non-canonical miracles. At the same time Christian socio-political groups, brotherhoods and associations emerged, though with a quite modest scope and influence compared with Democratic Russia and the Liberal Democratic Party of Russia.

The most difficult situation for the Russian Orthodox Church lay in Ukraine where the Greek Catholic Church, long banned and forcibly incorporated in Russian Orthodoxy, successfully reclaimed many of its faithful and its churches, alongside a move to establish an anti-Moscow, pro-Ukrainian Orthodoxy. The Western Ukraine in particular experienced a ferment of national feeling. The details of the resulting disputes do not matter here, but the underlying forces at work reflected a classic tension between the politics of the centre and the politics of what had been the periphery. Of recent years the Moscow Patriarchate has become increasingly politicised, and has worked in alliance with the Russian state to support the Russian-speaking populations of the Eastern Ukraine. Inevitably the Russian Church itself splits into rival clerical clans under different Metropolitans, and those who lose easily find themselves exiled to the periphery. The Russian Church abroad also feels the pull of the centre; and in the sphere of ecumenical contacts there are currently moves to form an alliance with conservative elements within the Catholic Church.[12]

[11] Nikolai Mitrokhin, in Irina Prokhorova (ed.), *1990: Russians Remember a Turning Point* (London: Maclehose, 2013, p. 338).

[12] Hilarion Alfeyev, *Orthodox Witness Today* (Geneva: WCC Publications, 2006).

The South and East push back against the influence of the North and West, Eurasia against the Euro-Atlantic. Writing in *The Tablet*, Mary Dejevsky concluded: 'After toppling Soviet Communism, Russia has fallen back on an inner conservatism. Russian Orthodoxy is part of this, and one whose imprint on the national character will not be dislodged.'[13] Moreover, the relation of Orthodoxy to autocracy in Russia represents another persistent trait that emerges to a greater or lesser degree from Ivan the Terrible and the Romanovs to Stalin and Putin. The present regime is a milder version of something familiar over several centuries. It may take the form of religion or nationalism or political ideology, and it may define dissidence as heresy or treason or political deviation, but the structure of power exercised from the centre remains familiar. The present regime rests on the declining economic power given by Gazprom, and the Church has to be careful that it does not become implicated in its eventual downfall. For the moment Eisenstadt's notion of 'multiple modernities', designed to suggest a variety of ways of being modern, serves the ideological purpose in Russia, or Belarus, of legitimating its less attractive features as just part of the rich variety of global alternatives.

Clearly these changes amount to de-secularisation, though when seen as a partial recovery from forced secularisation they do not necessarily refute the secularisation thesis. All over the sometime Eastern bloc the revival of religion has been strongly correlated with a revival of national identity wherever religion and nationalism have been aligned. Andrew Greeley has provided an analysis of the rapid upward shifts in identification with Orthodoxy in Russia, now standing at between 70 per cent and 80 per cent, belief in God, monthly worship and above all the celebration of Easter. Religion is deeply embedded in gesture and obeisance rather than assent to propositions of belief: that embedded character distinguishes it from religion in Protestant Europe and even from Counter-Reformation Catholicism. Greeley comments that the changes beginning in the 1980s exhibit some traditional traits of Holy Russia, including pan-Slavism, imperialism and anti-Semitism.[14] At the same time, a large component of the population continues to regard religion as derived from the weaknesses of human nature, as opposed to science, and as more interested in power than in spirituality. Confidence in the organisation of the Church has not survived the initial enthusiasm of the post-Soviet period. Corruption is taken for granted even though Church and army are regarded more positively than other

[13]   Mary Dejevsky, 'Holy Russia's Bleeding Heart', *The Tablet* (28 September 2013).
[14]   Andrew Greeley, *Religion in Europe at the End of the Second Millennium: A Sociological Profile* (New Brunswick and London: Transaction, 2003, p. 103).

institutions. Atheistic positivism and an almost instinctive materialism still influence a significant section of the educated middle class. As late as 1988 the agents of scientific atheism used the days before Easter to prove experimentally to pupils in Russian schools that water cannot be turned into wine. It is hardly surprising that Richard Dawkins has an enthusiastic following in Russia, even though home-grown atheists wonder how he presumes to instruct people who in the name of state ideology propagated his principles long before he was born.

Whether these changes amount to what Jürgen Habermas has defined as the post-secular condition is a different matter. Religion in the Russian public sphere was privatised in a way very different from Western Europe, and the remarkable return of the traditional *symphonia* of Church and state can be seen as a form of post-secularity understood in Habermasian terms as admission of the Church under certain conditions as a partner in the debates of the public sphere. The sequence in Russia and Eastern Europe from dramatic and forced secularisation to de-secularisation and post-secularity is an historically quite specific sequence and not part of some universal trend. Religion never retired from the public sphere in Western Europe during the time of Christian Democracy; and the separation of the religious and secular, the Church and the state, in the USA is arguably a Christian project rooted in the Baptist and Anabaptist traditions.

Two recent scenarios from the 'bloodlands' of Eurasia illustrate key themes in this chapter and some of the fundamental arguments of this book. The first scenario relates once again to the Pussy Riot. Once one puts analytic pressure on the Pussy Riot case it emerges as rich in ambiguities. It could be interpreted as a religious protest within an understood Orthodox ritual frame, appealing to the Blessed Virgin for aid in the struggle against tyranny and the collusion of Church and state, or alternatively as a typical Western-style art-protest happening. The reactions to the riot covered the whole range from those who placed the protest within the radical tradition of the Gospels concerning what pertains to Caesar and what to God, to those who invoked the Durkheimian sacred and agitated for condign punishment.

The second scenario illustrates a malign continuity of response, whatever the ideological or religious colouring, and shows that when history repeats itself it does so not as farce, (as Marx famously asserted), but as tragedy all over again. After the Enlightened autocrat, Catherine the Great, annexed Crimea the Muslim Tatars, as the 'people of the land', found themselves expropriated and thereafter subject to various kinds of harassment that resulted in a decimation of the Tatar communities and a massive diaspora.

This is not to portray Tatars as collectively 'innocent victims' since all groups with access to power, and subject to the dynamics of pre-emptive attack as the best form of defence, have abused that power. There are, in terms of the long durance of history, no collective innocents.[15] There are only innocent people who at a particular time suffer unjustly. That is what makes collective apology, particularly over an extended time-scale, so dubious. Those who have not committed crimes apologise to those who have not suffered them, and the putative innocence of the victim or guilt of the oppressor is transmitted to new generations by the automatic taint of ethnicity or the mere possession of a passport.

The notion of our shared implication as humans, alike in moral ruination and moral grandeur, is very different from the notion of ethnic taint and effectively undergirds a moral perspective according to which we are, in our specific memberships, short of our common humanity, accounted neither inherently guilty nor inherently innocent. It must be clear to anyone with the slightest sensitivity to the nature and implications of language that the presence in sociological discourse of words like innocence and guilt, let alone words carrying the semantic aura of corruption and blood, speaks volumes about the character of the human sciences. Sociology is a discipline that cannot escape either moral saturation or the theological dimension. They are quite literally written in. My point here relates to what is also written in: the dynamics associated with perceived difference, with differential access to power, and to different ratios of majorities to minorities, often also associated with concentrations of the mistrusted minorities in particular areas or occupational niches.

Under Stalin's regime of scientific atheism precisely these dynamics came once more into play. Crosses were marked on the doors of Tatars before they were attacked and expelled under various, mostly fabricated, pretexts. They were to some extent allowed back from exile with *perestroika*. Now under the regime of Vladimir Putin Crimea appears effectively once more annexed to Russia. And in March 2014 the crosses have appeared again.

---

[15]   David Martin, 'Collective National Guilt: A Socio-Theological Critique', in Lawrence Osborne and Andrew Walker (eds.), *Harmful Religion: An Exploration of Religious Abuse*. London: SPCK 1997: 144-62.

Index